The Responsibility of Forms

Roland Barthes

The Responsibility
of Forms

Critical Essays on

Music, Art, and Representation

TRANSLATED FROM THE FRENCH BY

Richard Howard

BASIL BLACKWELL

British Library Cataloguing in Publication Data

Barthes, Roland
The responsibility of forms: critical essays
on music, art and representation.
1. Semiotics   2. Structuralism (Literary analysis)
I. Title   II. L'obvie et l'obtus. *English*
001.56   P99

ISBN 0-631-14746-2

Printed in Great Britain by T.J. Press Ltd, Padstow

Editor's Note

A word of explanation about this edition: five of the essays included here have already been published in the English-language volume *Image – Music – Test* (1977). To subtract them from this collection would be to distort its structure. Particularly with regard to "Writing the Visible," the absence of the first essays in that group would be troublesome, for their double movement—focusing and also transcending semiology—develops a method of "reading" which governs the subsequent essays and permits us to appreciate their brilliance. Indubitably, "The Third Meaning" is one of RB's most important writings—a nucleus of the Barthesian text—and it is no accident that the categories of *obvious* and *obtuse* defined there were chosen for the French title of this collection. We are grateful to our friend Arthur Wang for having understood this and for agreeing to respect the integral architecture of RB's work. Thus the reader can discern how inventively RB—perhaps better than anyone else—manages to articulate: *information*, the communication of knowledge; deciphering of *significations*, the circulation among all lexicons of the symbol, in the web of all languages; and the revelation of *signifying* [*signifiance*]—that apprehension, based on certain singular elements in the signifer, of an ''extra'' meaning which finds its place in no code of discourse, which evokes an entirely different, discontinuous, ironic structure—a site of the highest evaluation of the text (whether written, pictorial, or musical), and notably of its eroticism. Once conscious of this articulation, the reader will understand why Roland Barthes, like the third meaning itself, remains with us, ''like a guest who persists in staying at the party without uttering a word, even when we [imagine] we have no need of him.''

Editions du Seuil

Contents

I
Writing the
Visible

[*Image*]

The Photographic Message

The press photograph is a message. This message as a whole is constituted by a source of emission, a channel of transmission, and a medium of reception. The source of emission is the newspaper staff, the group of technicians of whom some take the photograph, others select it, crop and compose it, treat it, and then others title it with a caption and a commentary. The medium of reception is the public which reads the newspaper. And the channel of transmission is the newspaper itself, or, more precisely, a complex of concurrent messages of which the photograph is the center but whose environs are constituted by the text, the caption, the headline, the layout, and, more abstractly but no less "informatively," the name of the paper itself (for this name constitutes a knowledge which can powerfully inflect the reading of the message proper: the same photograph can change its meaning by shifting from the [conservative] *Aurore* to the [communist] *Humanité*). Such observations are not a matter of indifference, for they allow us to realize that the three traditional parts of the message do not call for the same method of exploration; both the emission and the reception of the message pertain to a sociology: a matter of studying human groups, defining motives, attitudes, and trying to link the behavior of these groups to the total society to which they belong. But, for the message itself, the method has to be a different one: whatever the origin and the destination of the message, the photograph is not only a product or a channel, it is also an object, endowed with a structural autonomy: without in any way claiming to sever this object from its use, we must provide here a specific method prior to sociological analysis—this method can only be the immanent analysis of that original structure which the photograph constitutes.

Of course, even from the viewpoint of an immanent analysis, the photograph's structure is not an isolated one; it communicates with at least one other structure, which is the text (headline, caption, or article) by which every press photograph is accompanied. The totality of information is thus supported by two different structures (of which one is linguistic); these two structures are concurrent, but since their units are heterogeneous, they cannot mingle; here (in the text) the message's substance is constituted by words; there (in the photograph) by lines, surfaces, shadings. Further, the two structures of the message occupy separate if contiguous spaces which are not "homogenized," as they are, for instance, in a rebus, which dissolves words and images into a single line of reading. Therefore, though a press photograph is never without written commentary, analysis must first of all deal with each separate structure; it is only once we have exhausted the study of each structure that we will be able to understand the way in which they complement each other. One of these structures is already known—that of language (but not, it is true, that of the "literature" constituted by the newspaper's particular language: a great deal of work still remains to be done in this connection); the other structure, that of the photograph proper, is virtually unknown. We shall limit ourselves here to defining the initial difficulties of a structural analysis of the photographic message.

The Photographic Paradox

What is the content of the photographic message? What is it that the photograph transmits? By definition, the scene itself, the literal reality. From the object to its image, there is of course a reduction: in proportion, in perspective, in color. But this reduction is at no point a *transformation* (in the mathematical sense of the term); to shift from reality to its photograph, it is not at all necessary to break down this reality into units and to constitute these units into signs substantially different from the object they represent; between this object and its image, it is not at all necessary to arrange a relay, i.e., a code; of course, the image is not the reality, but at least it is its perfect *analogon*, and it is just this analogical perfection which, to common sense, defines the photograph. Here appears the particular status of the photographic image: *it is a message without a code*; a proposition from which we must immediately extract an important corollary: the photographic message is a continuous message.

Are there other messages without a code? At first glance, yes: specifically, all analogical reproductions of reality; drawings, paintings, movies, theater performances. But, as a matter of fact, each of these messages develops in an immediate and evident fashion, beyond the analogical content itself (scene, object, landscape), a supplementary message which is what we commonly call the *style* of the reproduction; here we are concerned with a second meaning, whose signifier is a certain "treatment" of the image as a result of the creator's action, and whose signified, whether aesthetic or ideological, refers to a certain "culture" of the society receiving the message. In short, all these imitative "arts" comprise two messages: a *denoted* message, which is the *analogon* itself, and a *connoted* message, which is the way in which the society represents, to a certain extent, what it thinks of the *analogon*. This duality of messages is obvious in all reproductions which are not photographic: there is no drawing, however "exact," whose very exactitude is not turned into a style (the style of hyper-realism); there is no filmed scene whose objectivity is not finally read as the very sign of objectivity. Here again, the study of these connoted messages is still to be made (in particular we must decide if what is called the work of art can be reduced to a system of significations); we can only predict that for all these imitative arts, when they are common ones, the code of the connoted system is most likely constituted by either a universal symbolic or by a period rhetoric, in short by a stock of stereotypes (schemas, colors, graphisms, gestures, expressions, arrangements of elements).

Now, in principle, with regard to the photograph, we find nothing of the kind, in any case with regard to the press photograph, which is never "artistic." Since the photograph offers itself as a mechanical analogue of reality, its first message completely "fills" its substance and leaves no room for the development of a second message. In short, of all the structures of information,* the photograph is the only one to be exclusively constituted and occupied by a "denoted" message, which completely exhausts its being; in front of a photograph, the feeling of "denotation,"

---

* This is a matter of "cultural" or culturalized structures, of course, and not of operational structures: mathematics, for example, constitutes a denoted structure without any connotation; but if mass society takes it up, using an algebraic formula—for instance, in an article devoted to Einstein —this message, originally purely mathematical, assumes a very heavy connotation, since it *signifies* science.

or if you prefer, of analogical plenitude, is so powerful that the description of a photograph is literally impossible; for to *describe* consists precisely in joining to the denoted message a second message or relay, drawn from a code which is language and which inevitably constitutes, whatever care is taken to be exact, a connotation in relation to the photographic analogue: to describe, then, is not only to be inexact or incomplete, it is to change structures, it is to signify something other than what is shown.*

Now, this purely "denotative" status of the photograph, the perfection and the plenitude of its analogy, in short its "objectivity"—all this risks being mythical (these are the characteristics which common sense attributes to the photograph); for, as a matter of fact, there is a strong probability (and this will be a working hypothesis here) that the photographic message (at least the press message) is also connoted. The connotation is not necessarily immediately apprehensible on the level of the message itself (it is, one might say, both invisible and active, clear and implicit), but we can already infer it from certain phenomena occurring on the level of the message's production and reception: on the one hand, a press photograph is an object worked up, selected, composed, constructed, treated according to various professional, aesthetic, or ideological norms which are so many connotation-factors; and, on the other hand, this same photograph is not only perceived, received, it is *read*, attached—more or less consciously by the public which consumes it—to a traditional stock of signs; now, every sign supposes a code, and it is this code (of connotation) which we must try to establish. The photographic paradox would then be the coexistence of two messages, one without a code (this would be

---

* To describe a drawing is easier, since it ultimately involves describing an already connoted structure, one worked up with a view to a *coded* signification. It may be for this reason that psychological tests use a great many drawings and very few photographs.

the photographic analogue) and the other with a code (this would be the "art," or the treatment, or the "writing," or the rhetoric of the photograph); structurally, the paradox is not of course the collusion of a denoted message and a connoted message: this is the probably inevitable status of all mass communication; the paradox is that the connoted (or coded) message develops here from a message *without a code*. This structural paradox coincides with an ethical one: when we want to be "neutral, objective," we seek to copy reality meticulously, as if the analogical were a resistance factor against the encroachment of values (at least this is the definition of aesthetic "realism"): how then can the photograph be at once "objective" and "encroached upon," natural and cultural? It is by apprehending the mode of imbrication of the denoted message and the connoted message that we may ultimately be able to answer this question. But, to undertake this task, we must remember that in the photograph, since the denoted message is absolutely analogical—i.e., deprived of any recourse to a code, i.e., *continuous*—there is no need to look for the signifying units of the first message; on the contrary, the connoted message does comprise a level of expression and a level of content, of signifiers and of signifieds: hence it requires a veritable deciphering. This deciphering would be premature at present, for in order to isolate the signifying units and the themes (or values) signified, we should have to undertake (perhaps by tests) certain directed readings, making certain elements of the photograph vary artificially, in order to observe whether these variations of forms involve variations of meaning. But at least for the moment we can anticipate the main levels of analysis of photographic connotation.

Connotation Procedures

Connotation, i.e., the imposition of a second meaning upon the photographic message proper, is elaborated at different levels of photographic production (selection, technical treatment, cropping, layout): in short, it is a coding of the photographic analogue; hence it is possible to separate out certain connotation procedures; but we must remember that such procedures have nothing to do with units of signification, as a subsequent analysis of a semantic kind may one day define them: they do not strictly belong to the photographic structure. These procedures are well known; we shall limit ourselves to translating them into structural terms. Strictly speaking, we should clearly separate the first three (trick effects, pose, objects) from the last three (photogeny, aestheticism, syntax), since, in these first three procedures, connotation is produced by a modification of reality itself, i.e., of the denoted message (such methods are of course not peculiar to the photograph); if we include them nonetheless in the photographic connotation-procedures, it is because they, too, benefit from the prestige of denotation: the photograph permits the photographer to *evade* the preparation to which he subjects the scene he will take; the fact nonetheless remains that, from the point of view of a subsequent structural analysis, it is not certain that we can take into account the material they afford.

1. *Trick effects*

In 1951 a photograph widely circulated in the American press is said to have cost Senator Millard Tydings his seat; this photograph represented the senator in conversation with the communist leader Earl Browder. The photograph happened to have been faked, constituted by the artificial juxtaposition of the two faces. The methodological interest of trick effects is that they intervene without warning on the level of denotation itself, they utilize the special credibility of the photograph, which is merely, as we have seen, its exceptional power of denotation, in order to present as simply denoted a message which is in fact strongly connoted; in no other treatment does connotation assume so completely the "objective" mask of denotation. Of course, signification is possible only to the degree that there is a stock of signs, the rudiments of a code; here the signifier is the conversational attitude of the two figures; it will be noted that this attitude becomes a sign only for a certain society, i.e., with regard only to certain values; it is the hypersensitive anti-communism of the American electorate which makes the interlocutors' gesture the sign of a reprehensible familiarity—which is to say that the code of connotation is neither artificial (as in a true language) nor natural: it is historical.

2. Pose

Consider a press photograph widely circulated during the 1960 American elections: a profile bust shot of President Kennedy, eyes looking upward, hands clasped. Here it is the actual pose of the subject which prepares the reading of the signifieds of connotation: youth, spirituality, purity; the photograph signifies, obviously, only because there exists a stock of stereotyped attitudes which constitute ready-made elements of signification (eyes raised, hands clasped); a "historical grammar" of iconographic connotation would therefore have to seek out its materials in painting, in theater, in associations of ideas, in popular metaphors, etc., i.e., in *culture*. As we have said, the pose is not a specifically photographic procedure, but it is difficult not to mention it, insofar as it derives its effect from the analogical principle which establishes the photograph: the message here is not "the pose" but "Kennedy praying": the reader receives as a simple denotation what in fact is a double structure—denoted-connoted.

3. Objects

Here we must grant a particular importance to what we might call the pose of objects, since the connoted meaning derives from the objects photographed (either because they have been artificially arranged in front of the lens if the photographer has had the opportunity, or because the layout man has chosen one among several photographs for this particular shot of a certain object). The interest lies in the fact that these objects are acknowledged inductors of associations of ideas (book-case = intellectual) or, more obscurely, of actual symbols (the gas-chamber door for Chessman's execution refers to the funereal gateway of the ancient mythologies). Such objects constitute excellent elements of signification: on the one hand, they are discontinuous and complete in themselves, which is, for a sign, a physical quality; and, on the other hand, they refer to clear, known signifieds; hence they are the elements of a true lexicon, stable to the point where we can readily constitute them into a syntax. Here, for example, is a "composition" of objects: a window open on tile roofs, a landscape of vineyards; in front of the window, a photograph album, a magnifying glass, a vase of flowers; we are, in other words, in the country, south of the Loire (tiles and vines), in a bourgeois dwelling (flowers on the table), whose aged resident (the magnifying glass) is reliving his memories (photograph album): this is François Mauriac in Malagar (in *Paris-Match*); the connotation "emerges" from all these signifying units, "taken," however, as though the scene

involved were immediate and spontaneous, i.e., without signification; we find this made explicit in the text, which develops the theme of Mauriac's links to the land. The object may
not possess a *power* any longer, but it certainly possesses a
meaning.

4. Photogeny

The theory of photogeny has already been sketched by Edgar
Morin in *Le Cinéma ou l'Homme imaginaire*, but this is not
the place to discuss the general signification of this procedure.
It will suffice to define photogeny in terms of informational
structure: in photogeny, the connoted message is within the
image itself, "embellished" (i.e., in most cases, sublimated)
by techniques of lighting, exposure, and printing. These techniques need be inventoried only if there corresponds to each of
them a signified of sufficiently constant connotation to be incorporated into a cultural lexicon of technical "effects" (for
instance, the "blur of movement" proposed by Dr. Steinert's
team to signify space-time). This inventory, moreover, would
afford an excellent occasion for distinguishing aesthetic effects
from signifying effects—subject to recognizing perhaps that in
photography, contrary to the intentions of exhibition photog-
raphers, there is never *art* but always *meaning*—which would at
last furnish an exact criterion for the opposition between good
painting, however strongly figurative, and photography.

5. Aestheticism

For if we can speak of aestheticism in photography, it appears
that we do so ambiguously: when the photograph becomes a
painting, i.e., a composition or visual substance deliberately

treated in its own texture, either in order to signify itself as "art" (this is the case of the "pictorialism" of the beginning of the century) or in order to impose a usually more subtle and more complex signified than other connotation procedures would allow; thus, Cartier-Bresson constructed Cardinal Pacelli's reception by the faithful of Lisieux like a scene from an Old Master; yet this photograph is not a painting at all; on the one hand, its paraded aestheticism refers (mockingly) to the very idea of such a scene (which is contrary to any real painting), and, on the other hand, the composition here signifies in an explicit way a certain ecstatic spirituality, translated precisely in terms of an objective spectacle. Moreover, we see here the difference between photograph and painting: in the scene by some Primitive, "spirituality" is not a signified at all but, one might say, the very being of the image; of course, there can be, in certain paintings, code elements, rhetorical figures, period symbols; but no signifying unit refers to spirituality, which is a mode of being, not the object of a structured message.

6. Syntax

We have already mentioned a discursive reading of object-signs within one and the same photograph; naturally, several photographs can be formed into a sequence (as is commonly done in illustrated periodicals); the connotation-signifier is then no longer found on the level of any of the fragments of the sequence, but on that—the supra-segmental level, as we should say in linguistics—of the concatenation. Consider, for example, four shots of a presidential hunt at Rambouillet; in each, the illustrious huntsman (Vincent Auriol) is aiming his rifle in an unlikely direction, greatly endangering the keepers, who run away or drop to the ground: the sequence (and the sequence alone) represents a comic effect which derives, accord-

ing to a familiar procedure, from the repetition and the variation of attitudes. It will be noted in this regard that the single
photograph is very rarely (i.e., with great difficulty) comical,
contrary to the drawing; the comic requires movement, i.e.,
repetition (which is readily obtained in the cinema), or typi-
fication (which is possible in drawing), these two "connotations" being denied to the photograph.

Text and Image

Such are the chief connotation procedures of the photographic image (once again, we are concerned here with techniques, not with units). To them may be joined the text which
accompanies the press photograph. Three remarks should be
made at this point.

First: The text constitutes a parasitical message intended to
connote the image, i.e., to "enliven" it with one or more secondary signifieds. In other words, and this is an important historical reversal, the image no longer *illustrates* the words; it is
the words which, structurally, are parasitical on the image;
this reversal has its price: in the traditional modes of "illustration," the image used to function as an episodic return to
denotation, starting from a principal message (the text), which
was perceived as connoted, precisely because it needed an illustration; in the present relation, the image does not come to illu-
minate or "realize" the words; it is the words which come to
sublimate, patheticize, or rationalize the image; but since this
operation is performed accessorily, the new informational set
seems chiefly based on an objective (denoted) message, of
which words are only a sort of secondary, almost inconsequential vibration; in the past, the image used to illustrate the text
(made it clearer); today the text burdens the image, loads it

with a culture, a morality, an imagination; there used to be a reduction from text to image; today there is an amplification from the one to the other: connotation is now experienced only as the natural resonance of the fundamental denotation constituted by the photographic analogy; hence we confront a characteristic process of the naturalization of the cultural.

Second: The connotation-effect probably differs according to the mode of presenting the words; the closer the words are to the image, the less they seem to connote it; caught up by the iconographic message, so to speak, the verbal message seems to participate in its objectivity, the connotation of language is made "innocent" through the denotation of the photograph; it is true that there is never a real incorporation, since the substances of the two structures (here graphic, there iconic) are irreducible; but there are probably degrees of amalgamation; the caption probably has a less obvious effect of connotation than the headline or the article; headline and article are noticeably separate from the image, the headline by its emphasis, the article by its distance, the former because it breaks with, the latter because it distances, the content of the image; the caption, on the contrary, by its very placing, by its average dose of reading matter, seems to duplicate the image, i.e., to participate in its denotation.

Yet it is impossible (and this will be a third remark apropos of the text) for the words to "duplicate" the image; for in the shift from one structure to the other, secondary signifieds are inevitably elaborated. What is the relation of these connotation-signifieds to the image? What is involved here is apparently an explicitation, i.e., to a certain degree, a stress; in effect, in most cases the text merely amplifies a set of connotations already included within the photograph; but sometimes, too, the text produces (invents) an entirely new signified, one which is somehow projected retroactively onto the image, so that it seems denoted there: *"They have had a brush with death, as their faces show,"* says the headline of a photograph in which we see Elizabeth and Philip getting out of an airplane; yet at the moment of the photograph these two persons still knew nothing about the possibility of the accident they had just escaped. Sometimes, too, the words can even contradict the image so as to produce a compensatory connotation; one of Gerbner's analyses in *The Social Anatomy of the Romance Confession Cover Girl* shows that in certain romance magazines the verbal message of the headlines on the cover (of a gloomy and disturbing content) always accompanied the image of a radiant cover girl; the two messages here form a compromise; the connotation has a regulating function, it preserves the irrational movement of projection-identification.

Photographic Non-signification

We have seen that the code of connotation was apparently neither "natural" nor "artificial" but historical, or perhaps one should say "cultural"; its signs are gestures, attitudes, expressions, colors, or effects endowed with certain meanings by virtue of the practices of a certain society: the link between signifier and signified—i.e., strictly speaking, the signification—remains, if not unmotivated, at least entirely historical. Hence we cannot say that modern man projects into his reading of the photograph certain characterial or "eternal" feelings and values, i.e., infra- or trans-historical feelings and values, unless we make it clear that signification is always elaborated by a specific history and society; signification is, in short, the dialectical movement which resolves the contradiction between cultural man and natural man.

Thanks to its code of connotation, the reading of the photograph is therefore always historical; it depends on the reader's "knowledge," just as if this were a matter of a real language, intelligible only if one has learned its signs. All things considered, the photographic "language" does in fact suggest certain ideographic languages in which analogical units and signaletic units are mixed, with the difference that the ideogram is experienced as a sign while the photographic "copy" passes for the pure and simple denotation of reality. To recognize this code of connotation would therefore be to isolate, to inventory, and to structure all the "historical" elements of the photograph, all the parts of the photographic surface which derive their very discontinuity from a certain knowledge on the reader's part, or, one might say, from his cultural situation.

Now this is a task which may take us very far indeed. No one knows if there are "neutral" parts of a photograph, or at least it may be that utter non-signification in photographs is altogether exceptional; in order to solve this problem, we should first have to elucidate completely the mechanisms of reading (in the physical, and no longer semantic, meaning of the term), or, one might say, of perceiving the photograph; now, on this point, we do not know much: How do we read a photograph? What do we perceive? In what order, according to what itinerary? What is it, in fact, to "perceive"? If, according to certain hypotheses of Bruner and Piaget, there is no perception without immediate categorization, the photograph is verbalized at the very moment it is perceived; or better still: it is perceived only when verbalized (or, if verbalization is delayed, there is a disorder of perception, interrogation, anxiety of the subject, traumatism, according to the Cohen-Séat hypothesis apropos of filmic perception). In this perspective, the image, immediately apprehended by an interior metalanguage, which is language itself, actually has no denoted state; it exists socially only when immersed in at least a primary connotation, that of the categories of language; and we know that all language accommodates itself to things—that it connotes reality, even if only by articulating it; the connotations of the photograph would therefore coincide, *grosso modo*, with the major connotation levels of language.

Hence, beyond "perceptual" connotation, hypothetical but possible, we would then encounter more particular modes of connotation. First of all, a "cognitive" connotation, whose signifiers would be selected, localized in certain parts of the *analogon*: looking at this city view, I *know* that I am in a North African country, because I see on the left a road sign in Arabic script, in the center a man in a gandurah, etc.; here the reading closely depends on my culture, on my knowledge of the world; and it is likely that a good press photograph (and they are all good, since they are selected) readily relies on the supposed knowledge of its readers, choosing those prints which involve the greatest possible quantity of information of this kind, so as to "euphorize" the reading; if we photograph the destruction of Agadir, we had better scatter around a few signs of "Arabicity," although "Arabicity" has nothing to do with the disaster itself; for the connotation resulting from knowledge is always a reassuring power: man loves signs, and he loves them to be clear.

Perceptual connotation, cognitive connotation: there remains the problem of ideological (in the broadest sense of the term) or ethical connotation, the connotation which introduces reasons or values into the reading of the image. This is a strong connotation; it requires a greatly elaborated signifier, of a readily syntactical order: an encounter of personages (as we have seen apropos of *trick effects*), a development of attitudes, a constellation of objects; a son has just been born to the Shah of Iran; here in the photograph we have: royalty (cradle worshipped by a host of servants surrounding it), hygiene (white surgical gowns, Plexiglas lid of the cradle), the nonetheless human condition of kings (the baby is crying); i.e., all the contradictory elements of the princely myth as we consume it nowadays. Here we are concerned with apolitical values, and their lexicon is rich and clear; it is possible (but this is merely a hypothesis) that, on the contrary, a political connotation is generally entrusted to the text, insofar as political choices are always, so to speak, in bad faith: of a particular photograph I can give a rightist or leftist reading (see in this regard an IFOP survey published by *Les Temps Modernes* in 1955); denotation, or its appearance, is impotent to modify political options: no photograph has ever convinced or refuted anyone (but it can "confirm"), insofar as political consciousness is perhaps nonexistent outside of the *logos*: politics is what permits *all* languages.

Such remarks sketch a kind of differential table of photographic connotations; we see in any case that connotation reaches very far. Is this to say that a pure denotation is impossible? If it exists, it is perhaps not at the level of what ordinary language calls the non-signifying, the neutral, the objective, but quite the contrary at the level of strictly traumatic images; trauma is just what suspends language and blocks signification. Of course, certain normally traumatic situations can be apprehended in a photographic process of signification; but this is precisely because they are indicated through a rhetorical code which distances them, sublimates them, pacifies them. Strictly traumatic photographs are rare, the trauma is entirely dependent on the certainty that the scene has really occurred: *the photographer had to be there* (this is the mythical definition of denotation); but this granted (which, to tell the truth, is already a connotation), the traumatic photograph (fires, shipwrecks, catastrophes, violent deaths) is the one about which there is nothing to say: the shock photo is by structure non-signifying: no value, no knowledge, at the limit no verbal categorization can have any hold over the process instituting its signification. We might imagine a kind of law: the more direct the trauma, the more difficult the connotation; or even: the "mythological" effect of a photograph is inversely proportional to its traumatic effect.

Why? No doubt because, like any well-structured signification, photographic connotation is an institutional activity; on the scale of society as a whole, its function is to integrate, in other words to reassure, humanity; every code is both arbitrary and rational; all recourse to a code is therefore a way for humanity to prove itself, to test itself through a rationality and a liberty. In this sense, analyzing codes may permit us to define a society historically—more readily and more certainly than analyzing its signifieds, for the latter can often appear as transhistorical, deriving from an anthropological basis rather than from an authentic history: Hegel defined the ancient Greeks better by sketching the way in which they made Nature signify than by describing the sum of their "feelings and beliefs" on this subject. In the same way we can perhaps do better than to inventory directly the ideological contents of our age; for by trying to reconstitute in its specific structure the connotation-code of a communication as broad as the press photograph, we may hope to recognize in all their complexity the forms our society employs to reassure itself, and thereby grasp the extent, the detours, and the deep function of this effort: a perspective all the more appealing, as we said at the beginning, in that, with regard to the photograph, it develops in the form of a paradox: the paradox which makes an inert object into a language and which transforms the non-culture of a "mechanical" art into the most social of institutions.

1961

Rhetoric of the
Image

According to an ancient etymology, the word *image* should be linked to the root of *imitari*. This immediately takes us to the heart of the most important problem confronting the semiology of images. Can analogical representation (the "copy") produce true sign-systems and no longer merely simply agglutinations of symbols? Is an analogical—and no longer a digital—"code" conceivable? We know that linguistics denies all communication by analogy the status of language, from the "language" of bees to the "language" of gesture, whenever such communications are not doubly articulated, i.e., definitively based on a combinatory system of digital units, as phonemes are. Linguistics is not alone in doubting the linguistic nature of the image; public opinion as well vaguely regards the image as a site of resistance to meaning, in the name of a certain mythical notion of Life: the image is re-presentation, i.e., ultimately resurrection, and we know that the intelligible is reputed antipathetic to the experiential. Thus, from both sides, analogy is perceived as an inferior meaning: some believe that the image is a very rudimentary system in relation to language, and others that signification cannot exhaust the ineffable wealth of the image. Now, even and especially if the image is somehow the *limit* of meaning, it permits us to return to a veritable ontology of signification. How does meaning come to the image? Where does meaning end? And if it ends, what is there *beyond*? This is the question we should like to raise here, subjecting the image to a spectral analysis of the messages it can contain. We shall start by making matters considerably easier for ourselves: we shall study only advertising images. Why? Because, in advertising, the image's signification is assuredly intentional: it is certain attributes of the product which a priori form the signifieds of the advertising message, and these signifieds must be transmitted as clearly as possible; if the image contains signs, we can be sure that in advertising these signs are replete, formed with a view to the best possible reading: the advertising image is *frank*, or at least emphatic.

The Three Messages

Here is a Panzani ad: pasta in packages, a can, a bag, tomatoes, onions, peppers, a mushroom, everything coming out of a half-open string bag, printed in yellows and greens on a red background.* Let us try to "skim off" the different messages it can contain.

The image immediately yields a first message, whose substance is linguistic; its supports are the (marginal) caption and the labels which are inserted into the natural arrangement of the scene, as though *"en abime"*; the code from which this message

---

* We give the *description* of the photograph cautiously, for it already constitutes a metalanguage. See reproduction (XVII).

is taken is none other than that of the French language; in order to be deciphered, this message requires no knowledge except the knowledge of writing and of French. To tell the truth, this message itself can be decomposed further, for the sign *Panzani* yields not only the name of the firm but also, by its assonance, a supplementary signified which is, so to speak, "Italianicity"; the linguistic message is therefore double (at least in this image): of denotation and of connotation; nonetheless, since there is here only a single typical sign,* i.e., that of articulated (written) language, we shall count it as only a single message.

Setting aside the linguistic message, there remains the pure image (even if the labels participate anecdotally). This image immediately yields a series of discontinuous signs. Here, first of all (this order is a matter of indifference, for these signs are not linear), the notion that the represented scene has something to do with a return from shopping; this signifier itself implies two euphoric values: that of the freshness of the products and that of the purely household preparation for which they are destined; its signifier is the gaping string bag which lets the provisions spill out onto the table, as though "unpacked." In order to read this first sign, all that is required is a knowledge somehow "implanted" in the usages of a very widespread civilization in which "to do one's own shopping" is opposed to the hasty stocking up (canned goods, refrigerators) of a more "mechanical" civilization. A second sign is almost as obvious; its signifier is the congruence of the tomato, the pepper, and the tricolor (yellow, red, green) print of the ad; its signified is Italy, or rather *Italianicity*; this sign is in a relation of redundance with the connoted sign of the linguistic message (the Italian assonance of the name Panzani); the knowledge

---

* The sign of a system will be called a *typical* sign insofar as it is sufficiently defined by its substance: the verbal sign, the iconic sign, the gestural sign are so many typical signs.

mobilized by this sign is already more particular: it is a strictly "French" knowledge (Italians could scarcely perceive the connotation of the proper name, and probably not the Italianicity of the tomato and the pepper), based on a knowledge of certain touristic stereotypes. Continuing to explore the image (which does not mean that it is not entirely clear at first glance), we readily discern in it at least two further signs; in one, the closely packed nature of various objects transmits the idea of a total culinary service, as if, on the one hand, Panzani afforded everything necessary to a complicated dish, and as if, on the other, the concentrate in the can equalled the natural products surrounding it, the scene "bridging" the origin of the products and their final condition; in the other sign, the composition, evoking the memory of so many alimentary paintings, refers to an aesthetic signified: it is the "still life"; here the knowledge necessary is distinctly cultural. We might suggest that a further piece of information is added to these four signs: the one which tells us that we are here concerned with an ad, and which comes both from the image's place in the magazine and from the insistence of the Panzani labels (not to mention the caption); but this last bit of information is coextensive with the scene; it somehow escapes signification, insofar as the advertising nature of the image is essentially functional: to utter something does not necessarily mean I *am talking*, except in deliberately reflexive systems such as literature.

Thus, here are four signs for this image, signs which we shall presume form a coherent whole (for they are all discontinuous), which all require a generally cultural knowledge, and which refer to signifieds each of which is total or inclusive (*Italianicity*, for instance), steeped in euphoric values; here, then, a second message of an iconic nature will be seen after the linguistic message. Is this all? If we subtract all these signs from the image, it still retains a certain informational substance; without any knowledge at all, I continue to "read" the image, to "understand" that it collects in a certain space a certain number of identifiable (namable) objects, and not only shapes and colors. The signifieds of this third message are formed by the real objects of the scene, the signifiers by these same objects photographed, for it is obvious that since in analogical representation the relation of the thing signified and of the signifying image is no longer "arbitrary" (as it is in speech), it is no longer necessary to insert the relay of a third term in the form of the psychic image of the object. What specifies this third message is the fact that the relation of the signified and the signifier is quasi-tautological; doubtless the photograph implies a certain manipulation of the scene (cropping, reducing, flattening), but this transition is not a *transformation* (as a *coding* can be); here there is a loss of the equivalence characteristic of true sign-systems and a positing of a quasi-identity. In other words, the sign of this message is no longer drawn from an institutional stock, it is not coded, and we are faced with the paradox (to which we shall return) of a *message without a code*.* This peculiarity recurs on the level of the knowledge invested in the reading of the message: in order to "read" this last (or this first) level of the image, we need no other knowledge than what is involved in our perception: this knowledge is not nil, for we must know what an image is (children know this only at about the age of four) and what a tomato, a string bag, and a package of pasta are: however, this is virtually anthropological knowledge. This message corresponds in some sense to the letter of the image, and we can agree to call it the literal message, as opposed to the preceding message, which is a "symbolic" message.

If our reading is satisfactory, the analyzed photograph thus offers us three messages: a linguistic message, a coded iconic message, and a non-coded iconic message. The linguistic message is readily separated from the other two; but since these latter messages have the same (iconic) substance, to what degree are

---

* Cf. the preceding essay, "The Photographic Message."

we entitled to distinguish them? It is certain that the distinction of the two iconic messages is not made spontaneously on the level of ordinary reading: the spectator of the image receives *at the same time* the perceptual message and the cultural message, and we shall see later on that this confusion in reading corresponds to the function of the mass-culture image (with which we are concerned here). Yet the distinction has an operational validity, analogous to the one which permits distinguishing in the linguistic sign a signifier and a signified, though in fact no one can ever separate the "word" from its meaning, except by resorting to the metalanguage of a definition: if the distinction permits describing the structure of the image in a simple and coherent fashion, and if the description thus arrived at prepares an explanation of the role of the image in society, we shall regard it as justified. Hence we must return to each type of message so as to explore it in its generality, without losing sight of the fact that we are trying to understand the structure of the image as a whole, i.e., the final relation of the three messages among themselves. Nevertheless, since it is no longer a matter of a "naïve" analysis but of a structural description,* we shall somewhat modify the order of the messages, inverting the cultural and the literal messages; of the two iconic messages, the first is somehow imprinted within the second: the literal message appears as the *support* of the "symbolic" message. Now, we know that a system which takes over the signs of another system in order to make them into its signifiers is a system of connotation; hence, we shall say immediately that the literal image is *denoted* and the symbolic system *connoted*. Hence, we shall study in succession the linguistic message, the denoted message, and the connoted message.

---

* The "naïve" analysis is an enumeration of elements; structural description seeks to apprehend the relation of these elements by virtue of the principle of solidarity among the terms of a structure: if one term changes, the others change as well.

The Linguistic Message

Is the linguistic message constant? Is there always something textual within, beneath, or around the image? In order to discover images without words, we must doubtless go back to partially analphabetic societies, i.e., to a sort of pictographics of the image; actually, since the advent of the book, the link between text and image is frequent; this link seems to have been studied very little from the structural point of view. What is the signifying structure of "illustration"? Does the image duplicate certain items of information in the text, by a phenomenon of redundance, or does the text add a brand-new item of information to the image? The problem might be put historically apropos of the classical period, which had a passion for books with pictures (it was inconceivable in the eighteenth century that La Fontaine's *Fables* would not be illustrated), and during which certain authors like Father Ménestrier explored the relations between the figurative and the discursive.*
Today, on the level of mass communication, it appears that the linguistic message is present in all images: as a caption, as a headline, as a press article, as a film dialogue, as a comic-strip balloon; whereby we see that it is not quite accurate to speak of a civilization of the image: we are still and more than ever a civilization of writing,† because writing and speech are still the "full" terms of informational structure. As a matter of fact, only the *presence* of the linguistic message counts, for neither its position nor its length seems pertinent (a long text

---

* *L'Art des Emblèmes*, 1684.

† The wordless image is no doubt to be met with, but by way of paradox—in certain cartoons, for example; the absence of speech always covers an enigmatic intention.

may comprise only a total signified, thanks to the connotation, and it is this signified that is put in relation with the image). What are the functions of the linguistic message in relation to the (double) iconic message? There seem to be two: *anchoring* and *relaying*.

As we shall see more clearly in a moment, every image is polysemous; it implies, subjacent to its signifiers, a "floating chain" of signifieds of which the reader can select some and ignore the rest. Polysemy questions meaning, and this question always appears as a dysfunction, even if this dysfunction is recuperated by society as a tragic act (a silent God affords no way of choosing between signs) or a poetic one (the panic "shudder of meaning" among the ancient Greeks); even in cinema, traumatic images are linked to an uncertainty (to an anxiety) as to the meaning of objects or attitudes. Hence, in every society a certain number of techniques are developed in order to *fix* the floating chain of signifieds, to combat the terror of uncertain signs: the linguistic message is one of these techniques. On the level of the literal message, language answers, more or less directly, more or less partially, the question *What is it?* Language helps identify purely and simply the elements of the scene and the scene itself: it is a matter of a denoted description of the image (a description that is often partial), or, in Hjelmslev's terminology, of an *operation* (as opposed to a connotation). The denominative function corresponds nicely to an *anchoring* of every possible (denoted) meaning of the object, by recourse to a nomenclature; in front of a dish of something (in an Amieux ad), I may hesitate to identify the shapes and volumes; the caption (*"Rice and tuna with mushrooms"*) helps me choose *the right level of perception*; it allows me to accommodate not only my gaze but also my intellection. On the level of the "symbolic" message, the linguistic message no longer guides the identification but the interpretation; it constitutes a kind of vise which keeps the connoted meanings from proliferating either toward too individual regions (i.e., it limits the image's projective power) or toward dysphoric values; an ad (d'Arcy preserves) shows a few fruits scattered around a ladder; the caption ("As *if you had picked them in your own garden*") distances a possible signified (parsimony, poor harvest) because it would be an unpleasant one and orients the reading toward a flattering signified (natural and personal character of the fruits of the private garden); the caption here acts as a counter-taboo, it combats the disagreeable myth of the artificial, ordinarily attached to canned goods. Of course, outside of advertising, anchoring can be ideological; this is even, no doubt, its main function; the text *directs* the reader among the various signifieds of the image, causes him to avoid some and to accept others; through an often subtle dispatching, it teleguides him toward a meaning selected in advance. In all these cases of anchoring, language obviously has a function of elucidation, but such elucidation is selective; it is a matter of a metalanguage applied not to the whole of the iconic message but only to certain of its signs; the text is really the creator's (and hence the society's) right-of-inspection of the image: anchoring is a means of control, it bears a responsibility, confronting the projective power of the figures, as to the use of the message; in relation to the freedom of the image's signifieds, the text has a *repressive* value,* and we can see that a society's ideology and morality are principally invested on this level.

---

*This is evident in the paradoxical case where the image is constructed according to the text, and where consequently the control would seem to be unnecessary. An ad which wants to suggest that in a certain coffee the aroma is "locked in" the powdered form of the product, and therefore will be wholly there when used, shows above the caption a can of coffee with a chain and a lock around it; here the linguistic metaphor ("locked in") is taken literally (a familiar poetic procedure); but as a matter of fact it is the image which is read first, and the text which has generated it ends up being the simple choice of one signified among others: the repression is noted in the circuit as a banalization of the message.

Anchoring is the most frequent function of the linguistic message; we frequently encounter it in press photographs and in advertising. The relaying function is rarer (at least with regard to the fixed image); we find it mainly in cartoons and comic strips. Here language (generally a fragment of dialogue) and image are in a complementary relation; the words are then fragments of a more general syntagm, as are the images, and the message's unity occurs on a higher level: that of the story, the anecdote, the diegesis (which confirms that the diegesis must be treated as an autonomous system).* Rare in the fixed image, this word-as-relay becomes very important in cinema, where dialogue does not have a simple elucidative function but actually advances the action by inserting, in the sequence of messages, certain meanings which are not to be found in the image. The two functions of the linguistic message can of course coexist in the same iconic whole, but the dominance of one or the other is certainly not a matter of indifference to the work's general economy; when language has a relaying diegetic value, the information is more "costly," since it requires apprenticeship to a digital code (language); when it has a substitutive value (of anchoring, of control), it is the image which governs the informational charge, and since the image is analogical, the information is in some sense "lazier": in certain comic strips meant to be read rapidly, the diegesis is chiefly entrusted to the words, the image collecting the attributive information of a paradigmatic order (the stereotyped status of the characters): the "costly" message and the discursive message are made to coincide, so as to spare the hurried reader the bother of verbal "descriptions," here entrusted to the image, i.e., to a less "laborious" system.

* Cf. Claude Bremond, "Le Message narratif," *Communications* 4, 1964.

The Denoted Image

We have seen that, in the image proper, the distinction between the literal message and the symbolic message is operational; we never—at least never in advertising—encounter a literal image in the pure state; even if an entirely "naïve" image were to be achieved, it would immediately join the sign of naïveté and be completed by a third, symbolic message. Thus, the characteristics of the literal message cannot be substantial, but only relational; one might say that it is first of all a privative message, constituted by what remains in the image when we (mentally) erase the signs of connotation (it would not be possible to take them away in actuality, for they can impregnate the entire image, as in the case of the "still-life composition"); this privative state naturally corresponds to a plenitude of possibilities: it is a matter of an absence of meaning charged with all meanings; it is next (and this is no contradiction of the foregoing) a sufficient message, for it has at least one meaning on the level of the identification of the represented scene; the literalness of the image corresponds in short to the first degree of intelligibility (below which the reader would perceive only lines, shapes, colors), but this intelligibility remains possible by virtue of its very "poverty," for each of us, as the product of a real society, always possesses a knowledge higher than mere anthropological knowledge and perceives more than the literal; at once private and sufficient, it is understandable that in an aesthetic perspective the denoted message can appear as a kind of Adamic state of the image; utopianly rid of its connotations, the image would become radically objective, i.e., ultimately innocent.

This utopian character of denotation is considerably reinforced by the paradox already mentioned, which makes the photograph (in its literal state), by reason of its absolutely analogical nature, seem to constitute a message without a code. Yet the structural analysis of the image must here be specified, for, of all images, only the photograph possesses the power to transmit (literal) information without forming it with the help of discontinuous signs and rules of transformation. Hence, we must set the photograph, a message without code, in opposition to the drawing, which, even denoted, is a coded message. The coded nature of the drawing appears on three levels. First of all, to reproduce an object or a scene by drawing necessitates a set of *regulated* transformations; there is no such thing as a *nature* of the pictorial copy, and the codes of transposition are historical (notably with regard to perspective). Second, the operation of the drawing (the coding) immediately necessitates a certain division between what signifies and what does not: the drawing does not reproduce *everything*, and often very little, though without ceasing to be a powerful message, whereas the photograph, if it can select its subject, its framing, and its angle, cannot intervene within the object (except by trick effects); in other words, the denotation of drawing is less pure than photographic denotation, for there is never a drawing without style. Third, like all codes, drawing requires an apprenticeship (Saussure attributed a great importance to this semiological phenomenon). Does the coding of the denoted message have certain consequences for the connoted message? It is certain that the coding of the literal prepares and facilitates connotation, since it already establishes a certain discontinuity in the image: the "making" of a drawing already constitutes a connotation; but at the same time, insofar as the drawing parades its coding, the relation of the two messages is profoundly modified; it is no longer the relation between a nature and a culture (as in the case of the photograph) but the relation between two cultures: the "morality" of the drawing is not that of the photograph.

In the photograph, in effect—at least on the level of the literal message—the relation between signifieds and signifiers is not one of "transformation" but of "registration," and the absence of a code obviously reinforces the myth of photographic "naturalness": the scene *is there*, registered mechanically, but not humanly (the mechanical is here the warrant of objectivity); the human interventions in the photograph (framing, range, light, focus, speed, etc.) all belong as a matter of fact to the level of connotation; everything happens as if there were at the (even if utopian) outset a raw (frontal and distinct) photograph, upon which man might arrange, thanks to certain techniques, the signs resulting from the cultural code. Only the opposition of the cultural code and the natural non-code can account, it would appear, for the specific character of the photograph and permit us to measure the anthropological revolution which it represents in human history, for the type of consciousness it implies is indeed unprecedented; the photograph institutes, in fact, not a consciousness of the thing's *being-there* (which any copy might provoke), but a consciousness of the thing's *having-been-there*. Hence, we are concerned with a new category of space-time: immediately spatial and anteriorly temporal; in the photograph an illogical conjunction occurs between the *here* and the *then*. Hence, it is on the level of this denoted message or message without a code that we can fully understand the photograph's *real unreality*; its unreality is that of the *here*, for the photograph is never experienced as an illusion, it is in no way a *presence*, and we must deflate the magical character of the photographic image; and its reality is that of *having-been-there*, for in every photograph there is the always stupefying evidence of: *this is how it was*: we then possess, by some precious miracle, a reality from which we are sheltered. This kind of temporal equilibrium (*having-been-there*) probably diminishes the image's projective power (very few psychological tests resort to photography, many resort to drawings): the *this has been* triumphs over the *this is me*.

If these remarks have any accuracy, we must therefore link photography to a pure spectatorial consciousness and not to the more projective, more "magical" fictional consciousness on which cinema by and large depends; hence, we should be justified in seeing, between cinema and the photograph, no longer a simple difference of degree but a radical opposition: the cinema is not an animated photograph; in it the *having-been-there* vanishes, giving way to a *being-there* of the thing; this would explain how there can be a history of the cinema, without a real break with the previous arts of fiction, whereas photography somehow escapes history (despite the development of the techniques and ambitions of photographic art) and represents a "matte" anthropological phenomenon, at once absolutely new and never to be transcended; for the first time in its history, humanity knows *messages without a code*. Hence the photograph is not the last (improved) term of the great family of images, but corresponds to a crucial mutation of the economies of information.

In any case, the denoted image, insofar as it implies no code (this is the case of the advertising photograph), assumes in the general structure of the iconic message a particular role which we can begin to specify (we shall return to this question once we have discussed the third message): the denoted image naturalizes the symbolic message, it makes "innocent" the very dense (especially in advertising) semantic artifice of connotation; although the Panzani poster is full of "symbols," there nonetheless remains in the photograph a kind of natural *being-there* of objects, insofar as the literal message is sufficient: nature seems to produce the represented scene quite spontaneously; the simple validity of openly semantic systems gives way surreptitiously to a pseudo-truth; the absence of a code de-intellectualizes the message because it seems to institute in nature the signs of culture. This is doubtless an important historical paradox: the more technology develops the circulation of information (and notably of images), the more means it provides of masking the constructed meaning under the appearance of the given meaning.

Rhetoric of the Image

We have seen that the signs of the third message ("symbolic" message, cultural or connoted) were discontinuous; even when the signifier seems to extend to the entire image, it is nonetheless a sign separated from the rest; "composition" carries an aesthetic signified, somewhat the way intonation, though suprasegmental, is a signifier isolated from language; hence, we are here dealing with a normal system whose signs are drawn from a cultural code (even if the linkage of the sign's elements appears more or less analogical). What constitutes the originality of this system is that the number of readings of the same lexia (of the same image) varies according to individuals: in the Panzani ad here analyzed, we have located four signs of connotation; there are probably others (the string bag, for example, can signify the miraculous draught of fishes, plenty, etc.). Yet the variation in readings is not anarchic, it depends on the different kinds of knowledge invested in the image (practical, national, cultural, aesthetic knowledge), and these kinds of knowledge can be classified, can join a typology; everything occurs as if the image presented itself to several people who might very well coexist in a single individual: *the same lexia mobilizes different lexicons*. What is a lexicon? It is a portion of the symbolic level (of language) which corresponds to a body of practices and techniques;* this is certainly the case

* Cf. A. J. Greimas, "Les problèmes de la description mécanographique," in *Cahiers de lexicologie* (Besançon) 1, 1959.

for the different readings of the image: each sign corresponds to a body of "attitudes": tourism, housekeeping, knowledge of art, some of which can obviously be missing on the level of any one individual. There is a plurality and a coexistence of lexicons in the same person; the number and identity of these lexicons form in a sense each person's *idiolect*. The image, in its connotation, would thus be constituted by an architecture of signs drawn from a variable depth of lexicons (of idiolects), each lexicon, however "deep," remaining coded, if, as we now think, the *psyche* itself is articulated like a language; better still: the further we "descend" into an individual's psychic depth, the more the signs are rarefied and the more classifiable they become: what is more systematic than the readings of Rorschach tests? The variability of readings therefore need not threaten the image's "language," if we grant that this language is composed of idiolects, lexicons, or sub-codes: the image is crisscrossed by the system of meaning, exactly as man is articulated to his very depths in distinct languages. The language of the image is not merely the entirety of utterances emitted (for example, on the level of the combiner of signs or the creator of the message), it is also the entirety of the utterances received;* such language must include the "surprises" of meaning.

Another difficulty attached to the analysis of connotation is that no particular analytic language corresponds to the particularity of its signifieds; how to name the signifieds of connotation? For one of them, we have ventured the term *Italianicity*, but the others can only be designated by forms from the usual language (*culinary preparation, still life, plenty*); the metalanguage which must take them over at the moment of analysis is not particularized. Here is an obstacle, for such signifieds

* In the Saussurian perspective, speech is above all what is emitted, drawn from language (and constituting it in return). Today we must enlarge the notion of language, especially from the semantic point of view: language is "the totalizing abstraction" of the messages emitted *and received*.

have a particular semantic nature; as a *seme* of connotation, "plenty" does not exactly coincide with "plenty" in its denoted meaning; the signifier of connotation (here the profusion and condensation of the products) is a kind of essential cipher of all possible plenties, or better still of the purest idea of plenty; the denoted word never refers to an essence, for it is always caught up in a contingent speech, a continuous syntagm (that of verbal discourse), oriented toward a certain practical transitivity of language; the seme "plenty," on the contrary, is a concept in the pure state, cut off from any syntagm, deprived of any context; it corresponds to a kind of theatrical state of meaning, or better still (since we are dealing with a sign without syntagm) to an *exposed* meaning. In order to render these semes of connotation, then, we must resort to a particular metalanguage; we have ventured *Italianicity*; it is barbarisms of this sort which might best account for signifieds of connotation, for the suffix-*icity* served to produce an abstract substantive from the adjective: *Italianicity* is not Italy; it is the condensed essence of all that can be Italian, from spaghetti to painting. By agreeing to govern artificially—and if need be quite barbarously—the naming of the semes of connotation, we might facilitate the analysis of their form;* these semes are obviously organized in associative fields, in paradigmatic articulations, perhaps even in oppositions, according to certain paths, or as Greimas says, according to certain semic axes:† Italianicity belongs to a certain axis of nationalities, alongside Francicity, Germanicity, or Hispanicity. The reconstitution of these axes—which, moreover, can subsequently be in opposition to each other—will obviously be possible only when we have proceeded to a massive inventory of connotation systems, not only that of the image but also those of other substances,

---

* *Form*, in the specific meaning Hjelmslev gives it, as the functional organization of the signifieds among themselves.

† Greimas, *Cours de sémantique*, 1964, notes mimeographed by the Ecole Normale Supérieure de Saint-Cloud.

for if connotation has typical signifiers according to the substances used (image, language, objects, behavior), it puts all
its signifieds in common: they are the same signifieds that we
will recognize in the printed word, the image, or the actor's
gesture (which is why semiology is conceivable only in a context that would be, so to speak, total); this common realm of
the signifieds of connotation is that of *ideology*, which cannot
help being one and the same for a given history and society,
whatever the signifiers of connotation to which it resorts.

To the general ideology, then, correspond signifiers of connotation which are specified according to the substance chosen.
We shall call these signifiers *connotators* and the totality of
the connotators a *rhetoric*: thus, rhetoric appears as the signifying aspect of ideology. Rhetorics inevitably vary by their
substance (here articulated sound, there image, gesture, etc.),
but not necessarily by their form; it is even probable that there
exists a single rhetorical *form*, common, for example, to the
dream, to literature, and to the image.* Thus, the rhetoric
of the image (i.e., the classification of its connotators) is specific insofar as it is subject to the physical constraints of vision
(different from phonatory constraints, for instance), but general insofar as the "figures" are never anything but formal relations of elements. This rhetoric could only be constituted on
the basis of a very broad inventory, but we can foresee even
now that in it will be found several of the figures formerly identified by the Ancients and the Classics;† thus, the tomato signifies
Italianicity by metonymy; elsewhere, the sequence of three

* Cf. E. Benveniste, "Remarques sur la fonction du langage dans la
découverte freudienne," in *La Psychanalyse* 1, 1956; reprinted in *Problèmes de linguistique générale* (Paris: Gallimard, 1966).

† Classical rhetoric needs to be rethought in structural terms (the object
of a work in progress), and it will then perhaps be possible to establish a
general rhetoric or linguistics of the signifiers of connotation, valid for
articulated sound, image, gesture, etc. [See, subsequently, *L'Ancienne
rhétorique* (Aide-mémoire), in *Communications* 16, 1970.—Ed.]

scenes (coffee in the bean, powdered coffee, coffee sipped) reveals by simple juxtaposition a certain logical relation in the same manner as an asyndeton. It is probable, as a matter of fact, that among the metabolas (or figures of substitution of one signifier for another),* it is metonymy which furnishes the image with the greatest number of its connotators; and that among the parataxes (or syntagmatic figures), it is the asyndeton which predominates.

Yet the most important thing—at least for the moment—is not to inventory the connotators but to understand that they constitute within the total image *discontinuous features* or, better still, *erratic features.* The connotators do not fill the entire lexia; reading them does not exhaust it. In other words (and this would be a proposition valid for semiology in general), all the elements of the lexia cannot be transformed into connotators; there still remains in discourse a certain denotation without which, in fact, discourse would not be possible. This brings us back to the second message, or denoted image. In the Panzani ad, the Mediterranean vegetables, the color, the composition, the very profusion appear as erratic blocks, at once isolated and set in a general scene which has its own space and, as we have seen, its "meaning": they are "caught" in a syntagm *which is not theirs and which is that of denotation.* This is an important proposition, for it allows us to establish (retroactively) the structural distinction between the second or literal message and the third or symbolic message, and to specify the naturalizing function of denotation in relation to connotation; we now know that *it is specifically the syntagm of the denoted message which "naturalizes" the system of the connoted message.* Or again: connotation is only system, it

---

* We prefer to avoid here Jakobson's opposition between metaphor and metonymy, for if metonymy is a figure of contiguity by its origin, it nonetheless functions ultimately as a substitute for the signifier, i.e., as a metaphor.

cannot be defined except in paradigmatic terms; iconic denotation is only syntagm, it associates elements without any system; the discontinuous connotators are linked, actualized, "spoken" through the syntagm of denotation: the discontinuous world of symbols plunges into the narrative of the denoted scene as into a lustral bath of innocence.

Whereby we see that in the total system of the image the structural functions are polarized; on one hand there is a sort of paradigmatic condensation on the level of the connotators (i.e., by and large, of the "symbols"), which are strong, erratic, and one might say "reified" signs; and on the other there is a syntagmatic "flow" on the level of denotation; it will not be forgotten that the syntagm is always very close to speech, and it is indeed the iconic "discourse" which naturalizes its symbols. Without seeking to infer too quickly from the image to semiology in general, we can nonetheless venture that the world of total meaning is torn internally (structurally) between the system as culture and the syntagm as nature: the works of mass communication all conjugate, through diverse and diversely successful dialectics, the fascination of a nature, that of narrative, of diegesis, of syntagm, and the intelligibility of a culture, sequestered in a few discontinuous symbols which men "decline" in the shelter of their living speech.

1964

The Third Meaning

I

Here is an image from *Ivan the Terrible* (I): two courtiers, confederates, or supernumeraries (it doesn't matter whether or not I recall the story's details exactly) are showering the young tsar's head with gold. I believe I can distinguish three levels of meaning in this scene:

1. An informational level: everything I can learn from the setting, the costumes, the characters, their relationships, their insertion in an anecdote familiar to me (however vaguely). This level is that of *communication*. If I had to find a mode of analysis for it, I should resort to a primary semiotics (that of

the "message"), though I shall not deal with this level and this semiotics here.

2. A symbolic level: the shower of gold. This level is itself stratified. There is a referential symbolism: the imperial ritual of baptism by gold. Then there is a diegetic symbolism: the theme of gold, of wealth (assuming it exists) in *Ivan the Terrible*, which in this image would make a significant intervention. There is also an Eisensteinian symbolism—if, say, a critic decided to show that gold, or a shower of gold, or the curtain constituted by this shower, or the disfigurement it produces, can participate in a system of displacements and substitutions characteristic of Eisenstein. Finally, there is a historical symbolism, if it can be shown, in a manner even more generalized than the preceding, that gold introduces a (theatrical) function, a scenography of exchange which we can locate both psychoanalytically and economically, i.e., semiologically. This second level, in its totality, is that of *signification*. Its mode of analysis would be a more highly elaborated semiotics than the first, a second or neo-semiotics no longer accessible to a science of the message but to sciences of the symbol (psychoanalysis, economics, dramaturgy).

Is this all? No, for I cannot yet detach myself from the image. I read, I receive (probably straight off, in fact) a third meaning, erratic yet evident and persistent.* I do not know what its signified is, at least I cannot give it a name, but I can clearly see the features—the signifying accidents of which this heretofore incomplete sign is composed. There is a certain density of the courtiers' makeup, in one case thick and emphatic, in the other smooth and "distinguished"; there is the "stupid"

* In the classical paradigm of the five senses, the third is hearing (the most important in the Middle Ages); this is a fortunate coincidence, for we are here concerned with *listening*, first because Eisenstein's remarks used here come from a consideration of the advent of sound in film; then because listening (without reference to the *phoné* alone) potentially releases the metaphor best suited to the "textual": orchestration (Eisenstein's word), counterpoint, stereophony.

nose on one and the delicate line of the eyelids on the other, his dull blond hair, his wan complexion, the affected smoothness of his hairstyle which suggests a wig, the connection with chalky skin tints, with rice powder. I am not certain whether my reading of this third meaning is justified—if it can be generalized—but already it seems to me that its signifier (the features I have just attempted to express, if not to describe) possesses a theoretical individuality. For, on the one hand, this signifier cannot be identified with the simple *Dasein* of the scene; it exceeds the copy of the referential motif, it compels an interrogative reading—an interrogation bearing precisely on the signifier, not on the signified, on the reading, not on intellection: it is a "poetic" apprehension. On the other hand, it cannot be identified with the episode's dramatic meaning. To say that these features refer to a significant "expression" of the courtiers, here remote and bored, there diligent (*"They are simply doing their job as courtiers"*), does not altogether satisfy me. Something in these two faces transcends psychology, anecdote, function, and, in short, meaning, though without being reduced to the persistence which any human body exerts by merely being present. In opposition to the first two levels, that of communication and that of signification, this third level— even if my reading of it is still uncertain—is that of *signifying* [*signifiance*], a word that has the advantage of referring to the field of the signifier (and not of signification) and of approaching, along the trail blazed by Julia Kristeva, who proposed the term, a semiotics of the text.

Signification and signifying—and not communication—are what concern me here. I must therefore name as economically as possible the second and the third meaning. The symbolic meaning (the shower of gold, power, wealth, the imperial rite) compels my recognition by a double determination. It is intentional (it is what the author has meant) and it is selected from a kind of general, common lexicon of symbols; it is a meaning which seeks me out—me, the recipient of the message, the subject of the reading—a meaning which proceeds from Eisenstein and moves *ahead of me*. It is evident, of course (as is the other meaning, too), but evident in a *closed* sense, participating in a complete system of destination. I propose to call this complete sign *the obvious meaning. Obvius* means *moving ahead*, which is just the case with this meaning, which seeks me out. In theology, we are told, the obvious meaning is the one "which presents itself quite naturally to the mind," and this, too, is the case: to me the symbolics of a shower of gold has always seemed endowed with a "natural" clarity. As for the other, the third meaning, the one which appears "in excess," as a supplement my intellection cannot quite absorb, a meaning both persistent and fugitive, apparent and evasive, I propose calling it *the obtuse meaning*. This word readily comes to my mind, and miraculously, upon exploring its etymology, I find it already yields a theory of the supplementary meaning; *obtusus* means *blunted, rounded*. Now, the features I have indicated—makeup, whiteness, false hair, etc.—are they not a kind of blunting of a too evident meaning, a too violent meaning? Do they not give the obvious signified a kind of ineffable roundness, do they not cause my reading to *skid*? An obtuse angle is greater than a right angle: *an obtuse angle of* 100°, says the dictionary; the third meaning, too, seems to me greater than the pure perpendicular, the trenchant, legal upright of the narrative. It seems to me to open the field of meaning totally, i.e., infinitely. I even accept, for this obtuse meaning, the word's pejorative connotation: the obtuse meaning seems to extend beyond culture, knowledge, information. Analytically, there is something ridiculous about it; because it opens onto the infinity of language, it can seem limited in the eyes of analytic reason. It belongs to the family of puns, jokes, useless exertions; indifferent to moral or aesthetic categories (the trivial, the futile, the artificial, the parodic), it sides with the carnival aspect of things. *Obtuse* therefore suits my purpose well.

The Obvious Meaning

A few words here about the obvious meaning, though it is not the object of these notes. Here are two images which present it in the pure state: the four figures of image II "symbolize" three ages of life, the unanimity of mourning (Vakulinchuk's funeral); the clenched fist of image III, a close-up shot, signifies indignation, controlled or channeled anger, determined opposition; joined metonymically to the entire *Potemkin* story, it "symbolizes" the working class, its power, and its will; for— a miracle of semantic intelligence—this fist *seen upside down,* kept by its owner in a kind of secrecy (it is the hand which *first of all* hangs naturally alongside the trousers and which *then* closes, tightens, conceives at one and the same time its future combat, its patience, and its discretion), cannot be read as some brawler's fist, I might even say as a fascist's fist: it is *immediately* a proletarian fist. Whereby we see that Eisenstein's "art" is not polysemous: it selects meaning, imposes it, belabors it (if signification is encroached on by the obtuse meaning, it is not thereby denied or blurred). The Eisensteinian meaning overwhelms ambiguity. How? By the addition of an aesthetic value, emphasis. Eisenstein's "decorativeness" has an economic function: it proffers truth. Consider image IV: grief emanates, quite classically, from the bent heads, the suffering faces, the hand over the mouth choking back a sob; but once all this has been said, quite adequately, it is repeated all over again by a decorative feature: the superimposition of the two hands, aesthetically arranged in a delicate, maternal, floral ascension toward the bending face. Within the general detail (the two women), another detail is inscribed *en abîme*; derived from a pictorial order like a quotation of gestures from

II

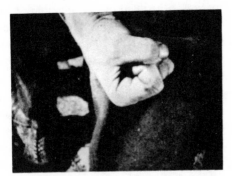

III

IV

icons and the Pietà, it does not distract meaning but accentuates it. This accentuation (characteristic of all realistic art) has some connection here with "truth," the truth of *Potemkin*. Baudelaire spoke of "the emphatic truth of gesture in the great circumstances of life"; here it is the truth of the "great proletarian circumstance" which requires emphasis. The Eisensteinian aesthetic does not constitute an independent level: it participates in the obvious meaning, and the obvious meaning is always, in Eisenstein, the Revolution.

The Obtuse Meaning

I first had the conviction of the obtuse meaning with regard to image V. A question occurred to me: What is it about this old woman weeping that raises the question of the signifier for me? I quickly decided that, however perfect they might be, it was neither the countenance nor the gestural repertoire of grief (closed eyelids, drawn mouth, fist over the breast): all that belongs to full signification, to the obvious meaning of the image, to Eisensteinian realism and decorativeness. I felt that the

V   VI

penetrating feature—disturbing as a guest who persists in staying at the party without uttering a word, even when we have no
need of him—must be located in the area of the forehead: the
kerchief had something to do with it. Yet in image VI the
obtuse meaning vanishes, there is no more than a message of
grief. I realized then that the "scandal," the supplement or
deviation imposed upon this classical representation of grief,
derived quite explicitly from a tenuous relation: that of the low
kerchief, the closed eyes, and the convex mouth, or rather, to
adopt Eisenstein's own distinction between "the shadows of
the cathedral" and "the shadowy cathedral," from a relation
between the "lowness" of the kerchief, worn abnormally close
to the eyebrows as in those disguises which seek to create a
foolish and stupid expression, the circumflex accent formed by
the old, faded eyebrows, the excessive curve of the lowered eyelids, close-set but apparently squinting, and the bar of the half-
open mouth corresponding to the curve of the kerchief and to
that of the brows, metaphorically speaking, "like a fish out of
water." All these features (the absurdly low kerchief, the old
woman, the squinting eyelids, the fish) have as a vague reference a somewhat low language, the language of a rather
pathetic disguise. United with the noble grief of the obvious
meaning, they form a dialogism so tenuous that there is no
guarantee of its intentionality. The characteristic of this third
meaning—at least in Eisenstein—actually blurs the limit separating expression from disguise, but also presents this oscillation quite succinctly: an elliptical emphasis, so to speak, a
complex, very intricate arrangement (for it implies a temporality of signification), which is perfectly described by Eisenstein himself when he jubilantly quotes old King Gillette's
golden rule: "Just short of the cutting edge."

The obtuse meaning, then, has something to do with disguise. Consider Ivan's beard, promoted, as I see it, to the status
of an obtuse meaning in image VII: it calls attention to itself

as false yet nonetheless refuses to abandon the "good faith" of its referent (the tsar's historical countenance). An actor disguises himself twice over (once as actor in the anecdote, once as actor in the dramaturgy), without the one disguise destroying the other; a layering of meanings which always allows the previous one to subsist, as in a geological formation; to speak the contrary without renouncing the thing contradicted: Brecht would have enjoyed this (two-term) dramatic dialectic! Eisensteinian "falsification" is both a false version of itself, i.e., a pastiche or parody, and a ridiculous fetish, since it exposes both severance and suture. What we see, in image VII, is the reattachment, hence the previous detachment, of the beard perpendicular to the chin. That the top of the head (the most "obtuse" part of the human person), that no more than a hank of hair (in image VIII) can be the *expression* of grief—that is what is ridiculous (about the expression, not about the grief). Hence, there is no parody, no trace of burlesque; grief is not aped (the obvious meaning must remain revolutionary, the general mourning which accompanies Vakulinchuk's death has a historical meaning), and yet, "incarnate" in this chignon, grief affords a severance, a rejection of contamination. The folk significance of the wool scarf (obvious meaning) *stops* at the chignon; here begins the fetish—the hank of hair—a kind of *non-negating mockery* of expression. The entire obtuse meaning (its power to disturb) functions in the excessive wad of hair. Consider another chignon (that of the woman in image IX): it contradicts the tiny raised fist, atrophies it without this reduction having the slightest symbolic (intellectual) value; prolonged by ringlets, drawing the face toward an ovine model, it gives the woman something *touching* (as a certain generous stupidity can often be touching) or even something *sensitive*. These outdated words—they are, in fact, anything but political or revolutionary, being adjectives of a certain mystification— must nonetheless be assumed; I believe that the obtuse mean-

VII

VIII

IX

ing carries a certain *emotion*; caught up in the disguise, this emotion is never viscous; it is an emotion which simply *designates* what is loved, what is to be defended; it is an emotion-as-value, an evaluation. Everyone, I think, can agree that Eisenstein's proletarian ethnography, fragmented throughout Vakulinchuk's funeral, is constantly suffused with love (taking the word without specification as to age or sex): maternal, heartfelt, virile, "sympathetic" without resorting to stereotypes, the Eisensteinian "people" is essentially *lovable*: we relish, we love the two round-capped men in image X, we enter into a complicity, an *intelligence* with them. Beauty can doubtless function as an obtuse meaning. This is the case in image XI, where the very dense obvious meaning (Ivan's gesture, young Vladimir's half-wit stupidity) is fixed and/or shifted by Basmanov's handsomeness: but the eroticism included in the obtuse meaning (or rather: the eroticism this meaning manages to assume) does not constitute an aesthetic acceptance. Euphrosyne is ugly, "obtuse" (images XII and XIII), like the monk in image XIV, but such obtuseness transcends the anecdote, it becomes the blurring of meaning, its deflection: there is, in the obtuse meaning, an eroticism which includes the opposite of the beautiful and even what is external to such opposition, i.e., in the limit case, inversion, discomfort, and perhaps sadism: consider the soft innocence of the *Children in the Furnace* (XV), the schoolboy absurdity of their mufflers diligently wrapped around their throats, that curds-and-whey texture of their skin (and their eyes and mouths set in that skin) which Fellini seems to have borrowed for the hermaphrodite of his *Satyricon*: this is just the kind of thing Georges Bataille could have meant, particularly in that text in *Documents* which for me situates one of the possible regions of the obtuse meaning: *The queen's big toe* (I don't remember the exact title).

To continue (if these examples suffice to lead on to a few remarks of a more theoretical nature). The obtuse meaning **is**

X

XI

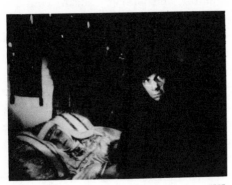

XII

XIII

XIV

XV

not in the language system (even that of symbols). Remove
it and communication and signification remain, circulate, pass.
Without it I can still speak and read, but it is not in speech
either; it may be that there is a certain constant in the Eisensteinian obtuse meaning, but then this is already a thematic
speech, an idiolect, and this idiolect is temporary (simply determined by some critic writing a book about Eisenstein); for
there are obtuse meanings not everywhere (the signifier is a
rare thing, a future figure) but *somewhere*: in other *authors* of
films (maybe), in a certain way of reading "life" and hence
"reality" (here understood in its simple opposition to the deliberately fictive). In this documentary image (XVI) from *Ordinary Fascism* I readily read an obvious meaning, that of fascism
(an aesthetic and symbolics of strength, the theatrical hunt),
but I also read an obtuse supplement; the (again) disguised
blond stupidity of the youth carrying the arrows, the slackness
of his hands and his mouth (I am not describing, I cannot
manage that, I am merely designating a site), Goering's coarse
nails, his trashy ring (here we are already at the limit of the
obvious meaning, like the vapid smile of the man in glasses in
the background, obviously an ass-kisser). In other words, the
obtuse meaning is not structurally situated, a semantologist

XVI

would not acknowledge its objective existence (but what is an objective reading?), and if it is evident to me, this is *still* perhaps (for the moment) because of the same "aberration" which *compelled* the unfortunate Saussure alone to hear an enigmatic, obsessive, and unoriginated voice, that of the anagram in ancient poetry. The same uncertainty when it is a matter of *describing* the obtuse meaning (of giving some idea of where it is going, where going away); the obtuse meaning is a signifier without signified; whence the difficulty of naming it: my reading remains suspended between the image and its description, between definition and approximation. If we cannot describe the obtuse meaning, this is because, unlike the obvious meaning, it copies nothing: how describe what represents nothing? Here the pictorial "rendering" of words is impossible. Consequently, if we remain, you and I, on the level of articulated language in the presence of these images—that is, on the level of my own text—the obtuse meaning will not come into being, will not enter into the critic's metalanguage. Which means that the obtuse meaning is outside (articulated) language, but still within interlocution. For if you look at these images I am talking about, you will see the meaning: we can understand each other about it "over the shoulder" or "on the back" of articulated language: thanks to the image (frozen, it is true: I shall return to this), indeed thanks to what in the image is purely image (and which, to tell the truth, is very little indeed), we do without speech yet continue to understand each other.

In short, what the obtuse meaning disturbs, sterilizes, is metalanguage (criticism). We can offer several reasons for this. First of all, the obtuse meaning is discontinuous, *indifferent* to the story and to the obvious meaning (as signification of the story); this dissociation has a *contra naturam* or at least a distancing effect with regard to the referent (to "reality" as nature, a realist instance). Eisenstein would probably have acknowledged and accepted this incongruity, this im-pertinence of the signifier, for it is he who remarks, apropos of sound and color: "Art begins the moment the creaking of a boot (on the sound track) accompanies a different visual shot and thereby provokes corresponding associations. The same is true of color: color begins where it no longer corresponds to natural coloration . . ." Thereupon, the signifier (the third meaning) is not filled; it is in a permanent state of *depletion* (a term from linguistics which designates the empty, all-purpose verbs—for example, the French verb *faire*); we might also say, on the other hand—and this would be quite as true—that this same signifier is not emptied (cannot be emptied); it maintains itself in a state of perpetual erethism; in it desire does not attain that spasm of the signified which usually causes the subject to sink voluptuously into the peace of nomination. Ultimately the obtuse meaning can be seen as an *accent*, the very form of an emergence, of a fold (even a crease) marking the heavy layer of information and signification. If it could be described (a contradiction in terms), it would have exactly the being of the Japanese haiku: an anaphoric gesture without significant content, a kind of gash from which meaning (the desire for meaning) is expunged; thus in image V:

> *Drawn mouth, squinting eyes,*
> *Kerchief low over her forehead,*
> *She weeps.*

This accent (whose simultaneously elliptical and emphatic nature we have discussed) does not tend toward meaning (as in hysteria); it does not theatricalize (Eisenstein's decorativeness belongs to another realm); it does not even indicate an *elsewhere* of meaning (another content, added to the obvious meaning), but baffles it—subverts not the content but the entire practice of meaning. A new—rare—practice affirmed against a majority practice (that of signification), the obtuse meaning inevitably appears as a luxury, an expenditure without exchange; this luxury does not *yet* belong to today's politics, though it is *already* part of tomorrow's.

A word remains to be said about the syntagmatic responsibility of this third meaning. What is its place in the anecdote's succession, in the logico-temporal system, without which, apparently, it is not possible for a narrative to be understood by the "mass" of readers and spectators? The obtuse meaning is clearly the epitome of counter-narrative; disseminated, reversible, trapped in its own temporality, it can establish (if followed) only an altogether different "script" from the one of shots, sequences, and syntagms (whether technical or narrative): an unheard-of script, counter-logical and yet "true." Imagine "following" not Euphrosyne's machinations or even the character (as a diegetic entity or as a symbolic figure), not even, further, the countenance of the Wicked Mother, but only, within this countenance, that grimace, that black veil, the heavy, ugly dullness of that skin. You will have another film. A theme with neither variations nor development (the obvious meaning, on the other hand, is thematic: there is a theme of the Funeral), the obtuse meaning can proceed only by appearing and disappearing; this operation of presence/absence undermines the character by making it a simple site of facets: a disjunction expressed on another point by Eisenstein himself: "What is characteristic is that the different positions of one and the same tsar . . . are given without transition from one position to another."

For that is the whole point: the supplementary signifier's *indifference*, or freedom of position with respect to narrative, permits locating Eisenstein's historical, political, theoretical achievements quite precisely. In his work, the story, the anecdotal, diegetic representation, is not destroyed; quite the contrary: what finer story than that of *Ivan*, that of *Potemkin*? This stature of narrative is necessary *in order to be understood* in a society which, unable to resolve the contradictions of history without a long political process, draws support (provisionally?) from mythic (narrative) solutions. The *present* problem is not to destroy narrative but to subvert it; to dissociate subversion from destruction is today's task. Eisenstein makes, it seems to me, just this distinction. The presence of a supplementary, obtuse, third meaning—even if only in a few images, but then as an imperishable signature, like a seal which endorses the entire work—and the entire oeuvre—this presence profoundly alters the theoretical status of the anecdote. The story (diegesis) is no longer merely a powerful system (an age-old narrative system), but also and contradictorily a simple space, a field of permanences and permutations; it becomes that configuration, that stage whose false limits multiply the signifier's permutative play; it is that vast outline which, by difference, compels a *vertical* reading (Eisenstein's word); it is that *false* order which permits us to avoid pure series, aleatory combination (chance is only a crude, a cheap signifier), and to achieve a structuration which *leaks from inside*. Hence, we can say that with Eisenstein we have to reverse the cliché which holds that the more gratuitous the meaning, the more it appears to be simply parasitic on the story told: on the contrary, it is this story which becomes somehow parametric to the signifier, of which it is no more than the field of displacement, the constitutive negativity, or again: the fellow traveler.

In short, the third meaning structures the film *differently*, without subverting the story (at least in Eisenstein), and for this reason, perhaps, it is at this level, and only here, that the "filmic" at last appears. The filmic is what, in the film, cannot be described, it is the representation that cannot be represented. The filmic begins only where language and articulated metalanguage cease. Everything we can *say* about *Ivan* or *Potemkin* can be said about a written text (which would be called *Ivan the Terrible* or *The Battleship Potemkin*), except this—which is the obtuse meaning; I can provide commentary for everything in Euphrosyne, except for the obtuse quality of her face: hence the filmic is precisely here, at this point where articulated language is no more than approximative and where another language begins (a language whose "science" cannot therefore be linguistics, soon discarded like a booster rocket). The third meaning, which we can locate theoretically but not describe, then appears as the *transition* from language to *signifying* [*signifiance*] and as the founding act of the filmic itself. Obliged to emerge from a civilization of the signified, it is not surprising that the filmic (despite the incalculable quantity of films in the world) should still be rare (a few flashes in Eisenstein; perhaps elsewhere?), to the point where we might assert that the film, like the text, does not yet exist: there is only "cinema," i.e., there is language, narrative, poetry, sometimes very "modern," "translated" into "images" said to be "animated." Nor is it surprising that we can perceive the filmic only after having traversed—analytically—the "essential," the "depth," and the "complexity" of the cinematic work—all riches belonging only to articulated language, out of which we constitute that work and believe we exhaust it. For the filmic is different from the film: the filmic is as far from the film as the novelistic is from the novel (I can write novelistically without ever writing novels).

The Still

This is why, to a certain extent (which is that of our theoretical approximations), the filmic, quite paradoxically, cannot be grasped in the projected film, the film "in movement," "*au naturel*," but only, as yet, in that major artifact which is the still. I have long been intrigued by this phenomenon: being interested and even obsessed by photographs from films (outside a theater, in the pages of *Cahiers du Cinéma*), and losing everything about these photographs (not just their immobilization but the very memory of the image itself) upon going inside the theater: a mutation which can lead to a complete reversal of values. I first attributed this preference for the still to my lack of cinematic culture, to my resistance to film; it seemed to me I was like those children who prefer "illustration" to text, or those consumers who cannot afford certain items and must be content with inspecting a choice of samples or a department-store catalogue. This explanation merely reproduces the common notion of the still as a remote sub-product of the film, a sample, a pornographic extract, and, technically, a reduction of the work through immobilization of what is supposed to be the cinema's sacred essence: the movement of the images.

If, though, the authentically filmic (the filmic of the future) is not in movement but in a third meaning, an inarticulate meaning which neither the simple photograph nor the figurative painting can assume because they lack the diegetic horizon, the possibility of configuration mentioned above,* then the "move-

---

* There are other "arts" which combine the still (or at least the drawing) and the story: these are the photo novel and the comic strip. I am convinced that these "arts," born in the lower depths of high culture, possess a theoretical qualification and afford a new signifier (related to the obtuse meaning); this is now acknowledged with regard to the comic strip; but I myself experience that minor trauma of signifying [signifiance] when looking at certain photo novels: "their stupidity touches me" (which might be a certain definition of the obtuse meaning); hence, there would be a future truth (or a truth from a very remote past) in these absurd, vulgar, stupid, dialogic forms from the subculture of consumption. And there would be an autonomous "art" (a "text"), that of the pictogram ("anecdotalized" images, obtuse meanings placed in a diegetic space); this art would cut across historically and culturally heteroclite productions: ethnographic pictograms, stained-glass windows, Carpaccio's Legend of Saint Ursula, images d'Epinal, photo novels, comic strips. The innovation represented by the movie still (in relation to these other pictograms) would be that the filmic (which it constitutes) is doubled by another text, the film.

ment" which is taken for the essence of film is not animation, flux, mobility, "life," copy, but merely the armature of a permutational unfolding, whereupon a theory of the still becomes necessary, whose possible points of departure must be indicated here, in conclusion.

The still gives us the *inside* of the fragment. We must here adopt, a little modified, Eisenstein's own formulations in discussing the new possibilities of audio-visual montage: ". . . the basic center of gravity . . . shifts to *inside* the fragment, into elements included within the image itself. And the center of gravity is no longer the element 'between shots'—the shock, but the element 'inside the shot'—the accentuation within the fragment . . ." Of course there is no audio-visual montage within the still, but Eisenstein's formulation is a general one, insofar as it establishes a right to syntagmatic disjunction of images and demands a *vertical* reading, as Eisenstein calls it, of the articulation. Moreover, the still is not a sample (a notion which assumes a kind of homogeneous, statistical nature of film's elements) but a quotation (we know how important this concept has become in today's theory of the text): it is therefore at once parodic and disseminative. It is not a specimen chemically extracted from the film's substance, but rather the trace of a superior *distribution* of features of which the film, experienced in its animated flow, would really be no more than one text among others. The still, then, is the fragment of a second text *whose existence never exceeds the fragment*; film and still meet in a palimpsest relation, without our being able to say that one is *above* the other or that one is *extracted* from the other. Finally, the still dissolves the constraint of filmic time; this constraint is a powerful one, it continues to obstruct what we might call the adult birth of film (born technically, sometimes even aesthetically, film is yet to be born theoretically). For written texts—unless they are extremely conventional, utterly committed to the logico-temporal order—reading time is free; for film, this is not so, since the image cannot move faster or slower without losing its perceptual figure. The still, by instituting a reading which is at once instantaneous and vertical, flouts logical time (which is only an operational time); it teaches us to dissociate technical constraint (the film's "projection") from the authentically filmic, which is the "indescribable" meaning. Perhaps it is *this other text* (here in stills) whose reading Eisenstein called for when he said that film is not to be simply seen and heard but *scrutinized* and closely listened to, *studied* by eye and ear alike. Such attention does not postulate, of course, a mere application of the mind (which would be no more than a banal requirement, a pious hope) but rather an authentic mutation of reading and its object, text or film: a major problem of our time.

1970

The Greek Theater

Toward the end of the seventh century B.C., the cult of Dionysus had produced, chiefly in the Dorian region between Corinth and Sicyon, a flourishing genre, half religious and half literary, consisting of choruses and dances—the dithyramb. Dithyrambic performances were said to have been introduced into Attica around 550 B.C. by a lyric poet, Thespis, who carted his effects from village to village and recruited his choruses on the spot. Some say that it was Thespis who created tragedy by introducing the first actor, others that it was his successor, Phrynichus. In any case, the new drama quickly received state consecration: it was sponsored by a strictly civic institution, the competition. The first Athenian tragedy contest apparently took place in 538 B.C. under Pisistratus, who wanted to embellish his tyranny with rites and festivals. The sequel is known: the theater was established on ground sacred to Dionysus, who remained the genre's patron: great poets (or, more accurately, great theatrical entrepreneurs), virtually contemporary with one another, gave dramatic performance its mature structure and its profound historical meaning; this flowering coincided with the triumph of democracy, the hegemony of Athens, the birth of history as a genre, and the sculpture of Phidias; this was the fifth century, the age of Pericles, and Greece's classical age. Then, from the fourth century to the end of the Alexandrian period, except for a few inspired resurgences about which we know very little (Menander and the New Comedy), there was a decline: mediocrity of the works, which vanished for that reason, and the gradual abandonment of the choral structure, which had been the specific feature of the Greek theater.

As "history," such an account remains somewhat mythic. Certain features are obscure, or at least hypothetical: we know nothing certain about how the Greek theater was related to the worship of Dionysus and we have lost—it must not be forgotten—almost its entire repertoire: whole genres, the dithyramb, Sicilian comedy, Epicharman comedy, the satyr play, of which virtually nothing remains; works by the hundreds: of several generations of dramatic authors, we know only three tragic poets and one comic poet: Aeschylus, Sophocles, Euripides, Aristophanes; and not only is the surviving work by each of these authors highly anthological (for example, seven tragedies out of the seventy Aeschylus is known to have written), but it is mutilated as well: all the tragic trilogies are incomplete, except for the *Oresteia*; without *Prometheus Unbound* we do not know the outcome Aeschylus assigned to the conflict between man and the gods. Other, better-known features are distorted by our image of classical synchrony: in its prestigious period, the fifth century, the Greek theater possesses only rudimentary techniques: its materiality is refined and enriched (or rather, complicated) precisely when the works themselves become mediocre; further, this theater continued to enjoy a great public success during its entire period of decline, so that if we were to apply to it sociological and no longer aesthetic criteria, the whole historical perspective would be altered.

The myth of the fifth century thus produces an image which is in need of many modifications. At least there is one truth in the image, which accounts for the fact that such a theater is constituted by an organized group of works, institutions, protocols, and techniques—it possesses a structure. And this structure is all the more important in that this theater's special feature was synthesis, the coherence of different dramatic codes. By immobilizing the Greek theater in the fifth century, we may lose a historical dimension, but we gain a structural truth, i.e., a signification.

Works

In the classical period, Greek spectacles included four chief genres: dithyramb, satyr play, tragedy, comedy. To which might be added the cortege which served as a prelude to the festivities, the *komos*, probably a survival of the processions (or more precisely, of the dionysiac *monomoi*); and, though these were more likely a kind of concert than a staged work, the thymelic entertainments, a kind of oratorio whose performers sat in the *orchestra* around the *thymele* or altar dedicated to Dionysus.

The dithyramb derives from certain episodes in the worship of Dionysus, in the seventh century B.C., probably near Corinth, a commercial and cosmopolitan city-state. It very soon took two forms: one literary and one popular, in which the text remained (largely) improvised. Brought to Athens by Thespis, the dithyramb was there regularized; the flowering of the dramatic genres (tragedy and comedy) in no way competed with it; dithyrambic performances took up the first two days of the Great Dionysia, before the days dedicated to the contests of tragedy and comedy. It was a kind of lyric drama whose subjects, mythological or occasionally historical, bore a close relation to those of tragedy. The (crucial) difference was that the dithyramb was performed without actors (even if there were soloists), and above all without masks and without costumes. The chorus was numerous: fifty performers, youths (under eighteen) or men. This was a cyclical chorus, that is, the choral dances were performed in the *orchestra* around the *thymele*, and not down front, facing the public, as in tragedy. The music used chiefly Oriental modes, and had a riotous signification (as opposed to the Apollonian paean); this music took increasing precedence over the text, which brings the dithyramb close to our opera. None of these dithyrambs survive, except a few mutilated fragments of Pindar.

We know almost as little about the satyr play, which is all the more inopportune since one invariably followed every tragic trilogy. Of this genre there survive only Sophocles' *Ichneutae*, Euripides' *Cyclops*, and some recently discovered fragments by Aeschylus. Also originating in Dorian regions, the satyr play was said to have been brought to Athens by Pratinas at about the beginning of Aeschylus' career; it was quickly incorporated into the tragic complex (three tragedies performed in sequence), thereby converted into a tetralogy. The satyr play is very close to tragedy; it has the same structure, and its subject is mythological. What differentiates and consequently constitutes it is that the chorus is always composed of Satyrs under the leadership of Silenus, adoptive father of Dionysus (in Athens the satyr play was also called a Silenic drama). This chorus has great dramatic importance and is the chief actor; it gives the genre its tone and makes it an "amusing tragedy," for these Satyrs are "rascals," "good-for-nothings," revelers who play tricks and tumble about (the satyr play ends happily); their dances have a grotesque character; they are costumed and masked.

Every work in this theater has a fixed structure, the occurrence of its parts is determined, and variations in order are insignificant. A Greek tragedy includes: a prologue, a preparatory scene of exposition (monologue or dialogue); the *parodos* or song for the entrance of the chorus; *episodes,* analogous to the acts of our plays (though of extremely various length), separated by danced choral songs known as *stasima* (half the chorus sang the strophes, the other half the antistrophes); the final episode, often formed by the chorus's exit, was called the *exodos.* Comedy reveals an analogous disposition of choral songs and recitation. Its structure, however, was somewhat different; in relation to tragedy, it includes two original elements: first of all, the *agon* or debate; this scene, which corresponds to the first episode of tragedy, is necessarily a scene of dispute, at the end of which the actor representing the poet's ideas vanquishes his adversary (for Athenian comedy is always a thesis play); and then, especially, the *parabasis;* this section follows the *agon*: the actors being (temporarily) absent from the stage, the chorus remove their cloaks, turn, and address the spectators directly; an (ideal) *parabasis* included seven pieces: a very brief song, the *kommation*; the *anapestes,* the speech of the coryphaeus (or leader of the chorus) to the public; the *pnigos* (suffocation), a long period spoken without taking a breath; finally, four symmetrical pieces, of strophic structure. Neither in tragedy nor in comedy (even less in comedy) were the unity of place and the unity of time necessary (though favored): in Aeschylus' (lost) *Aetnaeae,* the action shifted four times.

Whatever the variations may have been (either from author to author or historical), this structure has one constant feature, i.e., one meaning: the fixed alternation of the spoken and the sung, of action and commentary. Indeed, there may be better reason to call it "narrative" than "action"; in tragedy (at least), the episodes (our acts) are far from representing actions, that is, immediate modifications of situations; the action is generally refracted through intermediate modes of exposition which distance it by *telling* it: narratives (of battle or of murder), assigned to a typical role, that of the Messenger, or scenes of verbal dispute, which in a sense referred the action to its conflictual surface (the Greeks were very fond of these scenes, and it is virtually certain that public readings of them were given, outside of the actual performance). Here we see the dawn of the formal dialectical principle which establishes this theater: speech expresses action, but also screens it: "what happens" always tends toward "what has happened."

This narrated action is periodically suspended by the choral commentary which obliges the public to collect its thoughts in a simultaneously lyric and intellectual mode. For if the chorus comments on what has just happened before its eyes, this commentary is essentially an interrogation: the actor's "What has happened?" is answered by the chorus's "What is going to happen?" so that Greek tragedy (with which we are chiefly concerned) is always a triple spectacle: of a present (we are watching the transformation of a past into a future), of a freedom (what is to be done?), and of a meaning (the answer of gods and of men).

Such is the structure of the Greek theater: the organic alternation of what is being interrogated (the action, the scene, the dramatic speech) and of the man doing the interrogating (the chorus, the commentary, the lyric speech). And this "suspended" structure is the very distance which separates the world from the questions put to it. Already mythology itself had been the imposition of a vast semantic system upon nature. The Greek theater seizes upon the mythological answer and makes use of it as a reservoir of new questions: for to interrogate mythology is to interrogate what had been in its time a fulfilled answer. Itself an interrogation, the Greek theater thus takes its place between two other interrogations: one, religious, is mythology; the other, secular, is philosophy (in the fourth century B.C.). And it is true that this theater constitutes the path of art's gradual secularization: Sophocles is less "religious" than Aeschylus, Euripides than Sophocles. As the interrogation shifts to increasingly intellectual forms, tragedy evolves toward what we today call drama, even bourgeois comedy, based on conflicts of characters, not on conflicts of fate. And what marks this change of function is specifically the gradual atrophying of the interrogative element, i.e., of the chorus. The same evolution occurs in comedy; abandoning the interrogation of society (even if this contestation was regressive), political comedy (that of Aristophanes) becomes the comedy of plot, of character (with Philemon and Menander): tragedy and comedy then take human "truth" for their object; which is to say, for the theater the time of questions has passed.

Institutions

Religious theater or civic theater? Both together, of course: it could not be otherwise in a society where the notion of secularity was unknown. But the two elements do not have the same value: religion (it would be better to say *cult*) dominates the origin of the Greek theater, it is still present in the institutions which govern its mature phase; yet it is the city-state which gives the theater its meaning: its acquired characteristics create its being more than its innate ones. And if we are willing to leave aside, for the moment, the question of the chorus (which is, moreover, a transposed religious element), it can be said that the Dionysiac worship is present in the spectacle's coordinates (time and space), not in its substance.

We know that the theatrical performances could take place only three times a year, on the occasion of the festivals in honor of Dionysus. These were, in order of importance; the Great Dionysia, the Lenaean Dionysia, the Rural Dionysia. The Great (or City) Dionysia was a major Athenian festival (but the hegemony of Athens soon gave it a pan-Hellenic character) which took place in early spring, at the end of March; this festival lasted six days and normally included three contests (dithyramb, tragedy, comedy); it was during the Great Dionysia that most of the premieres of Aeschylus, Sophocles, and Euripides occurred. The Lenaean Dionysia occurred in January and was an exclusively Athenian festival, simpler than the Great Dionysia; it lasted only three or four days and did not include a dithyrambic competition. The Rural Dionysia occurred at the end of December, in the demes (townships) of Attica; the poor demes honored the god by a simple procession; the richer ones organized contests of tragedy and comedy; but only revivals were given on these occasions, except in the richest demes, such as Piraeus, where, according to Socrates, one of Euripides' premieres occurred.

For all these festivals, the theater (i.e., literally: *the place where one sees*) was built on ground dedicated to Dionysus. The consecration of the theater site involved a consecration of everything which occurred there: the spectators wore religious garlands, the performers were anointed, and conversely, misdemeanors became sacrileges. On this consecrated ground, two sites testified more specifically to the worship of the god: in the *orchestra*, probably dominated by the statue of Dionysus which had been installed there with great ceremony at the beginning of the festival, the *thymele*; what was the *thymele*? probably an altar, perhaps a trench to receive the blood of the victims; in any case, a sacrificial place; and in the *cavea*, which is to say the series of rows, certain places reserved for the clergy of the various Athenian cults (invariably an *occasional* clergy, since the priesthood was elective, either by lot or purchase, never vocational); the right to such places of honor was known as the *proedria*: it was extended to high dignitaries and to certain guests.

Evidently these were marginal institutions: once the performance was under way, no ritual element of worship intervened further (except perhaps for certain evocations of the dead, certain divine invocations). Yet a religious origin is commonly attributed to the very substance of the Greek spectacle, manifestly secularized in the classical period. What is the precise nature of this? Its origin is not arguable; what is hypothetical is the mode of filiation. The most familiar hypothesis is Aristotle's; tragedy is born of the satyr play, and the satyr play of the dithyramb; comedy followed a different path, deriving from certain phallic songs; Aristotle does not deal with the dithyramb's link to the cult of Dionysus; hence, this is the link which modern scholars have long attempted to explain. But is the internal filiation of the first three genres a precise one? Nowadays this has been cast into doubt; it is thought that only the dithyramb, the satyr play, and comedy can be linked to Dionysus (tragedy constituting a case apart), and that the filiation, for each genre, is direct: in short, tragedy is no longer, as Aristotle claimed, the gradual revelation of an essence (that of serious imitation or *mimesis*).

We know that the cult of Dionysus, interfused with Oriental elements, included veritable dances of possession to which the god's *thiasos* (or confraternity) was subject—they were the very symbol of his procession. Similarly, the dithyramb's cyclic dance reproduced the collective rounds of those possessed by the divine *mania*, and we know from other Oriental customs still observed by Islam in the last century that such whirling figures were both the expression and the exorcism of collective hysteria. As for the satyr play, its cultural heredity was apparently a double one: on one hand, its dances, consisting of wild leaps, reproduced the individual (and no longer the collective) *mania*, which has been identified with Charcot's convulsive *grande attaque*; on the other, its costumes (for the Satyrs were disguised and masked) derived from extremely ancient revels, including the use of horse-masks (the horse was then the animal of the underworld). Comedy, lastly, at least in its initial segments (*parodos, agon,* and *parabasis*), extended the *komoi,* which were scenarios of strolling revelers, performed by masked youths who opened the cult ceremonies.

As can be seen, and to summarize drastically, the link uniting Dionysiac worship to these three genres is of a more or less physical order: it is possession, or, to be even more precise, it is hysteria (whose "natural" relation to theatrical practices we are familiar with), of which dance is at once the fulfillment and the release. It is perhaps in this context that the notion of theatrical *catharsis* should be understood; we know that this notion, taken from Aristotle, has served as a theme for most discussions of tragedy's goal and purpose, from Racine to Lessing. Is it tragedy's more or less utilitarian task to "purge" all our passions by provoking pity and terror in us, or merely to rid us of that pity and that terror? There has been a great deal of dispute as to the nature of these passions, the objects and goals of theatrical imitation. Yet it is the notion of *catharsis* itself which remains most ambiguous: is passion to be "deracinated" (in Corneille's fine word), or, more modestly, is it to be purged, sublimated by ridding it of all irrational excess (Racine)? It would be futile to deny this debate whatever authenticity history has afforded it, but from a historical viewpoint, it is somewhat futile in the first place. Neither Corneille nor Racine nor Lessing could have any idea of the context, at once mystical and medical, so to speak, which probably confers its true meaning upon the notion of dramatic *catharsis;* in medical terms, *catharsis* is virtually the dénouement of the hysterical crisis; in mystical terms, it is both possession by and deliverance from the god—possession with a view to deliverance; it is difficult for today's "scientistic" vocabulary to accommodate such experiences, particularly when they must be associated with a theatrical performance (although psychodrama and sociodrama are restoring a certain currency to them); we can merely speculate that the ancient theater, insofar as it resulted from the cult of Dionysus, constituted a "total experience," mingling and summarizing certain intermediary, even contradictory states—in short a concerted practice of "dispossession" or, to use a more insipid but more contemporary term, of "alienation."

And tragedy? Paradoxically, this genre, the most prestigious of all the genres of which Dionysus was the patron, owed nothing—at least directly—to the cult of the god; through the strictly dionysiac genres, the city-state simply became receptive to a new dramatic form, elaborated by its poets; tragedy was, in its essence, a strictly Athenian creation to which the god, by mere proximity, accorded his theater and his patronage. If this is the case, we no longer need imagine a characterial relation between Dionysus and tragedy (such a relation has always been forced). Dionysus is a complex god—one might even call him dialectical: simultaneously a god of the underworld (of the world of the dead) and a god of renewal; he is, one might say, the very god of this contradiction. Of course, in the process of civilization, i.e., of accommodation to civic institutions, the dionysiac genres (dithyramb, satyr play, and comedy) purified, simplified, and moderated the god's disturbing character: this was a matter of emphasis. But, for tragedy, the autonomy is flagrant: nothing, in tragedy, can derive from dionysiac irrationality, whether demoniac or grotesque.

All this leads us to accentuate the civic character of the Greek theater, particularly with regard to tragedy: it is the city-state which accorded that theater its essence. The city-state, i.e., Athens, at once municipality and nation, a limited and a "worldwide" society. How did the spectacle fit into such a society? By means of three institutions: the choregy, the theoricon, and the competition.

The Greek theater was a theater legally offered to the poor by the rich. The choregy was a liturgy, i.e., an obligation officially imposed on rich citizens by the state: the choregus had to train and equip a chorus. In the classical period, the number of citizens who could be made responsible for a liturgy by reason of their fortune was about 1,200, out of the 40,000 citizens of Attica; it was among these that the archon chose the choregi for the year, as well as the choruses admitted to the competition; financial burdens were very heavy: the choregus had to rent the rehearsal space, pay for the equipment, furnish refreshments for the performers, and assume the daily salary of the artists; the expenses of a tragic choregus have been estimated at twenty-five minae, those of a comic choregus at fifteen minae (the mina roughly corresponded to a hundred days' salary of a non-skilled worker). When the state grew poor (at the end of the Peloponnesian War), a single choregy could be shared by two citizens: this was known as the synchoregy. Then the choregy disappeared altogether, giving way to the *agonothesia*, a kind of general commission of spectacles whose budget was funded in principle by the state but in fact, at least partially, by the commissioner himself (designated for one year). Obviously, a relationship can be established between the gradual loss of wealth and the disappearance of the chorus.

In principle, all citizens could attend the theater gratis, but since this resulted in tremendous overcrowding, a charge of two obols was made for each day of performance (a third of an unskilled workman's daily salary). This scarcely democratic charge—from which only the poor suffered—was quickly abolished and replaced by a state subvention for poor citizens; this subvention of two obols a head (diobelia) was determined around 410 by Cleophon, and the institution was given the name *theoricon*.

Choregy and theoricon assured the spectacle's material existence. A third—and no less important—institution would assure the democracy's control of its value (and we must not forget that the control of value is always a form of ideological censorship): the competition. We know the importance of the *agon*, the debate, in the public life of the ancient Greeks; it is virtually comparable to that of our own sports events.

From society's viewpoint, what is the function of the *agon?* No doubt, to mediate conflicts without censoring them. The competition permits retaining the question asked by the ancient duels (which is better?) but grants it a new meaning: which is better in relation to things, which is the better in order to master not man but nature? Here nature is art, i.e., a complete representation of religious and historical, moral and aesthetic values, and this phenomenon remains if not singular at least rare: art has rarely been subjected to such a system of disinterested competition.

The mechanism of the dramatic contests was complex, for the Greeks were very sensitive about the sincerity of their competitions. The archon, as we have seen, designated the choregi; he also established the list of poets qualified to compete (the poet was initially author and actor, then the poet himself selected his actors, and eventually a contest of tragedians was even instituted at the Great Dionysia); the distribution of the choregi (and of their chorus), on the one hand, and of the poets (and of their troupe), on the other, was governed by a lottery, democratically, i.e., by popular assembly. There were three contestants for tragedy (each offered a tetralogy), and three (later five) for comedy. Each work was performed only once, at least in the fifth century; later on, there were revivals: each competition was preceded by the performance of a classic (Euripides, above all).

The decision, which followed the festival, was entrusted to a jury of citizens, chosen by lot (we must not forget that for the Greeks a decision by lottery was a sign from the gods), in two stages: at the moment of the constitution of the jury (of ten citizens), i.e., before the performances, and after the vote, from which a new lottery retained only five final votes. There were prizes for the choregus, the poet, then later on for the protagonist (tripod or crown). The competition was closed by an official record engraved on marble.

It is difficult to imagine more powerful institutions, closer links between a society and its spectacle. And since this society was democratic precisely at the moment when the art of spectacle attained its peak, it is easy to make the Greek theater into the very model of a popular theater. Yet we must remember that, admirable as it was, Athenian democracy corresponded neither to the requirements nor to the conditions of a modern democracy. It has been called an aristocratic democracy: it excluded foreigners and slaves: there were only forty thousand citizens out of four hundred thousand inhabitants of Attica; these citizens could freely and abundantly participate in the festivals, and in the spectacles, insofar as other men worked for them. But in this limited group, where everyone knew everyone else, once it was constituted—and this again is what contrasts Athenian democracy to our own—a civic responsibility prevailed whose power is inconceivable nowadays; it is little enough to say that the Athenian citizen participated in public affairs: he *governed,* entirely immersed in power thanks to the numerous executive assemblies to which he belonged. And above all—another singularity—this responsibility was obligatory, i.e., constant, unanimous; it was the very framework of his mentality, nothing could be done, felt, or thought outside of a civic horizon. A popular theater? No. But a civic theater of the responsible state.

Protocols

This array of institutions must be completed by a list of uses, for a spectacle assumes its meaning only when it is integrated into the material life of its users.

The Greek theater was an essentially festive theater. The festival which brought it into being was an annual one lasting several days. Now, the formality and the extent of such a ceremony involves two consequences: first of all, a suspension of time; we know that the Greeks did not observe a weekly day of rest, a notion of Hebrew origin; they left off work only on the occasion of religious festivals, though these were numerous. Associated with the "loosening" of work time, the theater installed another time, a time of myth and of consciousness, which could be experienced not as leisure but as another life. For this suspended time, by its very duration, became a saturated time.

Here we must recall to what degree these feast days were *filled*. Before the festival itself, there was the *proagon*, a kind of pre-show in which the chosen poets and their troupe were presented to the crowd. The first day was dedicated to a procession which removed the statue of Dionysus from its temple and formally installed it in the theater; this procession was interrupted by a hecatomb of bulls, whose flesh, distributed to the crowd, was cooked on the spot. There followed two days of dithyrambic performances; a *komos* or cortege, the evening of the second day; then three days of dramatic performances: a tertralogy each morning (three tragedies and a satyr play, separated by a half-hour intermission) and a comedy each afternoon. Before the performance itself, other formalities, i.e., other spectacles: the entrance of honored personages into the *proedria*; the exhibition in the *orchestra* of the tribute of gold offered by allied city-states; the procession of the "pupils of the nation" in complete armor; the proclamation of honors awarded to certain citizens; a lustration, consisting of the blood of a young hog; and the trumpet call which announced the beginning of the spectacle proper. These festivals of ancient Greece were thus veritable "sessions" (the Great Dionysia lasted six days; each morning of tragedies about six hours, from dawn to noon, and of course the performances began again in the afternoon) during which the city-state lived theatrically, from the mask which was donned to attend the inaugural procession to the *mimesis* of the spectacle itself.

For here, contrary to our bourgeois theater, there was no physical break between the spectacle and its spectators; this continuity was assured by two basic elements, which our theater has recently attempted to rediscover: the circularity of the stage site and its openness.

The Greek theater's *orchestra* was perfectly circular (about twenty yards in diameter). The rows, usually built into a hillside, formed slightly more than a semicircle. Behind the *orchestra* was a structure whose interior served as wings and whose frontal wall as a support for the sets: the *skene*. Where did the performers act? At first, always in the *orchestra*, chorus and actors mingling (perhaps the actors possessed a low dais, several steps high, placed in front of the *skene*); then, later on (toward the end of the fourth century), a high but narrow *proskenion* was placed in front of the *skene*, to which the action was shifted, precisely when the chorus was losing its importance. The entire structure was first made of wood, the *orchestra* floor of beaten earth; the first stone theaters date from the middle of the fourth century. As we see, what is today called the stage (the entirety of the *skene* or of the *proskenion*) did not have a truly organic function in the Greek theater: as a pedestal for the action, it was a belated appendage. Now the stage, in our theaters, is the entire frontality of the action, the inevitable distribution of the spectacle into a front and back. In the ancient theater, nothing of the kind: the stage space was *voluminous*: there is an analogy, a community of experience between the spectacle's "outside" and the spectator's: this theater is a liminary theater, it is played on the threshold of tombs and palaces; this conic space, widening toward the top, open to the sky, has as its function to amplify the news (i.e., fate) and not to smother the plot.

Circularity constitutes what we might call an "existential" dimension of the ancient spectacle. Another is the open air.

It is tempting to imagine the picturesque nature of this morning theater—this theater of the dawn: the brightly dressed crowd (the spectators were in festival costume, heads garlanded as in every religious ceremony), the purple and gold of the stage costumes, the sunshine, the sky of Attica (though here we should observe a nuance: the festivals of Dionysus occurred in winter or at winter's end, rather than in spring). But we must not forget that the meaning of "open air" is its fragility. In the open air, the spectacle cannot be a habit, it is vulnerable, hence irreplaceable: the spectator's immersion in the complex polyphony of the open air (shifting sun, rising wind, flying birds, noises of the city) restores to the drama the singularity of an event. The open air cannot have the same image-repertoire as the dark theater: the latter is one of evasion; the former, of participation.

As for the public which sits in these tiers—a phenomenon familiar today in our sports events—it is itself transformed by its very mass; the number of seats is considerable, especially in relation to the rather modest total of citizens: about fourteen thousand seats in Athens (the main hall of the Palais de Chaillot seats between two and three thousand). This mass was structured, differently from our theaters or our modern stadiums: aside from the proedric seats, which could be installed in front of the first row, the regular seats themselves were frequently reserved in groups to certain categories of citizens: to members of the senate, to ephebi, to foreigners, to women (usually seated in the upper rows). Thus, a double cohesion was established: massive on the scale of the entire theater; special on that of homogeneous groups according to age, sex, function; and it is well known how much a group's integration fortifies its reactions and structures its affectivity: there was a veritable "installation" of the public in the theater; to which must be added the last of the protocols of possession: food; spectators ate and drank at the theater, and the generous choregi distributed wine and cakes to the audience.

Techniques

The fundamental technique of the Greek theater is one of synthesis: it is the *choreia*, or consubstantial union of poetry, music, and dance. Our theater, even our lyric theater, cannot give any idea of *choreia*, for with us music predominates to the detriment of the text and of the dance, which are relegated to interludes (ballets); now, what defines the *choreia* is the absolute equality of the languages which constitute it: all of them are, so to speak, "natural"; i.e., derived from the same mental framework, formed by an education which, under the name of "music," included letters and song (the choruses were, of course, composed of amateurs, and there was no difficulty in recruiting them). Perhaps, in order to approach an accurate image of the *choreia*, we must refer to the meaning of Greek education (at least as Hegel defines it): by a complete representation of his corporality (song and dance), the Athenian manifests his freedom: specifically the freedom to transform his body into a spiritual organ.

As for the poetry—or rather, as for speech itself, for here we are concerned to define a technique—we know that it was distributed among three modes of utterance: a dramatic, spoken expression, monologue or dialogue, composed in iambic trimeter (this was the *kataloguè*); a lyric, sung expression, written in various meters (the *melos*, or song); finally, an intermediate expression, the *parakataloguè*, composed in tetrameters: more rhetorical than the spoken language, but not so melodic as song, the *parakataloguè* was probably a melodramatic declamation on an elevated note, but *recto tono*, accompanied (as was the *melos*) by the flute.

The music was monodic, sung in unison or in octaves, with

the sole accompaniment (itself in unison) of the *aulos*, a kind of double-reed flute played by a musician seated on the *thymele*. The rhythm—and this was one of the notable aspects of the *choreia*—was absolutely based on the poetic meter: each measure corresponded to a foot, each note to a syllable, at least in the classical period; Euripides already uses an elaborate style of vocalism which soon obliges the poet to employ a professional composer. What must be said of this music (which is almost entirely lost to us: we have only a fragment of a chorus from Euripides' *Orestes*), what distinguishes it from ours, is that its expressivity was codified by a whole lexicon of musical modes: Greek music was eminently, openly *signifying*, its signification based less on natural effect than on convention.

In the *choreia*, it is the dance which we have the greatest difficulty imagining. Real dances or simple rhythmic movements? We know only that it was necessary to distinguish steps (*phorai*) from figures (*schemata*); these figures could doubtless achieve pantomime: there were pantomimes of hands and fingers (*chironomy*): one of these was famous, which Pratinas' chorus leader had invented for *The Seven against Thebes* and which narrated the battle "as if one were there." Here again, what is notable is the expressivity, i.e., the constitution of a veritable semantic system whose elements each spectator knew very well: one "read" a dance: its intellective function was at least as important as its plastic or emotive function.

Such were the various "codes" of the *choreia* (we have seen how important its semantic element was). Were they confined to the appropriate performers? Not at all. No doubt the chorus never recited (contrary to what it is made to do in our modern reconstructions), it always sang; but the actors and the coryphaeus, though chiefly speaking in dialogue, could also sing and even, after Euripides, dance; in any case, they commonly made use of the *parakataloguè*; this is because, we must not forget, the "characters" (a modern notion—Racine still called his "the actors") gradually emerged from an undifferentiated mass, the chorus. The function of the leader of the chorus (*exarchon*) led to the institution of an actor; Thespis or Phrynichus crossed this threshold and invented the first actor, transforming narrative into imitation: theatrical illusion was born. Aeschylus created the second actor and Sophocles the third (both remaining dependent upon the protagonist); since the number of characters often exceeded that of the actors, the same actor had to play successive roles: thus, in Aeschylus' *Persians*, one actor played the Queen and Xerxes, another played the Messenger and the ghost of Darius; it was by reason of this particular economy that the Greek theater is readily articulated around scenes of news or debate, in which only two characters are necessary.

As for the chorus, its mass did not vary during the classical period: twelve to fifteen choreuts for tragedy, twenty-four for comedy, including the coryphaeus. Then its role (if not, immediately, its mass) lessened in importance: initially the chorus speaks with the actor by the voice of the coryphaeus, it surrounds him physically, supports or questions him, participates not by acting but by commenting—in short, the chorus is the human collectivity confronting the event and seeking to understand it; all these functions gradually atrophied, and the choral parts eventually became no more than interludes without organic links with the play itself; there is a triple convergence here: lessening of fortunes and of civic zeal (as we have seen), i.e., reluctance of the rich to undertake the choregy; reduction of the choral function to simple interludes; development of the actors' number and role, evolution of the tragic interrogation in the direction of psychological truth.

Except in the dithyramb, all these performers, chorus and actors, were masked. The masks were made of rags covered with plaster, painted, and extended by a wig and eventually by an artificial beard; the forehead was often of exaggerated height

—this was the *onkos*, a lofty frontal protuberance. The expression of these masks has a history, which is precisely that of ancient realism; in Aeschylus' day, the mask had no specific expression; it was a neutral surface, admitting of little more than a faint line or frown on the forehead; in the Hellenistic period, on the contrary, the tragic mask becomes exceedingly pathetic, its features convulsed; in comedy, by means of other features (complexion, hair color), masks are classified by types, each of which obviously corresponds to a specific role, an age, or a temperament: these are character masks. What were the masks for? We can list certain superficial uses: to show features at a distance, to conceal differences in sex, since women's roles were taken by men. But their profound function doubtless altered according to the period; in the Hellenistic theater, the mask's typology serves a metaphysic of psychological essences; it does not hide, it proclaims; it is truly the ancestor of our present-day greasepaint. But previously, in the classical period, its function was apparently quite different: it alienated; first of all by banning the face's mobility—nuances, smiles, tears— without replacing it by any sign, however generalized; then by altering the voice, rendered deep, cavernous, strange, as though coming from another world: a mixture of inhumanity and of rhetorical humanity, it is then a capital function of the tragic illusion, whose mission is to make legible the communication of gods and men.

The same function for the stage costume, at once real and unreal. Real because its structure was that of the Greek garment: tunic, cloak, chlamys; unreal, at least in its tragic version, because this costume was the very garment of the god (Dionysus), or at least of his high priest, of a richness (colors and embroideries) obviously unknown in daily life (the comic costume's unreality is of course a minor affair: a tunic shortened so as to reveal the leather phallos exhibited by the masculine characters). Aside from this basic costume, there were certain special "emblems," i.e., the sketch of a vestimentary code: the purple mantle of kings, the long woolen garment of soothsayers, the rags of poverty, the black of mourning and of misfortune. As for the cothurnus, at least in its meaning of high-soled boot, this was a belated appendage of the Hellenistic period; the actor's elevation subsequently involved a factitious increase in his corpulence: false belly, false chest, glued on underneath the gown, exaggeration of the *onkos*.

The realistic effort—since this is the question we moderns ask of such techniques—proceeded much more rapidly with regard to the setting. At the start, this was merely a wooden structure, signifying in a rudimentary fashion an altar, a tomb, or a rock. But Sophocles, followed by Aeschylus in his last plays, introduced a painted set on a movable canvas which hung down in front of the *skene*: a flat painting, but one soon entrusted to specialist designers, scenographers. To this central (and frontal) setting was added, toward the end of the fifth century, two lateral sets, the *periactoi*: these were revolving structures mounted on pivots, each surface of which could be matched to the central setting, according to the requirements of the piece. Starting with the New Comedy, the left side (in relation to the spectator) conventionally represented an alien distance (in Athens, this was the side of the Attic countryside), and the right side, the immediate vicinity (the direction of Piraeus). Of course, as with the masks, there rapidly developed a summary typology of the sites represented: wooded landscape for the satyr play; domestic interior for comedy; temple, palace, warrior's tent, countryside, or seascape for tragedy. In front of these sets, no curtain until the Roman theater, though there may have been a movable screen intended for the preparation of certain scenes.

This enormous realist development was elaborated from generation to generation; it was aided by a precious technique: machinery. In the Hellenistic period, such machines were quite complex; there was one to exteriorize indoor scenes of murder—this was the *ekkyklema*, a rolling platform which brought corpses outside the palace doors, into the spectators' view; another, the *mechane*, enabled gods and heroes to fly through the air: this was a crane whose carrying cable was painted gray to make it invisible; in repose, in their dwelling place, the gods appeared, above the *skene*, in the *theologeion*, or gods' parlor; the *distegia* (or "second story") was a doorway which permitted the actors to communicate with the roofs or the upper story of the rear structure (especially in the theater of Euripides and of Aristophanes); finally, trapdoors, underground stairs, and even elevators served for the apparition of the infernal gods and the dead. Despite its diversity, this machinery has a general meaning: "to reveal the interior," that of the underworld, of palaces, or of Olympus; it betrays a secret, intensifies the analogy, suppresses a distance between the spectacle and the spectator; it is therefore logical that this machinery be developed concurrently with the *embourgeoisement* of the ancient drama: its function is not merely realistic (at the beginning) or fantastic (at the end), but also psychological.

A realistic theater? In any case, it very quickly developed into one; from Aeschylus on, it tended toward realism, although this first tragic theater still involved many distancing features: impersonality of the mask, convention of the costume, symbolism of the setting, small number of actors, importance of the chorus; but in any case, the realism of an art cannot be defined apart from the degree of credulity of its spectators: it inevitably refers to the mental structures which receive it. Certain allusive techniques combined with a powerful credulity produce what we might call a "dialectical realism" in which the theatrical illusion follows an incessant oscillation between an intense symbolism and an immediate reality; it is said that the spectators of the *Oresteia* fled in terror at the entrance of the Erinyes, because Aeschylus, breaking with the tradition of the *parodos*, had made them appear one by one; this movement rather closely recalls, as has been noted, the recoil of the first cinema audiences at the arrival of the locomotive at the La Céotat station; in one case as in the other, what the spectator consumes is neither reality nor its copy; it is, one might say, a "surreality," the world doubled by its signs. This, no doubt, was the realism of the first Greek theater, that of Aeschylus, perhaps that of Sophocles as well. But highly developed analogical techniques (expressivity of masks, complexity of machinery, atrophy of the chorus), combined with a credulity that was if not weakened at least trained, produced a very different realism; this was probably the realism of Euripides and of his successors: here the sign no longer refers to the world but to an interiority; the very materiality of the spectacle becomes in its entirety a setting, and at the very moment when the *choreia* is dissolved, its elements become simple "illustrations" which are asked to be plausible: what happens on the stage is no longer the sign of reality but its copy; we can understand that it should be Euripides with whom Racine made contact and continued the dialogue, and that the theatrical academicism of the nineteenth century should have felt closer to Sophocles than to Aeschylus.

For, whatever we have found in it, this theater has not ceased to concern us for four centuries. In the Renaissance, the musicians, poets, and amateurs of the Camera Bardi, in Florence, took their inspiration from the principles of the *choreia* in order to create opera. In the seventeenth and eighteenth centuries, the dramatic oeuvre of the ancient Greeks is the chief source from which our French playwrights derived not only their texts but also the very principles of a tragic art, its ends and its means; we know that Racine carefully annotated the passages of Aristotle's *Poetics* devoted to tragedy, and that later the debate over *catharsis* continued with Lessing. What Aristotle contributed to the modern theater was less a tragic philosophy than a compositional technique based on reason (this is the meaning of the various *ars poetica* of the period): a kind of tragic *praxis* was released by Aristotelian poetics, accrediting the notion of a dramatic craftsmanship: Greek tragedy became the model, the exercise, and the *askesis*, one might say, for all poetic creation. In the nineteenth and twentieth centuries, it is the Greek theater's very materiality, neglected by our classics, which crystallizes most reflections; first of all, on the level of philosophy and of ethnology, from Nietzsche to George Thomson, there has been an impassioned interrogation as to the origin and nature of this theater which is both religious and democratic, primitive and refined, surreal and realistic, exotic and classical; then, on the stage itself, we have begun (since the middle of the nineteenth century) to perform the works, first of all as a more pompous bourgeois theater (such were the first "reconstructions" of our Comédie-Française), then in a style at once cruder and more historical, about which we must say a word in conclusion, for since certain meditations of Copeau at the Vieux-Colombier and the performances of the *Persians* by students of the Groupe de Théâtre Antique de la Sorbonne in 1936, contemporary experiments have been numerous, based on principles that are frequently contradictory.

For we have never quite managed to decide whether this theater should be reconstructed or adapted. Although we frequently perform Shakespeare today without bothering about the Elizabethan conventions, or Racine without referring to classical dramaturgy, the ghost of the ancient festivity is always there, it fascinates us: nostalgia for a total, violently physical spectacle at once excessive and human, the trace of an incredible reconciliation between the theater and the city. Yet one thing is clear: this reconstruction is impossible; first of all because our archaeology affords us incomplete information, notably with regard to the plastic function of the chorus, which is the stumbling block of all modern productions; and then especially because the facts exhumed by erudition were never anything but the functions of a total system, the mental framework of the period, and because on the level of totality, history is irreversible: this framework being inaccessible, the functions vanish, the isolated facts become essences, they are given, willy-nilly, an unforeseen signification, and the literal fact rapidly becomes a misinterpretation. For instance: Greek music was monodic, the Greeks knew no other kind; but for us moderns, whose music is polyphonic, all monody becomes exotic: hence a fatal signification, which the ancient Greeks certainly did not want. Thus, in the Greek spectacle, as archaeology grants it to us, there are certain dangerous facts, liable to misconstruction: these are precisely the literal facts, the substantial facts: the shape of a mask, the tone of a melody, the sound of an instrument.

But there are also certain functions, relations, phenomena of structure: for example, the rigorous distinction of the spoken, the sung, and the declaimed, or the massive, frontal plasticity of the chorus (Claudel was right to suggest cantors behind lecterns), its essentially lyric function. It is such operations which we must, and which we can, it seems to me, rediscover. For this theater concerns us not by its exoticism but by its truth, not only by its aesthetic but by its order. And this truth can only be a function, the relation which joins our modern outlook to a very ancient society: this theater concerns us by its distance. Hence, the problem is no longer to assimilate but to distance it: that is, to make it understood.

1965

Diderot, Brecht,
Eisenstein

Let us imagine that an affinity of status and of history has linked mathematics and acoustics since the ancient Greeks; let us imagine that this characteristically Pythagorean space has been somewhat repressed the last two or three millennia (Pythagoras is surely the eponymous hero of Secrecy); and finally let us imagine that since these same Greeks, another link has been set up in opposition to the first one, that it has won out over it, continuously taking the lead in the history of the arts: the link connecting geometry and the theater: certainly the theater is that practice which calculates the *observed* place of things: if I put the spectacle here, the spectator will see this; if I put it elsewhere, he won't see it and I can take advantage of that concealment to profit by the illusion: the stage is just that line which intersects the optic beam, tracing its end point and, in a sense, the inception of its development: here would be instituted, against music (against the text), *representation*.

Representation is not directly defined by imitation: even if

we were to get rid of the notions of "reality" and "verisimilitude" and "copy," there would still be "representation," so
long as a subject (author, reader, spectator, or observer) directed his *gaze* toward a horizon and there projected the base
of a triangle of which his eye (or his mind) would be the apex.
The Organon of Representation (which it becomes possible
to write today, because *something else* is intimated)—this
Organon will have for its double basis the sovereignty of that
projection and the unity of the subject doing the projecting.
The substance of the arts is of little importance here; of course,
theater and cinema are direct expressions of geometry (unless
they proceed from some abstruse exploration of the voice,
stereophony), but our classic literary discourse (the readable),
too, which has long since abandoned prosody and music, is a
representative, geometrical discourse, insofar as it projects fragments in order to describe them: to discourse (the classics
might have said) is merely "to paint the picture one has in
mind." The scene, the picture, the shot or frame, the projected
rectangle—that is the *condition* which enables us to conceive
the theater, painting, the cinema, literature, i.e., all the "arts"
other than music and which we might call *dioptric arts*.
(Counter-proof: nothing permits us to locate any picture whatever in the musical text, unless we subject it to the dramatic
genres; nothing permits us to project any fetish in it, unless we
bastardize it by the use of refrains, tunes-as-motifs.)

Diderot's entire aesthetic, as we know, is based on the identification of the theatrical scene and the pictorial tableau: the
perfect play will be a series of tableaux, i.e., a gallery, a salon:
the stage offers the spectator "as many real tableaux as there
are, in the action, moments which favor the painter." The
(pictorial, theatrical, literary) tableau is a pure projection,
sharp-edged, incorruptible, irreversible, which banishes into
nothingness everything around it, which is therefore unnamed,
and promotes to the status of essence, to light, to sight, every-

thing it brings into its field; this demiurgic discrimination implies a high level of thought: the tableau is intellectual, it has something (moral, social) to say, but it also says that it knows *how* this must be said; it is at once significative and propaedeutic, impressive and reflexive, moving and conscious of the means of emotion. Brecht's epic-theater, the Eisensteinian shot or frame are tableaux, they are *set scenes* (as we say a *table is set*) which correspond perfectly to the dramatic unity of which Diderot has given us the theory: clearly projected (let us not forget Brecht's tolerance for the Italian curtain-stage, his scorn of a vague theater: open-air, theater-in-the-round), privileging a meaning but manifesting the production of that meaning, achieving the coincidence of the visual projection and the ideal projection. Nothing separates the Eisensteinian frame from the Greuzean tableau (except, of course, the project itself—in the one case moral, in the other social), nothing separates the epic-theater scene from the Eistensteinian frame (except that with Brecht the tableau is offered the spectator for criticism, not for adherence).

Is the tableau (since it is the product of a projection) a fetish object? Yes, on the level of ideal meaning (Welfare, Progress, the Cause, the advent of the right History); no, on the level of its composition. Or, more precisely, it is *composition* itself which enables us to shift the fetish-term and to transfer the erotic effect of the projection. Diderot, once again, is here the theoretician of this dialectic of desire; in the article "Composition," he writes: "A well-composed picture [*tableau*] is an entirety enclosed within a single point of view in which the parts contribute to one and the same goal and by their mutual correspondence form an ensemble as real as that of the limbs in an animate body; so that a piece of painting consisting of many figures flung about at random, without proportion, without intelligence, and without unity, no more deserves the name *true composition* than scattered studies of a leg, an eye, a nose on the same sheet deserve the name *portrait* or even *human figure*." Here the body is intentionally introduced into the notion of the tableau, but the whole body; the organs, grouped and oriented by the projection, function in the name of a transcendence, that of the *figure*, which receives the entire fetish-responsibility and becomes the sublime substitute for meaning: it is this meaning which is fetishized. (It would probably not be difficult to collect, in the post-Brechtian theater and in the post-Eisensteinian cinema, certain productions and performances marked by the dispersion of the tableau, the disintegration of the "composition," the exhibition of "partial organs" of the figure, in short, the jamming of the work's metaphysical meaning, but also of its political meaning—or at least the transfer of this meaning toward a *different* politics.)

Brecht indicated clearly that in the epic theater (which proceeds by successive tableaux) the entire burden of meaning and of pleasure is conveyed by each scene, not by the whole; on the level of the play, no development, no ripening; an ideal meaning, of course (on the level of each scene, each tableau), but no *final* meaning, nothing but projections, each of which possesses a sufficient demonstrative power. The same with Eisenstein: the film is a contiguity of episodes, each of which signifies absolutely, being aesthetically perfect; this is a cinema whose vocation is anthological: it, too, offers the fetishist, on dotted lines, the fragment to be cut out and taken away for his delectation. (Haven't we heard that in some *cinémathèque* or other a piece of film is missing from the reels of *Potemkin*—the baby-carriage scene, of course—snipped and stolen by some film lover as if it were a lock of a woman's hair, her glove, or her underwear?) This is Eisenstein's primary power: *no single image is boring*, we are not forced to wait for the next one in order to understand and be delighted: no dialectic (that interval of patience necessary for certain pleasures), but a continuous jubilation, consisting of a summation of perfect moments.

Diderot had thought of that perfect moment, of course (and had experienced it). In order to tell a story, the painter possesses only one moment: the one he will immobilize on the canvas; hence, he must choose this moment well, affording it in advance the greatest possible yield of meaning and of pleasure: necessarily total, this moment will be artificial (unreal: this is not a realist art), it will be a hieroglyph in which can be read at a glance (in a single apprehension, if we turn to the theater, to the cinema) the present, the past, and the future, i.e., the historical meaning of the represented gesture. This crucial moment, totally concrete and totally abstract, is what Lessing will call (in the *Laocoön*) the *pregnant moment*. Brecht's theater, Eisenstein's cinema are sequences of pregnant moments: when Mother Courage bites the coin the recruiting sergeant offers her and, because of this tiny interval of mistrust, loses her son, she demonstrates both her past as a tradeswoman and the future in store for her: all her children dead because of her moneymaking blindness. When (in *The General Line*) the peasant woman lets her skirt be torn into the strips that will serve to repair the tractor, this gesture is big with an entire history: such pregnancy collects the past conquest (the tractor fiercely won from bureaucratic negligence), the present struggle, and the effectiveness of solidarity. The pregnant moment is certainly the presence of all the absences (memories, lessons, promises) to whose rhythm history becomes both intelligible and desirable.

With Brecht, it is the *social gestus* which takes up the notion of the pregnant moment. What is a *social gestus* (how much irony reactionary criticism has lavished on this Brechtian concept, one of the clearest and most intelligent which dramatic theory has ever produced!)? It is a gesture, or a set of gestures (but never a gesticulation), in which can be read a whole social situation. Not every *gestus* is social: nothing social in the movements a man makes to brush away a fly; but if this same man, raggedly dressed, fights off watchdogs, the *gestus* becomes social;

the gesture by which Mother Courage verifies the coin she is given is a social *gestus*; the excessive paraph with which the bureaucrat in *The General Line* signs his papers is a social *gestus*. How far can we go in our search for the social *gestus*? Very far: into language itself: a language can be gestual, Brecht says, when it indicates certain attitudes which the speaker adopts toward other men: "If thine eye offend thee, pluck it out" is more gestual than "Pluck out the eye that offends thee," because the order of the sentence, the asyndeton which governs it, refers to a prophetic and vengeful situation. Certain rhetorical forms can thus be gestual: so that it is futile to reproach Eisenstein's art (or Brecht's) for being "formalistic" or "aestheticizing": form, aesthetic, rhetoric can be socially responsible, if they are handled in a deliberate manner. Representation (since that is what we are concerned with here) must inevitably come to terms with the social *gestus*: as soon as one "represents" (as one projects, as one closes the tableau and thereby makes the totality discontinuous), a decision must be made as to whether the gesture is social or is not (whether it refers not to a specific society but to Humanity).

In the tableau (the scene, the frame, or the shot), what does the actor do? Since the tableau is the presentation of an ideal meaning, the actor must present his consciousness of the meaning, for the meaning would not be an ideal one if it did not involve its own "machination," but the knowledge or consciousness which the actor, by an unaccustomed supplement, must present is neither his human knowledge (his tears must not simply refer to the Victim's feelings) nor his professional knowledge (he must not show that he knows how to act well). The actor must prove that he is not subjugated by the spectator (bogged down in "reality," in "humanity") but that he is guiding the meaning toward its ideality. This sovereignty of the actor, who thus becomes the master of meaning, is quite apparent in Brecht, since he has theorized it as "distancing"; it is no less so in Eisenstein (at least in the creator of *The General*

Line, with which I am concerned here), not by the effect of a ceremonial, ritual art—which is what Brecht asked for—but by the insistence of the social *gestus*, which unremittingly stamps all the actor's gestures (closing fists, hands grasping tools, peasants lining up at the bureaucrat's window, etc.). However, it is true in Eisenstein as in Greuze (Diderot's exemplary painter) that the actor sometimes assumes an expression of the deepest pathos, and this pathos may seem anything but "distanced"; but distancing is a strictly Brechtian method, necessary to Brecht because he is representing a tableau which must be criticized by the spectator; in the other two, the actor does not necessarily have to "distance"—what he must present is an ideal value; hence, it suffices that the actor "detach" the production of this value, make it apparent, intellectually visible, by the very excess of his versions: the expression then signifies an idea—which is why it is excessive—not a nature; we are far from the mannerisms of the Actors' Studio, whose much-vaunted "restraint" has no meaning beyond the personal glory of the performer (take, for example, Brando's grimacing in *Last Tango in Paris*).

Has the tableau a subject—a topic? No, not at all; it has a meaning, not a subject. Meaning begins with the social *gestus* (at the pregnant moment); outside the *gestus*, there is only vagueness, insignificance. "In a certain manner," Brecht says, "subjects always have a certain naïveté, they rather lack qualities. In a way, because they are empty they are self-sufficient. Only the social *gestus* (criticism, cunning, irony, propaganda, etc.) introduces the human element"; and Diderot adds, if we may put it this way: the painter's or dramatist's creation is not in the choice of a subject, it is in the choice of the pregnant moment, of the tableau. It matters little, after all, that Eisenstein took his "subjects" from Russia's past and from the Revolution's, and not, "as he should have" (his critics now remark), from the present moment of socialist construction (except for

The General Line); it matters little that the battleship and the tsar are merely vague and empty "subjects"—all that matters is the *gestus*, the critical demonstration of the gesture, the inscription of this gesture, to whatever period it belongs, within a text whose social machination is visible; the subject adds nothing, takes nothing away. How many films are there today "about" drugs, of which drugs are the "subject"? But this is a hollow subject; without social *gestus*, drugs are insignificant, or rather their significance is that of a vague, empty, eternal nature: "drugs make you impotent" (*Trash*), "drugs make you suicidal" (*Absences repétées*). The subject is a false projection: why this subject rather than some other? The work begins only with the tableau, when the meaning is put into the gesture and into the coordination of gestures. Take *Mother Courage*: you can be sure there has been a misunderstanding if you think its "subject" is the Thirty Years' War, or even a denunciation of war in general; its *gestus* is not there: it is in the blindness of the tradeswoman who believes she is making a living from war and who is actually making a death from it; even more, the *gestus* is in my own *vision*, as a spectator, of that blindness.

In theater, in cinema, in traditional literature, things are always seen *from somewhere*; this is the geometric basis of representation: there must be a fetishistic subject in order to project this tableau. This point of origin is always the Law: law of society, law of struggle, law of meaning. Every militant art, therefore, must be representative, legal. For representation to be really deprived of origin and for it to transcend its geometrical nature without ceasing to be a representation, the price to pay is enormous: it is nothing less than death. In Dreyer's *Vampyr*, a friend reminds me, the camera tracks from the house to the graveyard and takes in *what the dead man sees*: this is the limit-point where representation can be baffled: the spectator no longer need occupy any specific point, for he cannot identify his eyes with the corpse's closed eyes; the tableau has no point of departure, no support, it is a gap. Everything that happens on this side of that limit (and this is Brecht's case, and Eisenstein's) can only be legal: it is ultimately the Law of the Party which projects the epic-theater scene, the filmic shot or frame, this is the Law which observes, frames, centers, enunciates. And here again Eisenstein and Brecht join Diderot (promoter of bourgeois domestic tragedy, as his two successors were the promoters of a socialist art). Diderot happened to distinguish in painting certain major practices, of a cathartic force, whose goal was the ideality of meaning, from certain minor practices which were purely imitative and anecdotal; on one side Greuze, on the other Chardin; in other words, in a period of ascendancy, every physics of art (Chardin) must be crowned with a metaphysics (Greuze). In Brecht, in Eisenstein, Chardin and Greuze coexist (more devious, Brecht leaves it to his public to be the Greuze of the Chardin he puts before them): in a society which has not yet found peace, how could art cease being metaphysical, i.e., signifying, readable, representative? Fetishist? How long till the music, the Text?

Brecht, it seems, knew virtually no Diderot at all (maybe the *Paradoxe sur le Comédien*). Yet it is Brecht who in an entirely contingent fashion authorizes the tripartite conjunction just proposed. In around 1937, Brecht had the idea of founding a Diderot Society, a place for pooling experiments and studies in theater practice, doubtless because he saw in Diderot, beyond the figure of a great materialist philosopher, that of a man of the theater whose theory aimed at presenting both pleasure and instruction. Brecht drew up the program for this Society and made it into a pamphlet which he planned to send . . . to whom? To Piscator, to Jean Renoir, to Eisenstein.

1973

*The Spirit of
the Letter*

Massin's book *Letter and Image* is a splendid encyclopedia of information and of images. Is its subject the Letter? Yes, of course: the Occidental letter, taken in its environment, whether of advertising or of illustration, and in its vocation of figurative metamorphosis. Only it happens that this apparently simple object, so easy to identify and to enumerate, is somewhat diabolical: it slips out from under itself in every direction, chiefly toward its own contrary: it is what we call a contradictory signifier, an enantioseme. For, on the one hand, the Letter decrees that Law in whose name every extravagance can be reduced ("Keep, I pray you, to the letter of the text"), but on the other, for centuries, as Massin shows, it tirelessly releases a profusion of symbols; on the one hand, it "keeps" language, the whole written language, within the yoke of its twenty-six characters, and these characters are themselves merely the disposition of a few lines, a few curves; but, on the other hand, it releases an imagery vast as a cosmography; on the one hand, it signifies the most extreme censorship (Letter, what crimes are committed in thy name!), and on the other, the most extreme pleasure (all poetry—the whole of the unconscious—is a return to the letter); it concerns simultaneously the designer, the philologist, the painter, the jurist, the creator of advertising, the psychoanalyst, and the schoolboy. *The letter killeth and the spirit giveth life?* How simple everything would be if there were not, precisely, a spirit of the letter which gives the letter life; or again: if the extreme symbol did not turn out to be the letter itself. It is this circular trajectory of the letter and of the figure which Massin enables us to glimpse. His book, like any successful encyclopedia (and this one is all the more valuable in that it includes over a thousand images), enables, indeed obliges us to correct a number of prejudices: it is a euphoric book (since it concerns the signifier), but it is also a critical book.

First of all, as one leafs through these hundreds of figured letters produced by every century, from the medieval copyists' workshops to the Beatles' *Yellow Submarine,* it is quite clear that the letter is not the sound; all linguistics derives language from speech, of which it declares writing to be merely a particular disposition; Massin's book protests: the letter's coming and becoming (its source and its perpetual goal) are independent of the phoneme. This impressive expansion of letter-figures says that the word is not the only limit, the only result, the only transcendence of the letter. Do letters serve to constitute words? Yes, but also something else. What? Abecedaria. The alphabet is an autonomous system, here supplied with sufficient predicates to guarantee its individuality: "grotesque, diabolic, comic, new, magical" alphabets, and even more; in short, the alphabet is an object whose function and whose technical locus do not exhaust it: it is a signifying chain, a syntagm outside of meaning but not outside of the sign. All the artists Massin cites—monks, lithographers, painters, designers—have blocked the road which seems to run so naturally from the first articulation to the second, from the letter to the word, and have taken *another* road, not of language but of writing, not of communication but of signification: an adventure located in the margin of the so-called finalities of language and thereby in the very center of its action.

Massin's book affords a second (and by no means a minor) object of meditation: metaphor. These twenty-six letters of our alphabet, animated, as Massin says, by hundreds of artists from every period, are put in a metaphoric relation with *something other* than the letter: animals (birds, fish, serpents, rabbits, some devouring others in order to form a D, an E, a K, an L, etc.), men (silhouettes, limbs, postures), monsters, vegetal structures (flowers, tendrils, trunks), instruments (scissors, sickles, tripods, etc.): a whole catalogue of natural and human products comes to double the alphabet's brief list: the entire world is incorporated into the letters, the letter becomes an image in the tapestry of the world.

Certain constitutive features of metaphor are thereby illustrated, illuminated, corrected. First of all, the importance of what Jakobson calls the diagram, which is a kind of minimal analogy, a merely proportional and not exhaustively analogical relation between letter and world. Thus, in general, calligrams or poems in the shape of objects, of which Massin furnishes a valuable collection (since such things are often mentioned but, except for Apollinaire's, almost never shown). Then the polysemic (we should be able to say *pansemic*) nature of the image-sign: freed from its linguistic role (participation in a particular word), a letter can say everything: in this baroque region where meaning is destroyed beneath symbol, one and the same letter can signify two contraries (apparently Arabic knows such contradictory signifiers, such *ad'dâd*, to which J. Berque and J. P. Charnay have devoted an important book): Z, for Hugo, is the lightning flash, God, while for Balzac Z is the bad letter, the letter of deviance. I rather regret that Massin has not provided a recapitulation of the entire paradigm, worldwide and age-old, of a single letter (he had the means to do so): all the figures of M, for instance, which here range from the three Angels of a Gothic master to two snowy peaks—in a travel poster—of the Megève, including, in between, a pitchfork; a prone man, thighs raised, presenting his rump; a painter and his easel; and two housewives hanging out a sheet.

For—and this is the third chapter of this lesson-in-images about metaphor—it is obvious that by dint of extravagances, of extraversions, of migrations and associations, the letter no longer exists, it is not the origin of the image: *all metaphor is unoriginated,* once we shift from utterance to speech-act, from language to writing; the analogical relation is circular, without preeminence; the terms it apprehends are *floating* terms: in the signs presented, which *begins,* the man or the letter? Massin enters metaphor by the letter: one must, alas, assign a "subject" to our books; but one could also enter from the other end and make the letter into a *species* of man, of object, of plant. The letter, after all, is only a paradigmatic, arbitrary bridgehead, since discourse must *begin* (a constraint which has not yet been explored), but this bridgehead can also be an exit, if we conceive, for instance, as the poets and mystagogues do, that the letter (writing) institutes the world. To assign an origin to metaphorical expansion is always a choice—metaphysical, ideological. Whence the importance of reversals of origin (such as the one psychoanalysis performs upon the letter itself). As Massin keeps telling us by his images, there are only floating chains of signifiers which pass and intersect each other: writing is *in the air.* Consider the relation of letter and figure—all logic is exhausted by it: (1) the letter is the figure, this I is an hourglass; (2) the figure is in the letter, slipped whole into its sheath, like these two acrobats coiled into an O (Erté has made great use of this imbrication in his precious alphabet, which Massin unfortunately does not cite); (3) the letter is in the figure (as in the case of all rebuses): if we do not stop the symbol, it is because it is reversible: the letter I can refer to a knife, but the knife in its turn is merely a point of departure, at the end of which (as psychoanalysis has shown) you can rediscover the I (caught in some word that matters to your unconscious): there are never anything but *avatars*.

All of which tells us how many elements Massin's book contributes to the current approach of the signifier. Writing consists of letters, granted. But what do the letters consist of? We can look for a historical answer—unknown with regard to our alphabet; but we can also make use of the question in order to shift the problem of origins, providing a gradual conceptualization of the *interspace*, the floating relation whose anchorage we always determine abusively. In the Orient, an ideographic civilization, it is what is *between* writing and painting which is traced, without the wielder of the brush being able to refer one to the other; this permits evading that criminal law of filiation, which is our Law, paternal, civil, mental, scientific: a segregative law, by virtue of which we set graphic artists on this side, painters on that; novelists on this side, poets on that; whereas writing is *one*: the discontinuity which everywhere establishes it makes whatever we write, paint, draw into a single text. This is what Massin's book has shown us. It is our task not to censor this material field by reducing the prodigious *summa* of these letter-figures to a gallery of dreams and extravagances: the *margin* we concede to what can be called the baroque (to permit us to understand the humanists) is the very site where the writer, the painter, and the graphic artist—in a word, *the performer of the text*—must function.

1970

Erté,
or À la lettre

The Truth

In order to be known, artists must suffer a minor mythological purgatory: we must be able to associate them quite mechanically with an object, a school, a fashion, a period of which we call them the precursors, the founders, the witnesses, or the symbols; in a word, we must be able to *classify* them easily, to subject them to a label, like a species to its genus.

Erté's purgatory is Woman. Granted, Erté has drawn a great many women; in fact, one might say he has never drawn anything else—as if he could never separate himself from them (soul or accessory, obsession or commodity?)—as if Woman signed each of his sketches more certainly than the delicate scribble of his name. Take any large-scale composition by Erté (there are a number): the decorative complexity, the precise and baroque exuberance, the abstract transcendence informing the lines nonetheless tell you, in the manner of a rebus: *Cherchez la Femme.* And you always find her; there she is, tiny if need be, reclining at the center of a motif which, once she is located in it, makes all space collapse and converge upon the altar where she is worshipped (if not tortured). This constant practice of the feminine figure no doubt results from Erté's career in fashion, but this career itself augments the artist's mythological consistency, for Fashion is one of the best sites in which to discern the spirit of modernity, its plastic, erotic, oneiric experiments; now, Erté has continuously occupied, for half a century, the territory of Fashion (and of Spectacle, which often inspires or depends on it); and this territory constitutes institutionally (i.e., enjoys the blessing and the gratitude of society as a whole) a kind of national park, a zoological reservation in which is preserved, transformed and refined—by controlled experiments—the species Woman. Rarely, in short, has an artist's situation (a combination of practice, function, and talent) been clearer: Erté is a pure and complete character, historically simple, entirely and harmoniously incorporated into a homogeneous world, defined at its cardinal points by the major activities of its period, Adventure, Fashion, Cinema, and the Press, themselves summarized under the names of their most glamorous mediators, Mata Hari, Paul Poiret, Hollywood, and *Harper's Bazaar*; and for its center this world has one of the most strongly individualized dates in the history of styles: 1925. Erté's mythology is so pure, so full, that we no longer know (we no longer think to wonder) if he created the Woman of his period, or if he managed to intercept her—if he is the witness of a history or its founder, a hero or a mythologist.

And yet is Woman really involved in this obsessional figuration of Woman? Is Woman the first and last object (since all signifying space is circular) of the story Erté has been telling from drawing to drawing over fifty years, from Paul Poiret's studio (1911) to New York television (1968)? One stylistic feature leads us to wonder: Erté doesn't *look for* Woman, he produces her on the spot, repeated, actually duplicated in the perspective of an exact mirror multiplying the same figure to infinity; in all these thousands of women there occurs no labor of *variation* bearing on the feminine body which might testify to its symbolic density and enigma. Is Erté's Woman at least an essence? Not at all: the Fashion model, from which Erté's iconography is derived (and this is not to diminish that iconography) is not an idea based on reason or nature, not a secret divined and incarnated after a long philosophical inquiry or a creative drama, but only a brand, an inscription, resulting from a technique and normalized by a code. Nor is Erté's Woman a symbol, the renewed expression of a body whose forms would preserve the fantasmal impulses of its creator or its reader (as is the case with the Romantic Woman of painters and writers): she is merely a cipher, a sign referring to a conventional femininity (the stake of a social pact), because she is a pure object of communication, information, transition to the intelligible, and not the expression of the sensuous: these countless women are not portraits of an idea, fantasmal experiments, but instead the return of an identical morpheme which takes its place in the language of a period and, constituting our linguistic memory, permits us to *speak* that period (which is a great boon): Could we speak without a memory of signs? And do we not need a sign of Woman, of Woman as sign, in order to speak of other things? Erté should be honored as the founder of a sign, creator of a language, like the Logothete whom Plato compared to a god.

The Silhouette

In order to construct this feminine sign, something tremendous must be sacrificed, which is the body (as secret, founding site of the unconscious). Of course, it is impossible to abstract a representation of the human body completely—to transform it into a pure sign: a child can attach his fantasies even to the anatomical plates in an encyclopedia. Hence, for all his elegant (but continuous) chastity, Erté's semantics—what we might call his somatography—involves several fetish sites (however rare): the finger, severed from the body (this is the characteristic of the fetish) and consequently designated by the jewel which decks its tip (instead of ringing it, in the usual manner), like a phallic (castrating) bandage, in the astonishing *Finger Jewel* (for the little finger: originally a burrowing digit, then symbolically promoted to the rank of a social emblem signifying the upper class among peoples who let the little fingernail grow excessively long, not to be broken by any kind of manual labor); the foot, of course, designated only once but exemplarily (is not to make an object into the *subject* of a painting invariably to fetishize it?) by the delicious slipper simultaneously docile and refined, painted and scrolled, oblique and vertical, offered in solitary splendor, in profile like a ship or a house, as receptive as the latter, as elegant as the former; finally the rump, emphasized by the effervescence of the train which departs from it (in the letter R of Erté's alphabet), but most often elided (and hence super-signified) by the negating displacement which the artist imposes on this same train by no longer attaching it at the hips but rather at the shoulders, as in the Guadalquivir costume. These are quite ordinary fetishes, indicated in passing, one might say, by the artist; but what is specifically a fetish for Erté, who has made it the specialty of his oeuvre, is a site of the body which escapes the classical collection of fetish organs, an ambiguous site, a limit-fetish, reluctant symbol but much more frankly a sign, a product of art much more than of nature: indubitably a fetish, since it permits the reader to manipulate the woman's body fantasmally, to do with it what he will, to imagine it in the future tense, caught up in a scene adapted to his desire and to his benefit, and yet a denial of the fetish, since instead of resulting from a fragmentation of the body (the fetish is by definition a *fragment*), it is this body's total, inclusive form. This intermediary site (or form) between the fetish and the sign, visibly privileged by Erté, who provides a continuous representation of it, is the *silhouette*.

The silhouette, if only by its etymology, is a strange object, at once anatomic and semantic: it is the body which has explicitly become a drawing, carefully outlined on one hand, entirely void on the other. This body-drawing is essentially (by function) a social sign (this was indeed the meaning which the artists of Finance Minister Etienne de Silhouette gave their drawings); all sexuality (and its symbolic substitutes) is absent from it; a silhouette, even substitutively, is never naked: we cannot undress it, not because it is excessively secret but because, contrary to a true drawing, it is only a line (sign). Erté's silhouettes (never sketched, but of an admirable finish) are at the genre's limit: they are *adorable* (can still be desired) and yet already entirely *intelligible* (they are admirably precise signs). Let us say that they refer to a new relation of body and garment. Hegel has noted that the garment is responsible for the transition from the sensuous (the body) to the signifier; the Ertéan silhouette (infinitely more thought-out than the Fashion mannequin) performs the contrary movement (which is much more rare): it makes the garment sensuous and the body into a signifier; the body is there (signed by the silhouette) in order for the garment to exist; it is not possible to conceive a garment without the body (without silhouette): the empty garment, without head and without limbs (a schizophrenic fantasy), is death, not the body's neutral absence, but the body decapitated, mutilated.

In Erté's work, it is not the feminine body which is dressed (gowns, furs, crinolines, trains, veils, jewels, and a thousand baroque trinkets, whose pleasure is as inexhaustible as their invention); it is the garment which is extended as a body (not *filled* by it, for Erté's figures, properly unrealistic, are indifferent to what is underneath: everything is invented, substituted, developed poetically on the surface). Such is the function of the silhouette in Erté: to pose and propose an object (a concept, a form) which is unitary, an indissociable mixture of body and garment so that we can neither undress the body nor abstract the garment: Woman entirely socialized by her adornment, adornment stubbornly "corporeified" by Woman's contour.

The Head of Hair

Why this object (which we have called, *faute de mieux*, a silhouette)? Where does this invention of a Woman-Garment who is no longer, to any degree, the Woman of Fashion—where does this invention lead? Before finding out (and in order to find out), we must say how Erté deals with that element of the feminine body which is precisely, in its nature and its very history, a kind of "promised" garment, i.e., the head of hair. We are familiar with its very rich symbolism.

Anthropologically, by a very old metonymy appearing out of the mists of time—since religion obliges Women to hide it (to desexualize it) upon entering a place of worship—her head of hair is Woman herself, in her instituting difference. Poetically, hair is a total substance, close to the great vital milieu, marine or vegetal, ocean or forest, the fetish-object par excellence in which man immerses himself (Baudelaire). Functionally it is that part of the body which can immediately become a garment, not so much because it can cover the body, but because it performs without preparation the neurotic task of any garment, which must, like the blush which reddens a shamed face, at once conceal and parade the body. Symbolically, finally,

the head of hair is "what can be braided" (like the hair of the pubis): a fetish which Freud places at the origin of weaving (institutionally devolving upon women): the braid is substituted for the missing penis (this is the very definition of the fetish), so that "to cut off braids"—whether the amusement of little boys with regard to their sisters or a social aggression among the ancient Chinese, for whom the braid of hair was the phallic attribute of their Manchu invaders and masters— is a castrating act. Now, there are virtually no heads of hair in Erté's gynecographies. Most of his women—a period feature— have short hair plastered down (*à la garçonne*), a black cap, attractively serpentine or mephistophelian, a simple graphic signature of the head; and elsewhere, if there should be any at all, the hair itself is immediately transformed into *something else*: into feathers, extravasated above the horizon of chorus girls to form a whole curtain of plumes; into beads, streaming from *Delilah*'s triple-looped diadem to form her train, wimple, bracelets, and even the double chain which keeps Samson crouching at her feet; into steles, in the alternating series of

Blondes and Brunettes (Curtain for *Manhattan Mary*) who offer the public only the front of their wavy tresses. Yet Erté knows what a head of hair is (symbolically): in one of his drawings, consisting of nothing but the face of a sleeping woman, drifts and floats a cascade of broad curls, doubled (and this is the *meaning* of the object) by black spirals, as if the head of hair were here reestablished in its natural milieu, seething life (does not the head of hair remain intact on the crumbling corpse?); but, for Erté, in the interest of his system (which we are here attempting to describe), the head of hair must visibly give way to a less symbolic and more semantic appendage (or at least one whose symbolism is no longer vegetal, organic): the coiffure.

The coiffure (as vestimentary appendage, and not as capillary arrangement) is treated by Erté in what we might call an implacable fashion: like Johann Sebastian Bach *exhausting* a motif in all its possible inventions, canons, fugues, ricercari, and variations, Erté initiates, from his beauties' heads, every possible derivation: horizontal veils held at arm's length above the head, thick tubes of fabric (or of hair?) spiraling down to the waist, then to the ground, crests, plumes, multiple diadems, aureoles of every shape and dimension, extravagant (but elegant) appendages contradicting the historical model of which they are the baroque and excessive reminiscence (busby, chaperon, fontange, Sevillian comb, schapska, pschent, etc.), these are not so much coiffures (we do not suppose for a moment that they can be worn, i.e., taken off; nor do we imagine how they can "stay put") as supplementary limbs intended to form a new body inscribed, without conflicting with it, within the essential form of the original one. For the role of these chimerical headdresses is to subject the feminine body to some new idea (which we shall shortly name) and consequently to *deform* it (stripping this word of any pejorative meaning), either because the coiffure, a kind of half-vegetal, half-solar flower, is repeated at the bottom of the body and thereby makes unreal the ordinary meaning of the human figure, or because, much more frequently, it extends the statue by its entire height, in order to double its power of extension and articulation; then the face is merely the impassive proscenium of this excessively high coiffure in which are situated the potential infinity of forms and, by a paradoxical displacement, the face's very expressivity: if the woman of *The Annunciation* has her "hair standing on end," it is because her hair is *also* the surplice of the angel spread above the composition in an apotheosis of wings. The coiffure's upper duplication of the figure interests Erté to the point where he makes it the cell of an endless movement: on the high pschent of *Pharaoh's Wife* is painted another Pharaoh's Wife *en abîme;* installed atop a pyramid of worshippers, the triumphant *Courtesan* is coiffed with a high tiara, but this tiara in its turn is a woman: the woman and her coiffure (we should be able to say: the coiffure and its woman) thereby continuously modulate toward each other, by means of each other. This preference for ascensional constructions (besides the scaffolded coiffures, we must consider *Princess Boudour al Badour* perched on her palanquin and surmounted by an infinitely aerial motif, or *Du Barry,* whose necklaces are supported by two angels) may well deserve a phenomenological psychoanalysis à la Bachelard; but the truth of our artist, as has been said, is not in the realm of the symbol; the ascensional theme is above all, for Erté, the designation of a *possible* space for the line where, starting from the body, it can multiply its power of signification. The coiffure, a major accessory (it has its minor substitutes in scarves, trains, necklaces, and bracelets, everything which *departs from* the body), is the means by which the artist *tries out* on the feminine body the transformations he needs in order to elaborate, like an alchemist, a new object that is neither body nor garment yet participates in both.

The Letter

This new object which Erté creates, a kind of chimera composed half of Woman and half of her coiffure (or her train)— this object is the Letter (this word must be understood *à la lettre*). Erté's alphabet is, I believe, quite famous: here each of our twenty-six letters, in its capital form, is composed (with very few exceptions, which we will mention at the end) of a woman or of two, whose postures and adornment are devised as a function of the letter (or of the figure) which they are to represent, and to which this woman or these women are subjugated. Once you have seen Erté's alphabet you cannot forget it. Not only does this alphabet force our memory in a rather mysterious fashion (who impels us to remember these Letter-Women so insistently?), but further, by a natural (inevitable) metonymy, it ultimately impregnates Erté's entire oeuvre with its meaning: behind each of Erté's women (Fashion mannequin, theater model) appears a kind of spirit of the Letter, as if the alphabet were the feminine body's natural, originating, and somehow domestic site, and as if the woman emerged from it, in order to occupy the stage or the fashion page, only temporarily and by a kind of momentary release, after which she must return to her place in her native ABC's: consider *Samson and Delilah*: nothing to do with an alphabet, and yet don't the two bodies lodge within the same space like two intertwining initials? Outside the alphabet he has conceived, Erté's women remain letters; let us say they are unknown letters, the letters of an alien language which our particularism happens to keep us from speaking; does not the series of metal cutout paintings have the homogeneity, the wealth of variation, and the formal spirit of an unpublished alphabet one would like to spell out? Such paintings are, as people say, non-figurative, which accounts for why they are dedicated to the alphabet (known or unknown): the letter is the site upon which all graphic abstractions converge.

In Erté's generalized alphabet, there is a dialectic exchange: Woman seems to lend her figure to the Letter; but in return, and much more certainly, the Letter gives Woman its abstraction: by *figuring* the letter, Erté *unfigures* the woman (this barbarism is necessary since Erté strips woman of her figure— or at least evaporates it—without *dis*figuring her): an incessant shift affects Erté's figures, transforms letters into women, but also (our language itself acknowledges their relationship) *jambes* (legs) into *jambages* (downstrokes). Now we understand the importance of the *silhouette* in Erté's art (we have spoken of its ambiguous meaning: symbol and sign, fetish and message): the silhouette is an essential graphic product: it makes the human body into a potential letter, it asks to be *read*.

This ecumenicity of the letter in Erté, who was originally a fashion designer, involves a salutary correction of a received opinion: that Fashion (the stylized figuration of innovations in feminine apparel) naturally invokes a certain philosophy of Woman: everyone (stylists and journalists) thinks that Fashion is in the service of eternal Woman, like a priestess who lends her voice to a religion. Are not couturiers the poets who, from year to year, from strophe to strophe, write the anthem of the feminine body, a song of glory? Is not the *erotic* relation of Woman and Fashion self-understood? Hence, each time Fashion notably changes (for instance, shifting from long to short), we find reporters eagerly questioning the psychologists and sociologists to discover what new Woman will be generated by the miniskirt or the sack. A waste of time, as it turns out: no one can answer. Outside certain stereotypes, no discourse can be based on Fashion, once it is taken as the symbolic *expression* of the body: Fashion stubbornly resists any such notion, and this is only natural: choosing to produce the *sign* of Woman (or Woman as sign), Fashion cannot traverse, develop, describe its symbolic capacity; contrary to what we are supposed to believe (and unless we have a very undemanding notion of it), Fashion is not erotic; it seeks clarity, not pleasure; the cover girl is not a good object for fantasy: she is too busy constituting herself as a sign: impossible to live (in imaginary terms) with her, she must merely be *decoded,* or more exactly (for there is no secret in her) she must be placed in the general sign-system which makes our world intelligible to us, i.e., livable.

Hence it is something of an illusion to suppose that Fashion is obsessed by the body. Fashion is obsessed by that other thing which Erté has discovered with the artist's final lucidity, and which is the Letter, the body's inscription in a systematic space of signs. It may be that Erté established a Fashion (that of 1925), in the contingent sense of the word; but what is much more important is that he has in his work (even if, on this point, like every true innovator, he is not imitated widely) re-formed the idea of Fashion, neglecting the "feminine" illusion in which public opinion indulges (the public opinion, for example, of mass culture) and tendentiously shifting the symbolic field from Woman to the Letter. Of course, Woman is present in Erté's oeuvre (and even omnipresent); but she is merely the *theme* of this oeuvre, not its symbolic site. To interrogate Erté's Women would be no use whatever; they would say nothing more than themselves, being scarcely more loquacious (symbolically) than a dictionary which gives the (generally tautological) definition of a word, and not its poetic future. The characteristic of the signifier is to be a *departure* (for other signifiers); and the signifying point of departure, in Erté, is not Woman (she becomes nothing, if not her own coiffure—she is the simple cipher of mythic femininity); it is the Letter.

The Letter, the Spirit, the Letter

For a long time, according to a famous aphorism of the Gospel, the Letter (which kills) has been set in opposition to the Spirit (which gives life). This Letter (which kills) has generated, in our civilization, a number of murderous censorships (how many men have died, in our history, beginning with the history of our religion, for *a* meaning?), which we might group, stretching matters a little, under the generic name of philology; severe guardian of the "true" (univocal, canonical) meaning, this Letter has all the functions of the superego, of which the first, denying task is obviously to reject all symbolism; he who practices this murderous Letter is himself stricken with a mortal disease of language, asymbolia (cut off from all symbolic activity, man would soon die; and if the asymbolist survives, it is because the denial of which he makes himself the high priest is itself a symbolic activity which dares not speak its name).

Hence it was, in its day, a vital measure to oppose this murderous letter by the rights of the *spirit*. The spirit here is not the space of symbol, but only that of meaning: the spirit of a phenomenon, of a speech, is simply its right to *begin* to signify (whereas literality is precisely the refusal to engage in a process of signification): the *spirit* (as opposed to the *letter*) has therefore become the fundamental value of liberal ideologies; the right to interpretation is of course put in the service of a spiritual truth, but this truth is gained *against* its appearance (against the *Dasein* of the thing), *beyond* that appearance, that garment which must be stripped off with no further respect.

By a second reversal, however, modernity returns to the letter—which is obviously no longer the letter of philology. On the one hand, correcting a postulate of linguistics which, governing all language by its spoken form, makes the letter into the simple transcription of sound, philosophy (with Derrida, author of a book specifically called *Of Grammatology*) sets in opposition to speech a *being of writing*: the letter, in its graphic materiality, then becomes an irreducible ideality, linked to the deepest experiences of humanity (this is readily seen in the Orient, where "graphism" possesses a veritable civilizing power). On the other hand, psychoanalysis (in its most recent investigations) reveals that the letter (as a graphic feature, even if of phonic origin) is a great intersection of symbols (a truth divined by a whole baroque literature and by the entire art of calligraphy), a point of convergence and departure of countless metaphors. The empire of this new letter, this second letter (opposed to the literal letter, the one that kills), is yet to be described: since the advent of written humanity, of what games has the letter not been the point of departure! Take a letter: you will see its secret deepen (and never come to an end) down through the infinite associations (metonymies) in which you will rediscover everything about the world: its history, yours, its great symbols, the philosophy of your own name (by its initials), etc. Before Erté (but this is virtually a new age, so completely has it been forgotten), the Middle Ages bequeathed us a thesaurus of experiments, of dreams, of meanings, in the labor of its uncials; and graphic art, if we can shake off our society's empiricist yoke, which reduces language to a simple instrument of communication, should be the major art which transcends the futile opposition of figurative and of abstract: for a letter, at one and the same time, *means* and *means nothing*, imitates nothing and yet symbolizes, dismisses both the alibi of realism and that of aestheticism.

R.T.

Saussure is known for his *Cours de linguistique générale,* from which has emerged a good share of modern linguistics. We are beginning to realize, however, by certain fragmentary publications, that the Genevan philosopher's grand design was not at all to establish a new linguistics (he thought rather little, we are told, of his *Cours*), but to develop and impose upon other (highly skeptical) philosophers a discovery he had made and which obsessed his life (much more than structural linguistics): i.e., that there exists, braided into the verse of the old (Vedic, Greek, Latin) poems, a certain name (of a god, of a hero) put there by the poet in a rather esoteric fashion—and yet in a regular fashion, this name making itself understood by the successive selection of several privileged letters. Saussure's discovery is, in short, that poetry is double: line over line, letter over letter, word over word, signifier over signifier. This anagrammatic phenomenon was what Saussure, once he perceived it, believed he could find everywhere; he was obsessed by it; he could not read a line of verse without hearing in the rustle of the first meaning a ceremonial name formed by the federation of several letters apparently scattered throughout the line. Divided between his philosopher's reason and the certitude of this second hearing, Saussure was greatly tormented: he feared to pass for a lunatic. Yet what an admirable symbolic truth! Meaning is never simple (except in mathematics), and the letters which form a word, though each of them is *rationally* insignificant (linguistics has sufficiently taught us that sounds form distinctive units and not signifying units, as opposed to words), keep searching, in us, for their freedom, which is to signify *something else.* It cannot be by chance that, on the threshold of his career, Erté took the initials of his two names and out of them made a third, which has become his name as an artist: like Saussure, he merely *listened to* this double—braided without his knowing it into the mundane, everyday utterance— of his identity; by this annunciatory procedure, he already designated the permanent object of his oeuvre, the letter: the letter, wherever it may be (and with all the more reason in our name), always makes us a sign, like that woman who, holding a splendid bird in each hand and raising her arms to different heights, forms the F of the Ertéan alphabet: the woman makes the sign and the sign makes a sign: a kind of scriptorial art is instituted in which the sign can infinitely regress.

The Alphabet

Erté has composed an alphabet. Taken in the alphabet, the letter becomes primordial (ordinarily it is a capital); given in its *princeps* state, it reinforces its essence *as letter*: here it is pure letter, sheltered from any temptation which would link it to and dissolve it into the word (i.e., into a contingent meaning). Claudel once said of the Chinese character that it possessed a schematic being, a scriptorial persona. By his poetic work, Erté makes each of our Occidental letters into an ideogram, i.e., into a "graphism" which is self-sufficient; he dismisses the word: who would want to write a word with Erté's letters? That would be a kind of misunderstanding, a solecism: the only word, the only syntagm Erté composes with his letters is his own name, which is still two letters. In Erté's alphabet there is a choice which denies the sentence, which repudiates discourse. Here again Claudel helps us shake off that indolence which leads us to suppose that letters are merely the inert elements of a meaning generated only by combinations and accumulations of neutral forms; he helps us understand what a solitary letter can be (whose solitude is guaranteed for us by the alphabet): "The letter is in essence analytic: every word it constitutes is a successive utterance of affirmations which the eye and the voice spell out: to the unit it adds, on the same line, another unit, and the precarious vocable is created and modified in a perpetual variation." Erté's letter is an affirmation (however full of amenity), it posits itself anterior to the word's *precarity* (which is undone from one combination to the next): alone, it seeks development not in the direction of its sisters (within the sentence) but in the endless metaphor of its individual form: a strictly poetic path which does not lead to discourse, to the *logos*, to the (always syntagmatic) *ratio*, but to the infinite symbol. Such is the alphabet's power: to rediscover a kind of natural state of the letter. For the letter, if it is alone, is innocent: the Fall begins when we *align* letters to make them into words (what better means of putting an end to the other's discourse than to undo the word and make it return to the primordial letter, as our popular locution has it in most languages (*N, O, NO!* or, in French, *n, i, ni, c'est fini!*).

I should like to digress briefly here, and personally. The author of these lines has always felt a deep dissatisfaction with himself at being unable to keep from making the same mistakes in retyping a text. These mistakes are commonly omissions or additions; diabolic, the letter is *too much* or *too little*; the wiliest mistake, however, and the commonest as well, is metathesis: how many times (doubtless animated by an unconscious irritation against the words which were familiar to me and of which I consequently felt myself to be a prisoner) have I not typed *sturcture* (instead of *structure*), *susbtitute* (instead of *substitute*), or *trasncription* (instead of *transcription*)? Each of these mistakes, by dint of repetition, takes on a bizarre physiognomy, personal and malevolent—it signifies to me that there is something inside me that resists the word and punishes it by distorting it. In a way, evil begins with the word, with the intelligible series of letters. Hence, anterior or exterior to the word, the alphabet achieves a kind of Adamic state of language: it is language before the Fall, because it is language before discourse, language before the syntagm, and yet, already, by the letter's substitutive richness, entirely open to the treasures of the symbol. This is why, aside from their grace, their inventiveness, their aesthetic quality, or rather *through* these very properties, which are dimmed by no intention of meaning (discourse), Erté's letters are *euphoric* objects. Like the good fairy who, touching the child with her wand, graciously causes roses to fall from her lips with every word (instead of the toads "uttered" by her nasty rival), Erté bestows upon us the pure letter not yet compromised in any association and thus untouched by any Fall: gracious and incorruptible.

Sinuous

The substance from which Erté makes the letter is, as we have said, a mixture of woman and adornment; body and garment supplement each other; the vestimentary appendage spares the woman any acrobatic strain and transforms her into a letter without her losing anything of her femininity, as if the letter were "naturally" feminine. The "operators" of Erté's letters are numerous and varied: wings, tails, crests, plumes, scarves, balloons, trains, belts, veils; these "mutants" (they govern the mutation of Woman into Letter) have not only a formative role (by their complements, their corrections, they help create the letter geometrically) but also a conjurative one: they make it possible, by recalling a charming or cultural (familiar) object, to exorcise the wicked letter (there are such): T is a deadly sign: a gibbet, a cross, a torture; Erté makes it into a vernal, floral nymph, her body naked, her head covered with a thin veil; where the literal alphabet says *arms crossed*, Erté's symbolic alphabet says *arms open*, engaged in a gesture at once modest and favorable. This is because Erté makes of the letter what the poet makes of the word: a game, a form of pun. The play on words is based on a very simple semantic mechanism: one and the same signifier (a word) simultaneously takes two different signifieds, so that audition of the word is divided: French appropriately calls this a *double entendre*, a double hearing. Installed within the visual field, Erté practices, one might say, a *double vision*: you perceive, as you like, the woman or the letter, and supplementarily, the arrangement of the one and of the other. Look at the figure 2: it is a kneeling woman, it is a long plume shaped like a question mark, it is 2; the letter is a total and immediate form which would lose its proper meaning if we were to analyze it (according to Gestalt theory), but it is at the same time a charade, i.e., an analytic combination of parts each of which already has a meaning. Like that of baroque poets or painters of superimpositions such as Arcimboldo, Erté's procedure is wily: he makes meaning function on levels which are rationally contradictory (because apparently independent): that of the whole and that of each part; Erté has, one might say, that *touch of mind* (as we might say *touch of the hand*) which in a single gesture opens up the world of the signifier, the world of play.

This play is constituted by several simple forms, arch-forms (every letter supposes them). Let us reread Claudel: "All writing begins by the stroke or line which, by itself, in its continuity, is the pure sign of the individual. Either, then, the line is horizontal, as is each thing which, in mere parallelism to its principle, finds a sufficient reason for being; or else, vertical as is the tree and the human being, it indicates action and posits affirmation; or again, oblique, it marks both movement and meaning." With regard to this analysis, Erté will appear un-

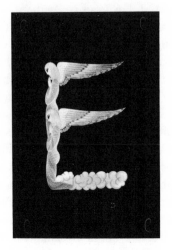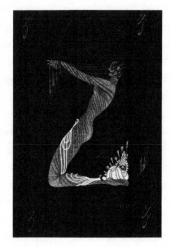

Claudelian (as we might have expected). In *his* alphabet there
are very few horizontals (perhaps two extended wings or birds
in the E and the F, a swirl of hair in the 7, a leg in the A);
Erté is not tellurian, not fluvial, not inspired by the arcana of
religious cosmogony; the extra-human *principle* is not his strong
point. As for verticals, they do not have, for him, the optimist,
voluntarist, humanist meaning which the Catholic poet assigned to this line, marked for him with an "inviolable rectitude." Consider the figure 1: this upright girl in her jar certainly
has something primordial about her, as if to be born were to be
first of all incarnated in the primary simplicity of the vertical;
but complement this figure 1 by the letter I which is close by:
here the woman is decapitated, the dot of the I separated from
its trunk: the vertical and naked—oversimple, one might say—
letters lack the "roundness" of life; they are, tendentiously, dead
letters; this meaning is corroborated by two explicit allegories:
Sadness and *Indifference* are for Erté excessive, paroxystic
verticals: what is sad and what rebuffs is too vertical, exclusively
straight: a good psychological intuition: the vertical straight line
is what cuts, it is the cutting edge which institutes the separa-

tion (*schizein* in Greek means *to split*) by which the sad and indifferent schizophrenic is marked. There are oblique lines in Erté's alphabet (how make letters without them?); obliquity leads Erté to unexpected inventions: N's transverse veil, Z's body flung back, K's broken and expulsed body; but this oblique line, which Claudel made into the natural symbol of movement and of meaning, is not the one Erté prefers. Well, then? Two indifferent lines (horizontal and oblique) and one bad one (vertical): where, then, is Erté's (and our) *euphoria*? The structure answers, corroborating the evidence: we know that in linguistics the ideal paradigm involves four terms: two polar terms (A is opposed to B), a mixed term (both A and B), and a neutral or zero term (neither A nor B); the primordial lines of writing are readily classified within this paradigm: the two polar terms are the horizontal and the vertical; the mixed term is the oblique, a compromise of the first two; but the fourth term, the neutral term, the line which rejects both the horizontal and the vertical? This is the one which Erté prefers, it is *the sinuous line*; it is visibly, for him, the emblem of life—not of raw, primary life, a metaphysical notion alien to Erté's universe, but of delicate, civilized, socialized life, which the feminine theme lets "sing" (as was said of ancient poetry; i.e., which Woman lets us speak of, which she opens to graphic speech): as a cultural (and no longer "natural") value, femininity is sinuous: the arch-form of S permits writing Love, Jealousy, the very dialectic of vital sentiment or, if you prefer a more psychological (and yet still material) term: *duplicity*. This philosophy of sinuosity is expressed in the Mask (*Mystery of the Mask*, says one composition by Erté): aside from the fact that the Woman is, so to speak, *on* the Mask (her body interrupts the bridge of the nose, her wings are its cheeks, and she is also lodged in the eye sockets), the entire Mask is like a piece of Chinese fabric into which is woven a symmetrical and inverted double S, whose four terminal volutes still stare at us (do we not say the *eye* of the volute?): for gaze is direct only by an optical abstraction: to look is also to be looked at, it is to posit a circuit, a *return*, as is said at once by the S of the eye and the Mask, a screen that looks at you.

Departures

Erté's letters are "poetic." What does this mean? The "poetic" is not some vague impression, a kind of indefinable value to which one might conveniently refer by subtraction of the "prosaic." The "poetic" is, very exactly, a form's symbolic capacity; this capacity has value only if it permits the form to "depart" in many directions and thereby potentially to manifest the *infinite* advance of the symbol, which one can never make into a final signified and which is, in short, always the signifier of another signifier (which is why the real antonym of the "poetic" is not the prosaic but the stereotyped). Hence it is futile to try to establish a canonical list of the symbols a work releases: only banalities are susceptible of being thus inventoried, for they alone are *finite* (and finished). We need not reconstitute an Ertéan thematics; it suffices to affirm the *departure potential* of his forms—which is also a potential for *returns*, since the symbolic path is circular, and what Erté leads us *toward* is perhaps the very thing *from which* invention of the letter is established: the O is a mouth, of course, but the two acrobats forming it add to it the very sign of effort, i.e., of the action of opening by which man supplements the closed line of his lips when he seeks to live; as for zero, another and different O, this is still a mouth, but this mouth holds a cigarette and can therefore be metonymically crowned with another mouth, a current of blue smoke which escapes from one corner and joins another: two departures for what is really the same form; K, occlusive, makes the two oblique lines of its form

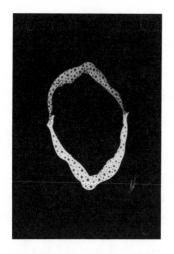 

depart from a *slap* which the rigid vertical of its downstroke imposes, by ricochet, on the woman's posterior (here it is the letter's phonetism which is exploited, since slap is an onomatopoeic word: a linguistic truth, for we know that there exists a phonetic symbolism, and even, for certain words, a semantics of sounds); L is the *link*, the lien (or liana), a woman holding a prone panther on a leash, a panther-woman, myth of fatal subjugation; D is Diana, nocturnal, lunar, musical—a huntress; more subtly in N, the specular letter par excellence (since, seen in a mirror, its oblique line would be inverted without modifying its general figure and without its ceasing to be legible), two steles, two symmetrical busts, exchange a mediating veil: one strips itself of what the other puts on, though this might be the contrary. Thus Erté's letters proceed, simultaneously women, adornments, coiffures, gestures, and lines: each is at once its own essence (in order to figure forth a letter, we must apprehend its archetype) and the point of departure of a symbolic adventure whose action the reader (or the amateur) must let develop in himself.

M

Yet, as we know, to release symbols is never a spontaneous action; poetic affirmation is based on certain denials, certain rejections imprinted by the artist in the form's baldly cultural meaning: symbolic creation is a battle against stereotypes. Erté undoes the primary meaning of certain letters. Consider his E (important because it participates in his own written name); this letter is graphically reputed to be open, by its three branches, toward the following part of the word; it proceeds, as we say, forward; without disfiguring it, Erté turns its tropism around; the back of the letter becomes its front; the letter looks to the left (a region already passed by, according to the direction of our writing), it frays out toward its future, as if the train and the wings of the two women constituting it were caught in a contrary wind. Or look at the Q, an inevitably offensive letter in French and consequently somewhat *taboo*: this is one of the most charming Erté has imagined: two birds form a circle, from their joined beaks to the tips of their long tails [*queues*] overlapping to form that tail of the letter which differentiates it from O. Beyond these euphoric accentuations, Erté keeps his distance with regard to a whole mythology of the letter which, though splendidly poetic, is nonetheless a little too familiar: the one Rimbaud has bequeathed us in his sonnet "Vowels": for Erté, A is not a "gulf of shadows," a "hairy black corset," but the yellow arching of two bodies face to face, whose legs at right angles gain from their acrobatic nature a notion of constructive tension; E, angelic and feminine, is not the "lance of proud glaciers"; I, if its head severed from its docile and modest body confers upon its rectitude, as we have remarked, a suspicion of anxiety, is certainly not purple (there is never any blood in Erté's oeuvre); U, whose two branches enclose, like those of two communicating vessels, two fierce women, is not the cyclic mark alchemy imprints on studious foreheads; and Erté's O, a line drawn in the air like the figure of two acrobats, is in no way the "supreme trumpet call of strange sonorities," is not Omega, hearth of the "Violet Ray of Her Eyes," but only a mouth, open for smiling, kissing, or speaking. This is because for Erté, we must insist, the space of the alphabet, even if the letter recalls its phonetism, is not phonic but graphic; he is chiefly concerned with a symbolism of lines, not of sounds: it is the letter which "departs," not the phoneme; or, if not the letter, at least that something which before being identified with a distinct sound is a muscular gesture marked in us by certain movements of occlusion, of concentration, and of release (this is the work of the acrobat, figured in O, in A, in X, in Y, in 4); Erté always looks for it in the realm of the line, the stroke, a graphic unit; his symbolism is limited, but it does apprehend an art abandoned by our high culture—the typographic art. Rooted in this art, the letter, detached from sound or at least mastering it, incorporating it in its lines, releases a symbolism of its own of which the feminine body becomes the mediator. Let us conclude with four of Erté's letters which exemplarily fulfill this metaphorical development, in which sound and line are braided together. R has, phonetically, a *rich* value (it is only exceptionally that the Parisians first of all, then the French evade it): R is a rural, earthy, *material* sound: R rolls (for Cratylus, the logothete god had made it into a fluvial sound); from the posterior of a naked woman, exposed on her high heels, despite the meditative gesture of her raised hand, spreads a broad stream of fabric (or of hair: we know that we cannot and must not distinguish) whose thick curve, supported on her buttocks like a bustle, forms the two scrolls of the R, as if the woman were abundantly designating in back what she seems to be withholding in front. The same materiality (which never ceases being elegant) occurs in S: this is a sinuous woman coiled within the shape of the letter, itself consisting of a pink effervescence—as if the young body were swimming in some primordial, seething yet smooth substance, and as if the letter as a whole were a kind of vernal hymn to the excellence of sinuosity, the line of life. Quite different is a nearby letter, S's twin yet foe: is not Z an inverted and angulated S, an S *belied*? For Erté, Z is a melancholy, crepuscular, veiled letter in which Woman inscribes both her submission and her supplication (for Balzac, too, Z was a "bad" letter, as he explains in his tale Z. *Marcas*).

Finally, in this alphabetic cosmography of Erté's, there is M: a singular letter, the only one, I believe, which owes nothing to Woman or to her favorite substitutes, angel and bird. This inhuman letter (since it is no longer anthropomorphic) consists of fierce flames: it is a burning door, devoured by wicks: the letter of love and death (at least in our Latin languages), the folk letter of black despair, flames alone amid so many Letter-Women (as we might say Flower-Maidens), like the mortal absence of that body Erté has made into the loveliest object imaginable: a script.

1973

Arcimboldo, or Magician
and Rhétoriqueur*

Officially, Arcimboldo was Maximilian's portraitist. His activity, however, far exceeded painting; he composed armorial bearings, ducal arms, designs for stained-glass windows and tapestry, he decorated organ panels and even proposed a colorimetric method of musical transcription by which "a melody could be represented by minuscule patches of color on a paper"; but, above all, he was an entertainer of princes, a showman: he organized and staged performances, invented tournaments (*giostre*). His composite heads, which he produced for twenty-five years at the court of the German emperors, functioned, generally speaking, as parlor games. In my childhood, we played a game called Families: each player, holding a hand of illustrated cards, took turns asking his partners for the members of the family he was collecting: the pork butcher, the pork butcher's wife, their son, their daughter, their dog, etc.; looking at

---

* Les Grands Rhétoriqueurs were a school of poets of the fifteenth and sixteenth centuries, though the word itself means *rhetorician*.—Trans.

Summer, *oil on canvas.*
Private collection, Bergamo

Autumn, *oil on canvas.*
Louvre, Paris

one of Arcimboldo's composite heads, I must in the same way reconstitute the family of, say, Winter: I ask for a tree stump here, a strand of ivy there, a mushroom, a lemon, a doormat, until I have the whole hibernal thematics before my eyes, the whole "family" of Villon's *morte saison*. Or again, with Arcimboldo, we are playing the game known as Chinese portraits: someone leaves the room, the others decide on someone to be identified, and when the questioner returns he must solve the riddle by the patient interplay of metaphors and metonymies: If it were a cheek, what would it be? —A peach. If it were a ruff? —Ears of ripe wheat. If it were an eye? —A cherry. I know: it's Summer.

In the figure of *Autumn,* the (terrible) eye consists of a little prune. In other words—in French, at least—the botanic *prunella* becomes the ocular *prunelle,* our word for eyeball. It is as if, like a baroque poet, Arcimboldo exploits the "curiosities" of language, plays on synonymy and homonymy. His painting has a linguistic basis, his imagination is, strictly speaking, poetic: it does not create signs, it combines them, permutes them, deflects them—precisely what the practitioner of language does.

One of the techniques of the poet Cyrano de Bergerac consists in taking a perfectly banal metaphor in the language and endlessly exploiting its literal meaning. If the language says "die of grief," Cyrano conceives the story of a condemned man whose executioners sing him tunes so lugubrious that he finally dies of grief over his own death. Arcimboldo proceeds in the same way as Cyrano: if ordinary discourse compares (as it often does) a headdress to an overturned dish of food, Arcimboldo takes the comparison literally, makes it into an identification: the hat becomes a dish, the dish becomes a helmet (a "salad," *celata*). The procedure functions in two time frames: at the moment of the comparison, it remains one of pure common sense, proposing the most ordinary thing in the world, an analogy; but in a second time frame the analogy goes wild because it is radically exploited, carried to the point where it destroys itself as analogy: comparison becomes metaphor: the helmet is no longer *like* a dish, it *is a* dish. However, by a final subtlety, Arcimboldo keeps the two terms of the identification, helmet and dish, separate: on one side I read a head, on the other the contents of a dish; the identity of the two objects does not depend on simultaneity of perception but on rotation of the image, presented as reversible. My reading oscillates continually: only the title manages to arrest it, makes the picture the portrait of a *Cook*, because from the dish we metonymically infer the man whose professional utensil it is. And then occurs a new repercussion of meaning: why does this cook have the fierce expression of a copper-complexioned old soldier? Because the metal of the dish necessitates armor, helmet, and the cooking of meats requires the swarthy red of open-air professions. A singular old soldier, moreover, whose helmet brim is embellished with a delicate slice of lemon. And so on: the metaphor turns on itself, but according to a centrifugal movement: the backwash of meaning never stops.

It is the dish which makes the hat, and it is the hat which makes the man. Curiously, this last proposition serves as the title of one of Max Ernst's collages (1920), in which human silhouettes result from a jointed pile of headgear. Here, too, baroque representation turns on language and its formulas. Under the picture hums the vague music of such ready-made phrases as *Le style, c'est l'homme,* or in Max Ernst's case, *The style is the tailor, The work shows the workman, The dish reveals the cook,* etc. Language discreetly affords these apparently whimsical, even surrealist paintings a rational point of reference. Arcimboldo's art is not extravagant; it remains within the rim of common sense, on the verge of the proverb; what mattered was that the princes for whom these entertainments were devised be amazed by them and yet recognize them for what they were; hence a sense of the marvelous rooted in certain customary propositions: *The cook prepares dishes.* Everything is elaborated within the field of commonplace metonymies.

There is a relation of these images to the language, but also to discourse: to the folk tale, for instance: they employ the same method of description. Mme d'Aulnay says of Laideronnette, Empress of the Pagodas ("tiny grotesque figures with movable heads"): "She undressed and stepped into the bath, whereupon pagodas and pagodines began to sing and to play their instruments: some had theorbos made of a walnut shell; others had viols fashioned from the hull of an almond; for their instruments had to match their size." Arcimboldo's composite heads thus participate in the fairy tale: of his allegorical personages we

Cook, *oil on wood. Civic Museum, Cremona*

might say; this one had mushrooms for lips and wore a lemon as a pendant; another had a squash for a nose; the neck of a third consisted of a heifer lying prone, etc. What circles vaguely behind the image, like a memory, the insistence of a model, is a fantastic tale: I seem to hear Perrault describing the metamorphosis of the words spoken by the good sister and the wicked one, after they have encountered the fairy: with each sentence, two roses, two pearls, and two big diamonds drop from the younger one's lips, while from the elder's mouth fall two vipers and two toads. The parts of speech are transmuted into objects; in the same way, Arcimboldo paints not so much things but rather the description a teller of fantastic tales might give of them: he illustrates what is already the linguistic copy of an amazing story.

Let us recall, once again, the structure of our human language: it is doubly articulated: the sequence of discourse can be divided into words, and the words divided in their turn into sounds (or into letters). Yet there is a great difference between these two articulations: the first produces units each of which already has a meaning (the words); the second produces non-signifying units (the phonemes: a phoneme, in itself, signifies nothing). This structure, we know, is not valid for the visual arts; it is quite possible to decompose the "discourse" of a picture into forms (lines and points) but these forms signify nothing before being assembled; painting knows only one articulation. Hence, we can readily understand the structural paradox of the Arcimboldesque compositions.

Arcimboldo makes painting into a veritable language, he gives it a double articulation: the head of *Calvin* first decomposes into forms which are *already* namable objects—in other words, *words*; a chicken carcass, a drumstick, a fishtail, scribbled pages: these objects in their turn decompose into forms which in themselves signify nothing: here we return to the double scale of words and sounds. Everything functions as if Arcimboldo had upset the pictural system, abusively doubled it, hypertrophying within it the signifying, analogical possibility, thereby producing a kind of structural monster, source of a subtle (because intellectual) uneasiness, even more penetrating than if the horror derived from a simple exaggeration or a simple mixture of elements: it is because everything signifies, *on two levels*, that Arcimboldo's painting functions as a rather alarming denial of pictural language.

In the West (contrary to Eastern practice), painting and writing have had relatively few relationships; letter and image have communicated only in the somewhat irresponsible margins of creation, outside of classicism. Without resorting to a single letter, Arcimboldo nonetheless constantly verges on the graphic experience. His friend and admirer Canon Comanini saw the composite heads as an emblematic writing (which is, after all, what Chinese ideography is); between the two levels of the Arcimboldesque language (that of the face and that of the signifying features which compose it) there is the same relation of *friction*, a grating relation, which we find in Leonardo da Vinci between the order of signs and the order of images: in the *Trattato della Pittura*, the mirror writing is sometimes interrupted by heads of old men or pairs of old women: writing and drawing are fascinated, caught up by each other. In the same way, looking at one of Arcimboldo's composite heads, we always feel a little as if it were *written*. And yet, no letter. This results from the double articulation. As in Leonardo's case, there is a duplicity of graphisms: they are deliberately half images, half signs.

A composite head is made with "things" (fruit, fish, babies, books, etc.). But the "things" which serve to compose the head are not diverted from another function (except perhaps in the *Cook*, where the animal which, upside down, produces the man's face is made to be eaten). These are things which are here *as things*, as if they came not from a familiar, everyday space but from a chart where objects are defined by their figurative analogon: here is the Stump, here is the Ivy, here is the Lemon, here is the Doormat, etc. The "things" are presented didactically, as in a book for children. The head is composed of lexicographic units which come from a dictionary, but this dictionary is of images.

Rhetoric and its figures: this was how the West meditated on language, for over two thousand years: it never stopped marveling that there could be in language certain transfers of meaning (*metabola*), and that these metabola could be coded to the point where they might be classified and named. In his fashion, Arcimboldo, too, is a rhetorician: by his composite heads, he casts into the discourse of the Image a whole bundle of rhetorical figures: the canvas becomes a real laboratory of tropes.

A shell stands for an ear: this is a *Metaphor*. A heap of fish stands for *Water*—in which they live: this is a *Metonymy*. *Fire* becomes a flaming head: this is an *Allegory*.

To enumerate peaches, pears, cherries, raspberries, and ears of wheat in order to signify *Summer*: this is an *Allusion*. To repeat the fish in order to make it here into a nose and there into a mouth: this is an *Antanaclasis* (I repeat a word while making it change its meaning). To evoke one name by another which has the same sound (*Tu es Petrus et super hanc petram . . .*): this is an *Agnomination*; to evoke one thing by another which has the same form (a nose by a rabbit's rump) is to make an agnomination of images, etc.

Rabelais made great use of certain comical languages artificially—but systematically—elaborated: these are *forgeries*, parodies of language itself, in a sense. There was, for instance, his *baragouin* or coding of an utterance by substitution of elements:

there was his *charabia,* or coding by transposition (Queneau, today, has derived certain comic effects from this cipher, writing for instance: *Kékcékça* for *"Qu'est-ce que c'est que ça?"*); finally there was, even crazier than the others, his *lanternois,* a magma of absolutely indecipherable sounds, a cryptogram whose key is lost. Now, Arcimboldo's art is an art of forgery. Suppose there is a message to deliver: Arcimboldo wants to signify the head of a cook, of a peasant, of a Reformation leader, or even of summer, water, fire; this message he encodes, for to encode means both to conceal and not to conceal; the message is concealed in that the eye is diverted from the total meaning by the meaning of the detail; at first I do not see that the fruits or the animals heaped up before me are anything but fruits or animals; and it is by an effort of distance, by changing the level of perception, that I receive another message, a hyper-metropic apparatus which, like a decoding grid, allows me suddenly to perceive the total meaning, the "real" meaning.

Thus, Arcimboldo imposes a system of substitution (an apple comes to stand for a cheek, as in a coded message; a letter or a syllable comes to mask another letter or another syllable), and, in the same way, a system of transposition (the whole figure is somehow drawn back toward the detail). However, and this is Arcimboldo's peculiarity, what is remarkable about the composite heads is that the picture *hesitates* between coding and decoding: even when we have displaced the screen of substitution and of transposition in order to perceive the head composed as an *effect,* our eyes retain the tracery of the first meanings which have served to produce this effect. In other words, from a linguistic point of view—which, indeed, is his own—Arcimboldo speaks a double language, both distinct and blurred; he produces "baragouin" and "charabia," but these forgeries remain entirely intelligible. In short, the only oddity which Arcimboldo does not produce is a totally incomprehensible language like "lanternois": his art is not insane.

. . .

Triumphant realm of metaphor: in Arcimboldo, everything is metaphor. Nothing is ever *denoted*, since all the features (lines, shapes, spirals) which serve to compose a head have a meaning *already*, and since this meaning is diverted toward another meaning, somehow cast beyond itself (this is, etymologically, what the word *metaphor* means). Often Arcimboldo's metaphors are *reasonable*. By which we mean that between the two terms of the transposition there subsists a common feature, a "bridge," a certain *analogy*: teeth "spontaneously" or "commonly" (since others besides Arcimboldo might have said it) resemble lily-of-the-valley blossoms on their stem, or peas in their pod; these different objects have shapes in common: they are fragments of substance singled out, made equal, and arranged—pigeonholed—in the same line: the nose resembles an ear of corn by its oblong and swelling shape; the fleshy mouth looks like a split fig whose whitish interior illuminates the red notch of the pulp. Yet, even when analogical, the Arcimboldesque metaphor is, so to speak, one-way: Arcimboldo persuades us that the nose *naturally* resembles an ear of corn, that the teeth *naturally* resemble seeds, that the flesh of fruit *naturally* resembles that of the lips: but no one would say the contrary *naturally*: the ear of corn is not a nose, the seeds are not teeth, the fig is not a mouth (unless it is mediated by another organ, this one female, as is attested by a folk metaphor which we find in many languages). In short, even when well founded, the Arcimboldesque metaphor depends on a *coup de force*. Arcimboldo's art is not indeterminate, it proceeds in a specific direction: this language is very affirmative.

Often, too, the metaphoric effort is so audacious (like that of an extremely *précieux* or extremely modern poet) that there is no "natural" relation between the thing represented and its representation: how can babies' legs or buttocks afford us an ear (*Herod*)? How can a common wax taper represent a man's forehead (*Fire*)? In any case, the procedure requires relays of great sophistication; the analogical link is farfetched (it becomes rare, *précieux*): it is the yellow color of the wax which suggests the smooth skin of the forehead, that part of human flesh where the blood is not abundant, or else the coil of wax suggests, at best, the frowning wrinkles of the human brow. We might say that in these extreme metaphors the two terms of the *metabola* are not in a relation of equivalence (of being) but actually of *praxis* (of doing): the flesh of the tiny naked body *makes* (fabricates, produces) the tyrant's ear. Arcimboldo thereby alerts us to the *productive*, transitive character of metaphors; his, in any case, are not simple observations of affinities, they do not register possible analogies which might exist in nature and which the poet would be responsible for making manifest: they *undo* certain familiar objects in order to produce new, strange ones from them by a veritable *coup de force* (still another), which is the visionary's *work*, and not merely his talent for collecting resemblances.

Perhaps, however, the greatest audacity of all is not in these improbable metaphors but in those we might call *offhand*. Such offhandedness means, not metaphorizing the object, but changing its place: when Arcimboldo replaces the teeth of the personage representing water by the teeth of a pike, he does not affect the object (it is still *teeth*), but he causes it to shift from one realm to another; the metaphor here is no more than the exploitation of an identity, even of a tautology (*teeth are teeth*), which has simply slipped and changed reference (context). This slight imbalance produces the strongest of alienations. As Magritte understood so well when he called one of his compositions, whose procedure is related to the Arcimboldesque "leap," *The Rape* (1934): here, too, what is in question is a duplicitous image, at once—and depending on the *turn* of the gaze—a woman's head and/or her bust: the breasts appearing, if the viewer so determines, in place of the eyes, the navel in place of the mouth. Here again the objects merely change places, leaving the realm of nudity for that of cerebrality—and this suffices to create a supernatural object, like the Aristophanic androgyne.

As a poet, i.e. a maker, a producer of language, Arcimboldo's verve is continuous; the synonyms are unremittingly flung on the canvas. Arcimboldo constantly employs different forms to say the same thing. If he chooses to "say" the nose, his reservoir of synonyms affords him a branch, a pear, a squash, an ear of corn, a flower's calyx, a fish, a rabbit's rump, a chicken's carcass. If he wants to "say" an ear, he need only draw upon a heteroclite catalogue, from which he extracts a tree stump, the underside of an umbellate mushroom, a rose, a carnation, an apple, a shell, an animal head, the crosspiece of an oil lamp. If he wants to give his character a beard, here is a fishtail, or a crayfish's antennae. Is this repertoire an infinite one? No, if we abide by the relatively infrequent allegories which have come down to us; almost always what is involved are fruits, plants, comestibles, since we are chiefly concerned with the seasonal figures of Mother Earth; but only the context limits the message; the imagination itself is indeed infinite, of an acrobatic application whose mastery is such that we feel it ready to seize upon any and every object.

It was a fashion of the period to produce reversible images: upside-down, the pope became a goat, Calvin a jester with bells; such diversions served as caricatures for the partisans or adversaries of the Reformation. We have one reversible image by Arcimboldo—in one direction a cook, in the other a simple dish of meat. In rhetoric this figure is called a palindrome; the true palindrome makes no change in the message, which is read identically in one direction and in the other: *Roma tibi subito motibus ibit amor,* Quintilian says; set a mirror at the end of the line and you will recover it intact, reading it in the opposite direction; the same is true for the figures on playing cards: the mirror bisects and repeats, it does not denature the image. On the contrary, when you reverse the Arcimboldesque image, you certainly rediscover meaning (and it is for this reason that you have a palindrome), but this meaning, in the movement of inversion, has changed: the dish becomes a cook. "Everything is always the same," says the true palindrome; whether you take things in one direction or the other, the truth remains. "Everything can assume an opposite meaning," says Arcimboldo's palindrome; i.e., everything always has a meaning, whichever way you read, but this meaning is never the same.

Everything signifies and yet everything is surprising. Arcimboldo makes the fantastic out of the familiar: the total has another effect than the adding up of the parts: we could say that it is the remainder. We must make an effort to understand these odd mathematics: they are mathematics of *analogy,* if we recall that etymologically *analogia* means *proportion:* meaning depends on the level you adopt. If you look at the image close up, you see only fruits and vegetables; if you step back, you no longer see anything but a man with a terrible eye, a ribbed doublet, a bristling ruff (*Summer*): distance and proximity are promoters of meaning. Is this not the great secret of every vital semantics? Everything proceeds from a *spacing out* or *staggering* of articulations. Meaning is born from a combination of non-signifying elements (phonemes, lines); but it does not suffice to combine these elements to a first degree in order to exhaust the creation of meaning: what has been combined forms aggregates which can combine again among themselves a second, a third time. I imagine that an ingenious artist could take all of Arcimboldo's composite heads, combine them with a view to a new effect of meaning, and from their arrangement produce, for instance, a landscape, a city, a forest: to defer perception is to engender a new meaning: perhaps the same principle applies in the historic parade of forms (to enlarge five square centimeters of Cézanne is in a way to come up with a canvas by Nicolas de Staël), and in that of the human sciences (historical science has changed the meaning of events by combining them *on another level*: battles, treaties, and reigns—the level where traditional history used to stop—when submitted to a perspective which would diminish their meaning, are now merely the signs of a new language, of a new intelligibility, of a new history).

In short, Arcimboldo's painting is *mobile*: it dictates to the "reader," by its very project, the obligation to come closer or to step back, assuring him that by this movement he will lose no meaning and that he will always remain in a vital relation with the image. In order to obtain mobile compositions, Calder freely articulated volumes; Arcimboldo obtains an analogous result while remaining on the surface of the canvas: it is not the support, it is the human subject that is asked to move. This choice, "entertaining" as it is (in Arcimboldo's case), is no less audacious for being so, or at least extremely "modern," for it implies a relativization of the space of meaning: including the reader's gaze within the very structure of the canvas, Arcimboldo virtually shifts from a Newtonian painting based on the fixity of the objects represented to an Einsteinian art according to which the observer's movement participates in the work's status.

Arcimboldo is animated by so great an energy of movement that, even when he affords several versions of the same head, he produces certain significant changes: from version to version, the head assumes different meanings. Here we are in a musical universe: there is certainly a basic theme (Summer, Autumn, Calvin), but each variation has a different effect. Here seasonal Man has just died, winter is still russet with a lingering autumn; he is already pale, but the eyelids, still swollen, have just closed; here (and if this second version preceded the first, it doesn't matter), the Winter-Man is now no more than a corpse in an advanced stage of decomposition; the face is gullied and gray; instead of the eye, even a closed one, there is no longer anything but a dark cavity; the tongue is livid. In the same manner, there are two versions of *Spring* (one is still timid, pale; the other, more cheerful, affirms the coming summer) and two of *Calvin*: the Bergamo *Calvin* is arrogant, the one in Sweden is hideous; it is as if from Bergamo to Stockholm (it does not matter whether or not this is the order of composition) the horrible countenance has turned gray, collapsed, fallen to pieces; the wicked eyes go dead, stupid; the rictus of the mouth grows more marked; the bundles which serve as a ruff turn from yellowed parchment to livid paper, the impression is all the more disgusting because this head is formed of edible substances: it then becomes, literally, inedible: the chicken and the fish turn into garbage, or worse: these are the discards of a bad restaurant. Everything happens as if, each time, the head were oscillating between marvelous life and horrible death. These composite heads are heads which are decomposing.

Let us once again turn to the question of meaning—for, after all, this is what interests, what fascinates and disturbs us in Arcimboldo. The "units" of a language are here on the canvas; unlike the phonemes of articulated language, they already have a meaning: they are namable things: fruit, flowers, branches, fish, sheaves, books, babies, etc.; combined, these units produce a unitary meaning; but this second meaning, as a matter of fact, doubles: on the one hand, I read a human head (a sufficient reading, since I can *name* the shape I perceive, can make it join the lexicon of my own language, where the word *head* exists), but on the other hand, I also and at the same time read an altogether different meaning which comes from a different region of the lexicon: "Summer," "Winter," "Autumn," "Spring," "Cook," "Calvin," "Water," "Fire"; now I can conceive this strictly allegorical meaning only by referring to the meaning of the first units: it is the fruits which make Summer, the stumps of dead wood which make Winter, the fish which make Water. Here already, then, are three meanings in one and the same image; the first two are, so to speak, denoted, for in order to be produced, they imply nothing other than the work of my perception, insofar as it is immediately articulated on a lexicon (a word's denoted meaning is the meaning given by the dictionary, and the dictionary suffices to make me read, according to the level of my perception: here fish, there a head). Quite different is the third meaning, the allegorical meaning: in order to read here the head of *Summer* or of *Calvin*, I require another culture than that of the dictionary; I require a metonymic culture, which makes me associate certain fruits (and not others) with Summer, or, more subtly still, the austere ugliness of a face with Calvinist puritanism; and as soon as we leave the dictionary of words for a chart of cultural meanings, of associations of ideas, in short for an encyclopedia of received ideas, we enter into the infinite realm of connotations. Arcimboldo's connotations are simple, they are stereotypes, yet connotation opens an interrogation of meaning; starting from the allegorical meaning, other meanings are possible, no longer "cultural," these latter, but proceeding from certain (attracting or repelling) movements of the body. Beyond perception and signification (itself lexical or cultural) develops a whole world of *value*: looking at one of Arcimboldo's composite heads, I find myself saying not only *I read, I divine, I find, I understand* but also *I like, I don't like* . . . Uneasiness, fear, laughter, desire join the party.

Doubtless, affect itself is cultural: Dogon masks strike us as having a panic expression because they are marked, for us Westerners, with exoticism, i.e., with the unknown; we perceive nothing of their symbolism, we are not *in league* with them (we are not *religious*); doubtless, they produce an altogether different effect on the Dogons themselves. So with Arcimboldo's heads: it is within our own culture that they provoke the affective meaning which we should, with etymological appropriateness, call the pathetic meaning; for we cannot find certain of these heads "nasty and stupid" without referring, by a training of the body—of language—to an entire sociality: as "expressions," stupidity and nastiness participate in a certain system of historical values: we may doubt that, looking at one of Arcimboldo's heads, an Australian aborigine experiences the vague dread which this head inspires in me.

The effects stirred up in us by Arcimboldo's art are often repulsive. Consider *Winter*: that fungus of the lips looks like a hypertrophied organ, cancerous and hideous: I see the face of a man who has just died, an asphyxiating gag thrust into his mouth. This same Winter, composed of dead bark, has a face covered with pustules and scales; he seems to be in the grip of a disgusting skin disease, pityriasis or psoriasis. The face of another one (*Autumn*) is merely a sum of tumors: the surface is bibulous, turgescent: it is an enormous inflamed organ whose brown blood is becoming congested. Arcimboldesque flesh is always *excessive*: either ravaged, or flayed (*Herod*), or swollen, or sunken, dead. Is there not a single pleasing head? At least there is Spring—doesn't it suggest a happy composition? True, *Spring* is covered with flowers; but we can say that Arcimboldo demystifies the flower, precisely to the degree (a logical scandal) that he does not take it literally; no doubt, seeing a flower, or a bouquet, or a meadow, is in itself an altogether vernal delight; but reduced to a surface, the floral extent readily becomes the efflorescence of a more disturbing state of matter; decomposition produces pulverulence ("flowers" of sulfur) and molds that resemble flowers; skin diseases often suggest tattooed flowers. Hence, Arcimboldo's *Spring* is incarnate in a big livid face tainted with some surface malady. What thereby dooms Arcimboldo's heads to an effect of *malaise* is precisely that they are composite: the more the form of the thing seems to have proceeded from a first impulse, the more euphoric it is (we know that a whole aspect of Oriental art has favored creation *alla prima*); in the immediate and so to speak *uncomposed* form there is the pleasure of a supernatural unit; some musicologists have even connected romantic melody, characterized precisely by its fine unitary development, with the world of the Mother, where the joy of fusion blooms for the child: we might attribute the same symbolic effect to the "beautiful form" seized by the artist on the paper, the canvas, at the first stroke, *alla prima*. Arcimboldo's art is a denial of this felicity: not only does the figured head proceed from a labor, but even the *complication* and hence the duration of this labor are represented: for, before "drawing" *Spring*, he must "draw" each of the flowers that will compose it. Hence, it is the very method of "composition" which disturbs and disaggregates the unitary development of form. Thematically, for instance, what could be smoother and more unified than Water? Water is always a maternal theme, fluidity is a felicity; but in order to produce the allegory of Water, Arcimboldo imagines certain contrary forms: *Water*, for him, is fish, shellfish, a whole heap of hard, discontinuous, sharp, or swollen shapes: Water is in fact monstrous.

Arcimboldo's heads are monstrous because they all refer, whatever the grace of the allegorical subject (Summer, Spring, Flora, Water), to a *malaise* of substance: *seething* or *swarming*. The swarm of living things (plants, animals, babies), arranged in a close-packed disorder (before joining the intelligibility of the final figure), evokes an entire larval life, the entanglement of vegetative beings, worms, fetuses, viscera which are at the limits of life, not yet born and yet already putrescible.

. . .

For Arcimboldo's century, the monster is a wonder, a marvel. The Habsburgs, the painter's patrons, had their cabinets of art and curiosities (*Kunst- und Wunderkammern*) which exhibited strange objects: accidents of nature, effigies of dwarfs, of giants, of hirsute men and women: anything "which amazed and inspired wonder"; these cabinets, it has been said, participated in the laboratories of Faust and of Caligari. Now, the "wonder" —or the "monster"—is essentially what transgresses the separation of realms, mingles animal and vegetable, animal and human; it is *excess*, insofar as it changes the quality of the things to which God has assigned a name: it is *metamorphosis* which causes one order to collapse into another; in short, to use another word, it is *transmigration* (it is said that in Arcimboldo's day there circulated throughout Europe certain Indian miniatures representing fantastic animals whose bodies were made "of a mosaic of human and animal shapes intertwined: musicians, hunters, lovers, foxes, lions, monkeys, rabbits"; each animal thus composed—camel, elephant, horse—represented the simultaneous regrouping of successive incarnations: what was apparently heteroclite referred in fact to the Hindu doctrine of the interior unity of beings). Arcimboldo's heads are, all in all, merely the visible space of a transmigration which leads, before our eyes, from fish to water, from the faggot to the fire, from the lemon to the pendant, and finally, from all substances to the human face (unless you prefer to take this route in the opposite direction and descend from the Winter-Man to the vegetal realm with which he is associated). The principle of the Arcimboldesque "monsters" is, in short, that *Nature does not stop*. Take Spring: it is normal, after all, that Spring should be represented in the form of a woman wearing a hat made of flowers (such hats have actually existed in fashion); but Arcimboldo *continues*; the flowers descend from the object to the body, they invade the skin, they *constitute* the skin: it is a leprosy of flowers which overtakes the face, the neck, the bust . . .

Now, the exercise of such an imagination relates not only to

"art" but also to knowledge: to "surprise" certain metamorphoses (as Leonardo da Vinci did on several occasions) is an act
of knowledge; all knowledge is linked to a classifying order: to
aggrandize or simply to change knowledge is to experiment, by
certain audacious operations, upon what subverts the classifica-
tions we are accustomed to: this is the noble function of magic,
"summa of natural wisdom" (Pico della Mirandola).

Thus Arcimboldo proceeds, from game to Grand Rhetoric,
from rhetoric to magic, from magic to wisdom.

1978

Is Painting a Language?

Since linguistics has attained its present extension—in any case, since the author of these lines first expressed his interest in semiology (now some dozen years ago), how many times has he been asked this question: Is painting a language? Yet, till now, no answer: we have not been able to establish either painting's lexicon or its general grammar—to put the picture's signifiers on one side and its signifieds on the other, and to systematize their rules of substitution and combination. Semiology, as a science of signs, has not managed to make inroads into art: an unfortunate obstruction, since it reinforces by default the old humanist superstition that artistic creation cannot be "reduced" to a system: system, as we know, is the declared enemy of man and of art.

As a matter of fact, to ask if painting is a language is *already* an ethical question, one which requires a mitigated, a censored answer safeguarding the rights of the creative individual (the artist) and those of a human universality (society). Like any innovator, Jean-Louis Schefer does not answer the rigged questions of art (of its philosophy or of its history); he substitutes for them an apparently marginal question, but one whose distance leads him to constitute an unexamined field in which painting and its relation (as we might say: the relation of a journey), structure, text, code, system, representation, and figuration, all these terms inherited from semiology, are distributed according to a new topology, which constitutes "a new way of feeling, a new way of thinking." His question is more or less the following: What is the connection between the picture and the language inevitably used in order to read it—i.e., in order (implicitly) to write it? *Is not this connection the picture itself?*

Obviously the question is not one that would limit writing the picture to the professional criticism of painting. The picture, whoever writes it, exists only in the *account* given of it; or again: in the total and the organization of the various readings that can be made of it: a picture is never anything but its own plural description. We see how this traversal of the picture by the text out of which I constitute it is both close to and remote from a painting presumed to be a language; as Jean-Louis Schefer says: "*The image has no a priori structure, it has textural structures . . . of which it is the system*"; so it is no longer possible (and this is where Schefer gets pictural semiology out of its rut) to conceive the description by which the picture is constituted as a neutral, literal, denoted state of language; nor as a pure mythic elaboration, the infinitely available site of subjective investments: the picture is neither a real object nor an imaginary object. Of course, the identity of what is "represented" is ceaselessly deferred, the signified always displaced (for it is only a series of nominations, as in a dictionary), the analysis is endless; but this leakage, this infinity of language is precisely the picture's system: the image is not the expression of a code, it is the variation of a work of codification: it is not the repository of a system but the generation of systems. To paraphrase a famous title, Schefer might have called his book *The Unique and Its Structure*; and this structure is structuration itself.

The ideological repercussions are evident: every effort of classical semiotics tended to constitute or to postulate—confronted with the heteroclite of works (pictures, myths, narratives)—a Model, in relation to which each product could be defined in terms of discrepancies. With Schefer, who extends Julia Kristeva's work in this fundamental area, semiology emerges a little further from the age of the Model, the Norm, the Code, the Law—or, one might say, from theology.

This *deviation*, or this reversal, of Saussurian linguistics obliges us to modify the very discourse of analysis, and this extreme consequence is perhaps the best proof of its validity and of its novelty. Schefer could express the shift from structure to structuration, from the remote, frozen, ecstatic Model of the work (of the system), only by analyzing *a single picture*; he has chosen the Venetian painter Paris Bordone's *Chess Game* (thereby affording us some admirable "transcriptions," writing of a quality which finally puts the critic on the writer's side); his discourse offers an exemplary break with the dissertation; his analysis does not furnish its "results," ordinarily induced from a total of statistical samplings; it is continuously *in the act of language*, since Schefer's principle is that the very practice of the picture is its own theory. Schefer's discourse reveals not the secret, the truth of this *Chess Game*, but only (and necessarily) the activity by which it is structured: the work of the reading (which defines the picture) is radically identified with the work of the writing: there is no longer a critic, nor even a writer talking painting, there is the *grammatographer*, someone who writes the picture's writing.

This book constitutes, in the order of what is commonly called aesthetics or art criticism, a *labor princeps*, but we must understand that this labor could be achieved only by subverting the context of our disciplines, the classification of the objects which define our "culture." Schefer's text in no way derives from that famous "interdisciplinary" program cooked up by our new academic culture. It is not the disciplines which need to be exchanged, it is the objects: there is no question of "applying" linguistics to the picture, injecting a little semiology into art history; there *is* a question of eliminating the distance (the censorship) institutionally separating picture and text. Something is being born, something which will invalidate "literature" as much as "painting" (and their metalinguistic correlates, "criticism" and "aesthetics"), substituting for these old cultural divinities a generalized "ergography," the text as work, the work as text.

1969

Masson's Semiography

From the start, Masson's semiograms, by a kind of unexpected precursion, "take up" in advance the chief propositions of a theory of the text which twenty years ago did not exist and which today constitutes the distinctive sign of the avant-garde: proof that it is the *circulation* of the "arts" (or elsewhere: of the sciences) which produces movement: "painting" here opens the way to "literature," for its seems to have postulated a new object ahead of itself, the Text, which decisively invalidates the separation of the "arts." Masson was fifty-four when he entered his Asiatic (or, as I should prefer to call it, his textural) period; most of our current theoreticians of the Text were just getting born. Here are the textural (and current) propositions already to be found in Masson's painting (I use the word *painting* to simplify matters; it would be better to say *semiography*):

First, Masson deliberately establishes what we call an *inter-text*: the painter circulates between (at least) two texts: on the one hand, his own (let us say: the text of painting, of its practices, its gestures, its instruments), and on the other, that of Chinese ideography (i.e., of a localized culture): as it turns out in any true inter-textuality, the Asiatic signs are not inspirational models, "sources," but conductors of graphic energy, distorted citations, identifiable according to line, not letter; what is henceforth displaced is the work's responsibility: it is no longer consecrated by a narrow ownership (that of its immediate creator), it journeys in a cultural space which is open, without limits, without partitions, without hierarchies, where we can recognize pastiche, plagiarism, even imposture—in a word, all forms of the "copy," a practice condemned to disgrace by so-called bourgeois art.

Masson's semiography also tells us this, which is capital in the current theory of the Text: that writing cannot be reduced to a pure function of communication (of *transcription*), as is claimed by the historians of language. Masson's work during this period demonstrates that the identity of written and painted features is not contingent, marginal, baroque (obvious only in calligraphy—a practice, moreover, virtually unknown to our civilization), but somehow persisted in, obsessive, including both the origin and the perpetual present of any *drawn line*: there is a unique practice, extensive to any functionalization, which is that of an undifferentiated "graphism." Thanks to Masson's dazzling demonstration, writing (imagined or real) appears, then, as the very *surplus* of its own function; the painter helps us understand that writing's truth is neither in its messages nor in the system of transmission which it constitutes for current meaning, still less in the psychological expressivity attributed to it by a suspect science, graphology, compromised by certain technocratic interests (expertise, tests), but in the hand which presses down and traces a line, i.e., in *the body which throbs* (which takes pleasure). This is why (Masson's complementary demonstration) color must not be understood as a background against which certain characters "stand out" but rather as pulsion's entire space (we know the pulsional nature of color: witness the scandal caused by the Fauve liberation): in Masson's semiographic work, color provokes the withdrawal of writing from its mercantile, bookkeeping basis (at least this is the origin assigned to our Syrio-Occidental writing). If something is "communicated" in writing (and hence exemplarily in Masson's semiograms), it is not a reckoning, a "reason" (etymologically, this is the same thing), but a desire.

Lastly, by turning (chiefly) to Chinese ideograms, Masson recognizes not only the astonishing beauty of such writing; he also supports the lapse which ideographic characters effect in what we might call the West's scriptory good conscience: are we not proudly convinced our alphabet is the best—the most rational, the most effective? Do not our most rigorous scholars maintain as "self-evident" that the invention of the consonantal alphabet (of the Syrian type) and then of the vocalic alphabet (of the Greek type) were irreversible kinds of progress, conquests of reason and economy over the baroque scribbling of ideographic systems? A fine testimony to that impenitent ethnocentrism which governs our very science! In truth, if we reject the ideogram, it is because we constantly try, in our Occident, to substitute the realm of speech for that of gesture; for reasons which derive from a truly monumental history, it is in our interests to believe, to maintain, to assert scientifically, that writing is but the "transcription" of articulated language: the instrument of an instrument: a chain along whose entire length it is the body which disappears. Masson's semiography, rectifying millennia of scriptorial history, refers us not to origins (what do we care about origins?) but to the body: it imposes upon us not the form (banal proposition of all painters) but the figure, i.e., the elliptical collision of two signifiers: the gesture beneath every ideogram as a kind of evaporated figurative outline, and the gesture of the painter, of the calligrapher, which makes the brush move according to his body. That is what Masson's work tells us: *for writing to be manifest in its truth* (and not in its instrumentality), *it must be illegible*: the semiographer (Masson) knowingly produces, by a sovereign elaboration, the illegible: he detaches writing's pulsion from the image-repertoire of communication (legibility). This is what the Text desires as well. But whereas the written text must still—and ceaselessly—struggle with an apparently signifying substance (words), Masson's semiography, directly resulting from a non-signifying practice (painting), achieves from the start the utopia of the Text.

1973

Cy Twombly:
Works on Paper

Who is Cy Twombly (hereinafter known as TW)? What is it he does? And what are we to call what he does? Words occur readily enough ("drawing," "graphism," "scratching," "clumsy," "childish"), immediately followed by an embarrassment of language: these words, at one and the same time (strangely enough), are *neither untrue nor satisfactory*; for, on the one hand, TW's work coincides with its appearance, which one must be bold enough to say is quite insipid; but on the other hand— and this is the enigma—this appearance does not coincide with the language so much simplicity and innocence should awaken in us, as we look at it. "Childish," TW's "graphisms"? Yes, why not? But also: something more, or less, or aside from that . . . We say: this canvas by TW is *this*, or *that*; but it is rather something very different, *starting from* this or that: in a word, ambiguous because literal and metaphoric, it is *displaced*.

To consider TW's work with the eyes and the lips is therefore continuously to disappoint *what it looks like*. This work does not ask us to contradict the words of culture (what is spontaneous in a man is his culture), simply to displace them, to detach them, to give them another light. TW compels us not to reject but—what is perhaps much more subversive—to traverse the aesthetic stereotype; in short, he calls forth from us a *work of language* (is it not just this work—*our* work—which constitutes the value of an oeuvre?).

Writing

TW's work—others have said as much—is a kind of writing; it has some relation with calligraphy. Yet this relation is one neither of imitation nor of inspiration; a canvas by TW is only what we might call the *allusive* field of writing (allusion, a rhetorical figure, consists in saying one thing with the intention of making another understood). TW alludes to writing (as he often does, as well, to culture, through words: *Virgil, Sesostris*), and then he goes off somewhere else. Where? Specifically, far away from calligraphy, i.e., from that formed, drawn, deliberate, shapely writing which in the eighteenth century was called *a fine hand.*

TW has his own way of saying that the essence of writing is neither a form nor a usage but only a gesture, the gesture which produces it by *permitting it to linger*: a blur, almost a blotch, a negligence. Let us make a comparison. What is the essence of a pair of pants (if it has such a thing)? Certainly not that crisp and well-pressed object to be found on department-store racks; rather, that clump of fabric on the floor, negligently dropped there when the boy stepped out of them, careless, lazy, indifferent. The essence of an object has some relation with its destruction: not necessarily what remains after it has been used up, but what is *thrown away* as being of no use. This is the case with TW's "writings"—they are the scraps of an indolence,

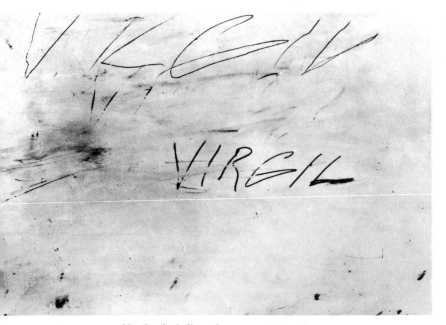

Virgil, *oil, chalk, and crayon on paper.*
Private collection, Berlin

hence of an extreme elegance; as if there remained, after writing, which is a powerful erotic action, what Verlaine calls *la fatigue amoureuse*: that garment dropped in a corner of the . . . canvas.

In TW, the letter—the very contrary of an illuminated initial —is produced without deliberation. Yet it is not *childish* in form, for the child applies himself, presses down, rounds off, sticks out his tongue in his efforts; the child works hard to join the code of the grown-ups. TW draws away from it, loosens, lags behind; his hand seems to levitate—as if the word has been written with his fingertips, not out of disgust or boredom, but out of a kind of caprice open to the memory of a defunct culture which has left no more than the trace of a few words. Chateaubriand: "On islands off the Norwegian coast have been exhumed certain urns engraved with indecipherable characters. To whom do these ashes belong? The winds know nothing of them." TW's writing is even more futile: it is decipherable, but not interpretable; the strokes themselves may well be specific, discontinuous; even so, their function is to restore that *vagueness* which in the army kept TW from being a good decoder of military ciphers ("I was a little too vague for that"). Now, it is the vague which paradoxically excludes any notion of the enigmatic; the vague is not allied with death—the vague is alive.

Of writing TW retains the gesture, not the product. Even if it is possible to consume aesthetically the result of his work (what is called the oeuvre, the canvas), even if TW's productions link up with (they cannot escape) a History and a Theory of Art, what is *shown* is a gesture. What is a gesture? Something like the surplus of an action. The action is transitive, it seeks only to provoke an object, a result; the gesture is the indeterminate and inexhaustible total of reasons, pulsions, indolences which surround the action with an *atmosphere* (in the astronomical sense of the word). Hence, let us distinguish the *message*, which seeks to produce information, and the *sign*, which seeks to produce an intellection, from the *gesture*, which produces all the rest (the "surplus") without necessarily seeking to produce anything. The artist (let us retain this somewhat kitsch term) is by status an "operator" of gestures: he seeks to produce an effect and at the same time seeks no such thing; the effects he produces he has not obligatorily sought out; they are reversed, inadvertent effects which turn back upon him and thereupon provoke certain modifications, deviations, mitigations of the line, of the stroke. Thus in gesture is abolished the distinction between cause and effect, motivation and goal, expression and persuasion. The artist's gesture—or the artist as gesture —does not break the causative chain of actions, what the Buddhist calls *karma* (the artist is not a saint, an ascetic), but he blurs, confuses it, he starts it up again until it loses its meaning. In (Japanese) Zen, this sudden (and sometimes very tenuous) break in our causal logic (I am simplifying) is called a *satori*: by some tiny, even ridiculous, aberrant, preposterous circumstance, the subject *wakens* to a radical negativity (which is no longer a negation). I regard TW's "graphisms" as so many little *satoris*: starting from writing (a causal field if ever there was one: we write, it is said, to communicate), various futile explosions, which are not even interpreted letters, suspend the active Being of writing, the tissue of its motivations, even its aesthetic motivations: *writing* no longer abides anywhere, it is absolutely *in excess*. Is it not at this extreme limit that "art" really begins, or the "text"—all that man does "for nothing," his perversion, his expenditure?

TW has been compared to Mallarmé. But what enables the comparison, i.e., a kind of higher aestheticism which would unite them, exists in neither one. To attack language, as Mallarmé did, implies a much more serious—much more dangerous —intention than that of aesthetics. Mallarmé wanted to deconstruct the sentence, that time-honored (for France) vehicle of ideology. In passing, in loitering (one might say), TW deconstructs writing. To deconstruct does not at all mean to make unrecognizable; in Mallarmé's texts, the French language is acknowledged, it functions—in fragments, it is true. In TW's "graphisms," writing, too, is recognized; it proceeds, it presents itself as writing. Yet the letters formed no longer participate in any graphic code, just as Mallarmé's large syntagmas no longer participate in any rhetorical code—not even that of destruction.

On certain surfaces of TW's there is nothing written, and yet these surfaces seem to be the repository of all writing. Just as Chinese writing was born, we are told, from the tiny cracks of an overheated tortoiseshell, so what appears to be writing in TW's work is born from the surface itself. No surface, wherever we consider it, is a virgin surface: everything is always, already, rough, discontinuous, unequal, set in motion by some accident: there is the texture of the paper, then the stains, the hatchings, the tracery of strokes, the diagrams, the words. At the end of this chain, writing loses its violence; what is imposed is not this writing or that, nor even the Being of writing, it is the idea of a graphic texture: *"for writing,"* says TW's work, as we might say elsewhere: *"for taking,"* *"for eating."*

Culture

Through TW's work, the germs of writing proceed from the greatest rarity to a swarming multiplicity: a kind of graphic pruritus. In its tendency, then, writing becomes culture. When writing bears down, explodes, pushes toward the margins, it rejoins the idea of the Book. The Book which is potentially present in TW's work is the old Book, the annotated Book: a super-added word invades the margins, the interlinea: this is *the gloss*. When TW writes and repeats this one word: *Virgil*, it is *already* a commentary on Virgil, for the name, inscribed by hand, not only calls up a whole idea (though an empty one) of ancient culture but also "operates" a kind of citation: that of an era of bygone, calm, leisurely, even decadent studies: English preparatory schools, Latin verses, desks, lamps, tiny pencil annotations. That is culture for TW: an ease, a memory, an irony, a posture, the gesture of a dandy.

Gauche

It has been said that TW's work looks as if it had been drawn by his left hand. The French language is right-handed: what moves with a certain vacillation, what makes detours, what is clumsy, embarrassed, it calls *gauche*, and out of this *gauche*, an ethical notion, a judgment, a condemnation, it has made a physical term, one of pure denotation, abusively replacing the old word *sénestre* and designating what is to the left of the body: here it is the subjective which, *on the level of language*, has established the objective (just as we observe, in another corner of our language, a sentimental metaphor gives its name to an entirely physical substance: the lover, the *amoureux* who feels love's flame, the *amado*, paradoxically becomes the name of any substance that conducts heat: the *amadou*). This scrap of etymological history reminds us that by producing a writing which seems *gauche* (or left-handed), TW disturbs the body's morality: a morality of the most archaic kind, since it identifies "anomaly" with deficiency, and deficiency with error. The fact that his "graphisms," his compositions, are "gauche" refers TW to the circle of the excluded, the marginal—where he finds himself, of course, with the children, the disabled: the "gauche" (or the "lefty") is a kind of blind man: he doesn't quite see the direction, the *bearing* of his gestures; only his hand guides him, or that hand's desire, not its instrumental aptitude; the eye is reason, evidence, empiricism, verisimilitude—everything which serves to control, to coordinate, to imitate; as an exclusive art of seeing, all our past painting has been subject to a repressive rationality. In a certain sense, TW liberates painting from seeing; for the "gauche" (the "lefty") undoes the link between hand and eye: he draws without light (as TW actually did, in the army).

.   .   .

TW, contrary to the venture of so many present-day painters, *shows* the gesture. We are not asked to see, to conceive, to savor the *product*, but to review, to identify, and, so to speak, to "enjoy" the *movement* which has ended up *here*. Now, as long as humanity has practiced a manual writing, to the exclusion of print, the trajectory of the hand, and not the visual perception of its work, has been the fundamental action by which letters were defined, studied, classified: this controlled action is what in paleography is called the *ductus*: the hand conducts the line or the stroke, from top to bottom, from left to right, turning, bearing down, breaking off, etc.); of course, it is in ideographic writing that the *ductus* has most importance: rigorously coded, it permits classifying the characters according to the number and direction of the brush strokes, it establishes the very possibility of a dictionary for writing without an alphabet. In TW's work the *ductus* prevails: not its rule, but its play, its whims, its explorations, its indolences. In short, it is a writing of which only the leaning, the cursivity remains; in the old "graphism," the cursive is born of the (economic) need to write quickly: to lift the pen is expensive. Here it is just the contrary: the writing falls like a fine rain, it lies flat like the grass, it scratches out from idleness, as if it were a matter of making time itself visible, the tremor of time . . .

Many of TW's compositions suggest, it has been said, the scrawls of children. The child is the *infans* who does not yet speak; but the child who conducts TW's hand already writes— he is a schoolboy: lined paper, colored pencils, ruler, repeated letters, little plumes of cross-hatching, like the smoke that comes out of the locomotive in children's drawings. Yet, once again, the stereotype ("what it looks like") subtly reverses. The child's (graphic) production is never a result of the idea alone: it immediately involves the objective mark of the instrument (a pencil, commercial object) and the *id* of the little subject who bears down, insists, on the sheet of paper. Between the tool and the fantasy, TW interposes the idea: the colored pencil becomes the pencil-color: the reminiscence (of the schoolboy) becomes a total sign: of time, of culture, of society (this is less Mallarméan than Proustian).

Clumsiness (*gaucherie*) is rarely a matter of lightness; generally, to be *gauche* is to press too hard; real awkwardness insists, stubbornly, wants to be loved (as the child wants *to show* what it makes, to exhibit it triumphantly to its mother). It is characteristic of TW to reverse this very cunning *gaucherie* I have spoken of: his does not press down, quite the contrary, his gradually erases itself, fades away, while retaining the delicate stain of the eraser's movement: the hand has drawn something like a flower and then has begun "dawdling" over this line; the flower has been written, then unwritten; but the two movements remain vaguely superimposed; it is a perverse palimpsest: three texts (if we add the kind of signature, caption, or citation: *Sesostris*) are here, one tending to efface the other, but only, one might say, in order to *show* that effacement: a veritable philosophy of time. As always, life (art, gesture, work) must without despair testify to an ineluctable disappearance: by engendering themselves (like those *a*'s linked by a single circling of the hand, repeated, translated), by *showing* their engendering (this was in earlier times the meaning of the *sketch*), the forms (at least, certainly, TW's) do not celebrate the wonders of generation any more than the grim sterilities of repetition— their task, one might say, is to link in a single state what appears and what disappears; to separate the exaltation of life and the fear of death is banality; the utopia of which art can be the language, but which all of human neurosis resists, is to produce a single affect: neither Eros nor Thanatos, but Life-Death, in a single thought, a single gesture. This utopia is approached by neither a violent art nor an icy one, but rather, to my taste, by TW's, unclassifiable because it unites, by an inimitable stroke, both inscription and erasure, childhood and culture, drift and invention.

Support?

It looks as if TW is an "anti-colorist." But what is color? A kind of bliss. That bliss is in TW. In order to understand him, we must remember that color is *also* an idea (a sensual idea): for there to be color (in the blissful sense of the word) it is not necessary that color be subject to rhetorical modes of existence; it is not necessary that color be intense, violent, rich, or even delicate, refined, rare, or again thick-spread, crusty, fluid, etc.; in short, it is not necessary that there be affirmation, *installation* of color. It suffices that color appear, that it be there, that it be inscribed like a pinprick in the corner of the eye (a metaphor which in the *Arabian Nights* designates the excellence of a story), it suffices that color lacerate something: that it pass in front of the eye, like an apparition—or a disappearance, for color is like a closing eyelid, a tiny fainting spell. TW does not paint color; at most, one might say that he *colors in*; but this coloring-in is rare, interrupted, and always instantaneous, as if one were trying out the crayon. This dearth of color reveals not an effect (still less a verisimilitude) but a gesture, the pleasure of a gesture: to see engendered at one's fingertip, at the verge of vision, something which is both expected (I know that this crayon I am holding is blue) and unexpected (not only do I not know which blue is going to come out, but even if I knew, I would still be surprised, because color, like the *event*, is new each time: it is precisely the *stroke* which makes the color—as it produces bliss).

. . .

Furthermore, one suspects, color is *already* in TW's paper insofar as that paper is *already* dirtied, tainted, with an unclassifiable luminosity. It is only a writer's paper which is white, which is "clean," and that is not the least of his problems (Mallarmé's problem of the white page: often this whiteness, this blank provokes a panic: how to corrupt it?); the writer's misfortune, his difference (in relation to the painter, and especially to a painter of writing, like TW), is that he is forbidden graffiti: TW is, after all, a writer who has access to graffiti, with every justification and in sight of everyone. We know that what constitutes graffiti is in fact neither the inscription nor its message but the wall, the background, the surface (the desktop); it is because the background exists fully, as an object which has already *lived*, that such writing always comes to it as an enigmatic surplus: what is *in excess*, supernumerary, out of place— that is what disturbs the order of things; or again: it is insofar as the background *is not clean* that it is unsuitable to thought (contrary to the philosopher's blank sheet of paper) and therefore very suitable to everything that remains (art, indolence, pulsion, sensuality, irony, taste: everything the intellect can experience as so many aesthetic catastrophes).

As in a surgical operation of extreme delicacy, everything occurs (in TW) at that infinitesimal moment where the crayon's wax approaches the paper's texture. Wax, a soft substance, adheres to the tiny asperities of the graphic field, and it is the trace of this light swarm of bees that constitutes TW's stroke, his line. An odd adherence, for it contradicts the very idea of adherence: it is like a contact of which the mere recollection would constitute the ultimate value; but this *past tense* of the stroke can also be defined as its *future*: the crayon, half soft, half pointed (we do not know how it will turn), is *going* to touch the paper: technically, TW's work seems to be conjugated in the past tense or in the future, never really in the present; one might say that there is never anything but the memory or

Mars and the Artist, *collage of oil, charcoal, and crayon
on paper. Alessandro Twombly collection*

the anticipation of the stroke: on the paper—on account of the paper—the tense is perpetually uncertain.

Take an architect's or an engineer's drawing, the diagram of a machine or of some building element; here it is not the drawing's materiality that we see but its meaning, entirely independent of the technician's performance; in short, we see nothing, if not a kind of intelligibility. Now let us take one step down into the graphic substance: confronting a writing drawn by the hand, it is still the intelligibility of signs that we consume, but certain opaque, non-signifying elements—or rather, elements of a different signification—catch our attention (and already our desire): the nervous turn of the letters, the spurt of the ink, the tensile quality of the strokes, all those accidents which are not necessary to the functioning of the graphic code and are consequently, already, surpluses. Now let us move still further away from meaning: a classical drawing shows no constituted sign; no functional message *passes*: I invest my desire in the *performance* of the analogy, the success of the making, the seduction of the style, in a word, in the final state of the product: it is truly an object which I am given to contemplate. In this chain, which proceeds from schema to drawing, and along which meaning gradually evaporates, to be replaced by an increasingly futile "profit," TW occupies the extreme term: signs, sometimes, but faded, clumsy (as we have said), as if he were quite indifferent to their being torn up, but especially painting's *final state*, its floor: the paper ("TW admits to having more of a sense of paper than of painting"). And yet there occurs a very strange reversal: because meaning has been extenuated, because paper has become what we must call *the object of desire*, drawing can reappear, absolved of any technical, expressive, or aesthetic function; in certain of TW's compositions, the architect's, the cabinetmaker's, the surveyor's drawing returns, as if we had freely recovered the origin of the chain, only purified, henceforth liberated from the reasons which for centuries seemed to justify the graphic reproduction of a *recognizable* object.

Body

The line—any line inscribed on the sheet of paper—denies the *important body*, the fleshly body, the humoral body; the line gives access neither to the skin nor to the mucous membranes; what it expresses is the body insofar as the line scratches, brushes over (one can go so far as to say: tickles); by the line, art *displaces itself*; its center is no longer the object of desire (the splendid body frozen in marble), but the subject of this desire: the line, however supple, light, or uncertain it may be, always refers to a force, to a direction; it is an *energon*, a labor which reveals—which makes legible—the trace of its pulsion and its expenditure. The line is a visible action.

TW's line is inimitable (try to imitate it: what you will make will be neither his nor yours: it will be: *nothing*). Now what is ultimately inimitable is the body; no discourse, whether verbal or plastic—if it is not that of anatomical science, exceedingly crude when all is said and done—can reduce one body to another body. TW's work reveals this fatality: my body will never be yours. From this fatality, in which a certain human affliction can be epitomized, there is only one means of escape: seduction: that my body (or its sensuous substitutes, art, writing) seduce, overwhelm, or disturb the other body.

In our society, the tiniest graphic feature, provided it derive from this inimitable body, from this certain body, is worth millions. What is consumed (since it is a consumer society which concerns us here) is a body, an "individuality" (i.e., what can be divided no further). In other words, in the artist's work, it is his body which is bought: an exchange in which we cannot help but recognize the contract of prostitution. Is this contract a characteristic of capitalist civilization? Can we say that it specifically defines the commercial *mores* of our art world (frequently shocking to many people)? In the Republic of China, I have seen the works of "rural" painters, whose labor was in theory free from any principle of exchange; yet there occurred here a curious redistribution: the most-admired painter had produced a correct and banal portrait (a cell secretary, reading): in the graphic stroke, no body, no passion, no indolence, nothing but the trace of an analogical operation (to produce a resemblance, to produce an expression); on the contrary, the exhibition abounded in other works, of a so-called naïve style, in which, despite their realistic subject, the amateur artist's body made itself felt, exploded, delighted (by the voluptuous fullness of the strokes, the unbridled color, the intoxicating repetition of motifs). In other words, the body always exceeds the exchange in which it is caught up: no commerce in the world, no political virtue can exhaust the body: there is always an extreme point where it gives itself *for nothing*.

This morning, a fruitful—in any case, an agreeable—occupation: I very slowly look through a book of TW's reproductions, and I frequently stop in order to attempt, quite quickly, on slips of paper, to make certain scribbles; I am not directly imitating TW (what would be the use of that?), I am imitating his *gesture*, which I, if not unconsciously, at least dreamily, infer from my reading; I am not copying the product, but the producing, I am putting myself, so to speak, *in the hand's footsteps*.

For such is (for my body, at least) TW's work: a *producing*, delicately imprisoned, enchanted within that aesthetic product which we call a canvas, a drawing, of which the collection (book, exhibition) is never anything but an anthology of *traces*. This oeuvre conducts TW's reader (I am saying: *reader*, though there is nothing to decipher) to a certain philosophy of time: he must retrospectively see a movement, what was the hand's *becoming*; but then—a salutary revolution—the product (any product?) appears as a kind of bait: all art, insofar as it is accumulated, acknowledged, published, is betrayed as *imaginary*: what is real, to which TW's work continuously recalls you, is producing: at each stroke, TW blows up the Museum.

There exists what we might call a sublime form of what is drawn, sublime because stripped of any scribbling, any lesion: the drawing instrument (brush, crayon, or pencil) descends on the sheet, makes contact—or hardens—there, that is all: there is not even the shadow of an incision, simply a *touch*: to the quasi-Oriental rarefaction of the slightly soiled surface (this is what the *object* is) corresponds the extenuation of the movement: it grasps nothing, it deposits, and everything is said.

If the distinction between *product* and *producing*, on which, as I see it, the whole of TW's work is based, seems somewhat sophisticated, let me recall the decisive light which certain terminological oppositions enable us to shed on some apparently confused psychic activities: the British analyst D. W. Winnicott has shown us that it is a mistake to reduce a child's play to a pure ludic activity; he reminds us of the opposition of *game* (a strictly regulated play) and *play* (which has no such rules). TW, of course, is to be found on the side of *play*, not of *game*. But this is not all; in a second phase of his procedure, Winnicott shifts from play—still too rigid—to *playing*: the child's—and the artist's—reality is the *process* of manipulation, not the object produced (Winnicott reaches the point of systematically substituting for concepts the verbal forms which correspond to them: *fantasying, dreaming, living, holding*, etc.). All of this is quite valid for TW: his work does not derive from a concept (*mark*) but from an activity (*marking*); or better still: from a field (the sheet of paper), insofar as an activity is deployed there. For Winnicott, the child's play disappears and gives way to his "playground"; for TW, "drawing" gives way to the surface it inhabits, mobilizes, torments, scores—or rarefies.

Morality

The artist has no morals, but he has a *morality*. In his work, there are these questions: *What are others for me? How am I to desire them? How am I to lend myself to their desire? How am I to behave among them?* Uttering each time a "subtle vision of the world" (thus speaks the Tao), the artist *composes* what is alleged (or rejected) by his culture and what his own body insists on: what is avoided, *what is evoked*, what is repeated, or again: forbidden/desired: that is the paradigm which, like two legs, enables the artist to walk, *insofar as he produces*.

How to draw a line that is not stupid? It is not enough to undulate it a little to make it a living thing: you must—as has been said—make it *gauche*: there is always a little *gaucherie* in intelligence. Consider these two parallel lines drawn by TW; they end by meeting, as if their creator could not *sustain* to the end the stubborn gap which mathematically defines them. What *seems* to intervene in TW's line and to conduct it to the verge of that very mysterious *dysgraphia* which constitutes his entire art is a certain indolence (which is one of the purest of the body's signs). Indolence: this is precisely what enables "drawing," but not "painting" (any color released, left behind, is violent), or writing (each word is born whole, deliberate, armed by culture). TW's "indolence" (I am speaking here of an effect, not of a disposition) is tactical, however: it allows him to avoid

24 short pieces, *crayon on paper. Private collection, Berlin*

the platitude of graphic codes, without yielding to the conformism of destructions: it is, in every sense of the word, a *tact.*

An extraordinary thing: TW's work manifests no aggression (a feature, it has been remarked, which differentiates him from Paul Klee). I believe I know the reason for this effect, so contrary to all art in which the body is engaged: TW seems to proceed in the manner of certain Chinese painters who must triumph over the line, the form, the figure, at the first stroke, without being able to correct themselves, by reason of the fragility of the paper, of the silk: this is painting *alla prima.* TW, too, seems to work *alla prima*, but while the Chinese touch involves a great danger, that of "spoiling" the figure (by missing the analogy), TW's line or trace involves nothing of the kind: it is without goal, without model, without instance; it is without *telos*, and consequently without risk: why "correct yourself," since there is no master? From which it follows that any aggression is somehow futile.

The *value* TW deposits in his work can reside in what Sade called *the principle of delicacy* ("I respect others' tastes, fantasies . . . I find them respectable . . . because even the strangest, properly analyzed, can always be traced back to a principle of delicacy"). As a principle, "delicacy" is neither moral nor cultural; it is a pulsion (why should a pulsion be innately violent, crude?), *a certain demand of the body itself.*

24 short pieces: this sounds like both Webern and the Japanese haiku. In all three cases, we are concerned with a paradoxical, even provocative (if it were not delicate) art, in that here concision frustrates depth. In general, what is succinct seems compact: rarity engenders density, and density gives birth to the enigma. In TW, there is a different development: of course there is a silence, or, to be more accurate, a very faint buzzing of the surface, but this ground itself is a positive power; inverting the usual relation of classical production, we might say that the line, the hatching, the shape, in short the graphic event, is what permits the surface or the sheet of paper to exist, to signify, to take pleasure ("Being," says the Tao, "offers possibilities, it is by non-being that one makes use of them"). The space treated is no longer reckonable, though it does not cease to be plural: is it not according to this barely tenable opposition (since it excludes both number and unity, dispersion and center) that we must interpret Webern's dedication to Alban Berg: "*Non multa, sed multum*"?

There are paintings which are excited, possessive, dogmatic; they impose the product, give it the tyranny of a fetish. TW's art—this is its morality, and also its greatest historical singularity —*does not want to take anything*; it hangs together, it floats, it drifts between desire, which subtly animates the hand, and politeness, which dismisses it; if we required some reference for this art, we could go looking for it only very far away, outside painting, outside the West, outside the historical period, at the very limit of meaning, and say, with the Tao Tê Ching:

He produces without taking for himself,
He acts without expectation,
His work done, he is not attached to it,
and since he is not attached to it,
his work will remain.

1979

The Wisdom of Art

Whatever the transformations of painting, whatever its substance and its context, the same question is always asked: *What is happening here?* Canvas, paper, or wall constitute a stage on which something happens (and if, in certain forms of art, the artist intends that nothing happen, that too is an occurrence, an adventure). Hence, we must take the picture (a convenient name, even if an old one) as a kind of theater *à l'italienne*: the curtain parts, we watch, we wait, we receive, we understand; and when the scene is over and the picture gone, we remember: we are no longer the same as we were before: as in ancient drama, we have been initiated. I should like to question Twombly in relation to the Event.

What happens on the stage proposed by Twombly (canvas or paper) is something which participates in several types of event, which the Greek vocabulary clearly distinguished: there occurs a fact (*pragma*), an accident (*tyché*), an outcome (*telos*), a surprise (*apodeston*), and an action (*drama*).

I

Before anything else, there occur . . . paper, canvas, pencil, crayon, oil paint. The instrument of painting is not an instrument. It is a fact. Twombly imposes his materials not as something which will serve some purpose but as an absolute substance, manifested in its glory (in the theological vocabulary, God's glory is the manifestation of his Being). The materials are what the Alchemists called *materia prima*—what exists prior to the division of meaning: a tremendous paradox, since in the human order nothing comes to man that is not immediately accompanied by a meaning, the meaning which other men have given it, and so on, back to infinity. The painter's demiurgic power is that he makes the materials exist as substance; even if meaning emerges from the canvas, pencil and color remain "things," stubborn substances whose persistence in "being-there" nothing (no subsequent meaning) can annul.

Twombly's art consists in making things seen—not the things he represents (that is another problem), but those he manipulates: these few pencil strokes, this graph paper, this patch of pink, that brown smudge. This art has its secret, which is in general not to flaunt substance (charcoal, ink, oil paint) but to *permit it to linger.* We might think that in order to express the pencil's character it would have to be pressed hard, emphasized, made thick, black, intense. Twombly thinks the opposite: by withholding the pressure of substance, by letting it come to rest quite casually, so that its texture is somewhat scattered, matter will reveal its essence, grant us the certainty of its name: *this is* pencil. If we were to philosophize (a little), we might say that the being of things is not in their heaviness but in their lightness; which would perhaps confirm Nietzsche's proposition: "What is good is light": nothing, as a matter of fact, is less Wagnerian than Twombly.

The task, then, is always, in every circumstance (in any work whatever), to make substance appear as a fact (*pragma*). To perform it, Twombly has, if not methods (and even if he had, in art *method* is noble), at least habits. We shall not ask whether other painters have had these habits; in any case, it is their combination, their distribution, their proportion which constitute Twombly's original art. Words, too, belong to everyone; but the sentence belongs to the writer: Twombly's "sentences" are inimitable.

It is through these gestures, then, that Twombly utters (could we say: spells out?) the substance of what is drawn: (1) *scratching*: Twombly scratches the canvas with a scribble of lines (*Free Wheeler, Criticism, Olympia*); the gesture is that of an occasionally intense oscillation of the hand, as if the artist were doodling, like someone bored during a union meeting and blackening a scrap of paper in front of him with apparently meaningless lines; (2) *clotting* (*Commodus II*): Twombly controls his clots, shifts them around as if he intervened with his fingers; the body, then, is here, close to the canvas, not by projection but, so to speak, by contact, though always light: nothing is ever *ground in* (see, for instance, *Bay of Naples*); hence, it might be better to speak of *maculae* rather than "clots"; for the *macula* is not just any stain or clot, it is (etymologically) the stain on the skin, but it is also the mesh of a net, suggesting the reticulation of certain animals; Twombly's *maculae*, as a matter of fact, do suggest a network; (3) *smearing*: my name for the streaks, of color or of pencil, often of indefinable substance, with which Twombly seems to cover up other marks, as if he wanted to erase them, without really wanting to, since these marks remain faintly visible under the layer covering them; this is a subtle dialectic: the artist pretends to have "spoiled" some piece of his canvas and to have wanted to erase it; but then he spoils this erasure in its turn; and these two superimposed "failures" produce a kind of palimpsest: they give the canvas the depth of a sky in which thin clouds pass in front of each other without canceling each other out (*View, School of Athens*).

We might observe that these gestures, which aim to establish substance as a fact, are all related to *dirtying*. A paradox: the fact, in its purity, is best defined by not being clean. Take an ordinary object: it is not its new, virgin state which best accounts for its essence, but its worn, lopsided, soiled, somewhat forsaken condition: the truth of things is best read in the cast-off. The truth of red is in the smear; the pencil's truth is in the wobbly line. Ideas (in the Platonic sense) are not shiny, metallic Figures in conceptual corsets, but somewhat shaky maculations, tenuous blemishes on a vague background.

So much for the pictural fact (*via di porre*). But there are other events in Twombly's work: written events, Names. These, too, are facts: they stand there on the stage, without settings or props: *Virgil, Orpheus*. But their nominalist glory (nothing but the Name) is also impure: the writing of it is a little childish, irregular, clumsy; nothing to do with the typography of conceptual art; the hand that writes them gives these names all the blunders of someone learning to write; and perhaps in this, once again, the Name's truth is more apparent: doesn't the schoolboy learn the essence of *table* by copying its name in his laborious handwriting? By writing *Virgil* on his canvas, it's as if Twombly were condensing in his handwriting the very immensity of the Virgilian world, all the references of which this name is the repository. This is why, in Twombly's titles, we must not look for any induction of analogy. If the canvas is called *The Italians*, do not look for the Italians anywhere except, precisely, in their name. Twombly knows that the Name has an absolute (and sufficient) power of evocation: to write *The Italians* is to see all Italians. Names are like those jars mentioned in one of the stories of the *Arabian Nights*: genii are shut up in them; open or break the jar and the genie comes out, looms up, changes shape like smoke, and fills the air: break the title and the whole canvas escapes.

A procedure quite as pure is evident in the dedications. There are several of these in Twombly: *To Valéry*, *To Tatlin*. Again, nothing here but the graphic action of dedicating. For "to dedicate" is one of those verbs linguists, following Austin, have called "performatives," because their meaning is identified with the very action of uttering them: "I dedicate" has no meaning other than the actual gesture by which I present what I have made (my work) to someone I love or admire. This is just what Twombly does: bearing only the dedication's inscription, the canvas "vanishes": all that is given is the action of giving—and this scrap of writing to say so. These are limit-canvases, not in that they involve no painting (other painters have explored this limit) but because the very notion of oeuvre is suppressed— but not the painter's relation to someone he loves.

2

Tyché, in Greek, is the event insofar as it occurs by chance. Twombly's canvases always seem to involve a certain power of accident, a *Bonne Chance*. Never mind if, in fact, the work is the result of precise calculation. What matters is the *effect* of change or, to put it more subtly (for Twombly's art is not aleatory), of *inspiration*, that creative force which is, in a sense, the euphoria of chance. Two movements and one state account for this effect.

The movements are: first, the impression of being "thrown": the materials seem thrown across the canvas, and *to throw* is an action in which are simultaneously inscribed an initial decision and a terminal indetermination: by throwing, I know what I am doing but I do not know what I am producing. Twombly's way of throwing is elegant, supple, "long," as we say in those games where a ball has to be tossed; second—this being a consequence of the first—a "scattered" look; on one of Twombly's canvases (or works on paper), the elements are separated from each other by space, a lot of space; in this they have some affinity with Oriental painting, to which Twombly is otherwise related by his recourse to a frequent mixture of painting and writing. Even when the accidents—the events—are strongly marked (*Bay of Naples*), Twombly's canvases remain absolutely aerated spaces; and their aeration is not merely a plastic value; it is a kind of subtle energy which makes it easier to breathe: the canvas produces in me what the philosopher Bachelard calls an "ascensional" imagination: I float in the sky, I inhale the air (*School of Fontainebleau*). The state linked to these two movements (throwing and scattering), a state found in all Twombly's canvases, is the *Rare*. "Rarus" in Latin means: presenting intervals or interstices, sparse, porous, scattered; and this indeed is Twombly's space (see especially *Untitled*, 1959).

How can these two ideas, that of empty space and that of chance (*tyché*), be related? Valéry, to whom one of Twombly's drawings is dedicated, can help us understand. In a lecture given at the Collège de France on May 5, 1944, Valéry examines the two possibilities for the creator of a work: in the first, the work answers to a predetermined plan; in the second, the artist fills in an imaginary rectangle. Twombly fills in his rectangle according to the principle of the Rare, i.e., of spacing. This notion is crucial in Japanese aesthetics, which does not acknowledge the Kantian categories of space and time but the subtler one of interval (in Japanese: *Ma*). The Japanese *Ma* is basically the Latin *Rarus*, and it is Twombly's art. The Rare Rectangle thus refers to two civilizations: on the one hand, to the "void" of Oriental compositions, merely accentuated here and there by some calligraphy; and on the other, to a Mediterranean space, which is Twombly's; curiously, as it happens, Valéry (again) has nicely accounted for this rare space, not apropos of the sky or the sea (as we might initially suppose), but apropos of old southern houses: "Those huge rooms of the Midi, very good for meditation—the big pieces of furniture lost in them. The great emptiness enclosed—where time doesn't count. The mind seeks to populate all this." Basically, Twombly's canvases are big Mediterranean rooms, warm and luminous, with their elements lost in them (*rari*), rooms the mind seeks to populate.

3

Mars and the Artist is an apparently symbolic composition: at the top, Mars, i.e., a conflict of lines and reds; at the bottom, the Artist, i.e., a flower and his (the artist's) name. The canvas functions like a pictogram in which figurative and graphic elements are combined. This system is very clear, and although it is quite exceptional in Twombly's work, its very clarity refers us to the double problem of figuration and signification.

Although abstraction (misnamed, as we know) has been under way a long time in the history of painting (since, some say, late Cézanne), each new artist unceasingly struggles with it: in art, the problems of language are never really settled: language always circles back on itself. Hence it is never naïve (despite the intimidations of culture, and above all, of specialist culture) to ask, in front of a canvas, *what it represents*. Meaning sticks to man: even when he wants to create non-meaning or extra-meaning, he ends by producing the very meaning of non-meaning or of extra-meaning. It is all the more legitimate to keep returning to the question of meaning, in that it is precisely this question which impedes the universality of painting. If so many men (because of cultural differences) have the impression of "understanding nothing" in front of a canvas, it is because they want meaning and because the canvas (they think) does not give it to them.

Twombly faces the problem squarely, if only in this: that most of his canvases are titled. From the very fact that they have a title, they offer us, who crave it, the bait of a signification. For, in classical painting, a picture's caption (that thin line of words which runs along the bottom of the work and on which museum visitors first fling themselves) clearly said what the picture represented: the analogy of the painting was doubled by the analogy of the title: signification seemed to be exhaustive, figuration exhausted. Now it is impossible, seeing one of Twombly's titled canvases, not to have this initial reflex: we look for the analogy. *The Italians? Sahara?* Where are the Italians? Where is the Sahara? Let's look for them—and, of course, we find nothing. Or at least—and it is here that Twombly's art begins—what we find, i.e., the canvas itself, the Event in its splendor and its enigma, is ambiguous: nothing "represents" the Italians, the Sahara—no analogical figure for these referents —and yet, we vaguely realize, nothing in these canvases contradicts a certain natural idea of the Sahara, of the Italians. In other words, the spectator has the presentiment of another logic (his gaze is beginning to work): although very obscure, the canvas has an outcome; what is happening in it conforms to a *telos*, a certain finality.

This outcome is not found immediately. In the first stage, the title seems to block access to the canvas, for by its specificity, its intelligibility, its classicism (nothing strange about it, nothing surrealistic), it leads us down an analogical path which very soon turns out to be barred. Twombly's titles have a labyrinthine function: having followed the notion they suggest, we are forced to retrace our steps and start out in another direction. Yet something remains—a kind of ghost—and pervades the canvas. They constitute the negative moment of all initiation. This art of very rare doctrine, simultaneously very intellectual and very sensuous, continuously submits to negativity, in the manner of those mystics known as "apophatic" (negative) because they advocate experiencing all that is not, in order to perceive in this absence a faint glow, flickering but also radiant, *because it does not lie.*

What Twombly's canvases produce (their *telos*) is very simple: it is an "effect." This word must here be understood in the very technical sense it had in the French literary schools of the late nineteenth century, from the Parnassians to the Symbolists. The "effect" is a general impression suggested by the poem—an eminently sensuous and generally visual impression. This is familiar enough. But the effect's characteristic is that its generality cannot really be decomposed: it cannot be reduced to a series of localizable details. Théophile Gautier wrote a poem, "Symphonie en blanc majeur," all of whose lines, in a simultaneously insistent and diffuse fashion, help establish one color, white, which is imprinted in us independently of the objects which "support" it. In the same way, Paul Valéry, in his Symbolist period, wrote two sonnets, both entitled "Féerie," whose effect is a certain color; but since, from Parnassians to Symbolists, sensibility had grown refined (under the painters' influence, moreover), this color cannot be spoken by name (as was the case for Gautier's white); probably it is *silvery* which prevails, but this shade is caught up in other sensations which diversify and reinforce it: luminosity, transparence, lightness, sudden sharpness, coldness: lunar pallor, silky feathers, diamond luster, pearly iridescence. Hence, the effect is not a rhetorical "device": it is a veritable category of sensation, defined by this paradox: indecomposable unity of impression (of the "message") and complexity of causes, of elements: the generality is not mysterious (entirely entrusted to the artist's power) yet it is *irreducible.* It is, in a way, another logic, a kind of challenge offered by the poet (and the painter) to the Aristotelian rules of structure.

Though many elements separate Twombly from French

Symbolism (art, history, nationality), they have something in common: a certain form of culture. This culture is classical: not only does Twombly directly refer to certain mythological facts transmitted by Greek or Latin literature, but even the "authors" (*auctores* means: authorities) he introduces into his painting are either humanist poets (Keats, Valéry) or painters nurtured by Antiquity (Raphael, Poussin). A single chain, ceaselessly evoked, leads from the Greek gods to the modern artist—a chain whose links are Ovid and Poussin. A kind of golden triangle joins the ancients, the poets, and the painter. It is significant that one of Twombly's canvases is dedicated to Valéry, and even more perhaps—because this coincidence doubtless occurred without Twombly's knowing it—that a canvas by this painter and a poem by this writer bear the same title: *Birth of Venus*; and these two works have the same "effect": of rising from the sea. This convergence, here exemplary, may provide the key to Twombly's "effect." It seems to me that this effect, constant in all Twombly's canvases, even those painted before he moved to Italy (for, as Valéry also said, it happens that the future is sometimes the cause of the past), is the very general one released in all its possible dimensions by the word *Mediterranean*. The Mediterranean is an enormous complex of memories and sensations: two languages, Greek and Latin, to be found in Twombly's titles, a mythological, historical, poetic culture, a whole life of forms, colors, and light which occurs at the frontier between land and sea. Twombly's inimitable art consists in having imposed the Mediterranean effect starting from materials (scratches, maculae, smears, dearth of color, no academic forms) which have no analogical relation with the great Mediterranean radiance.

I know the island of Procida, out in the Bay of Naples, where Twombly has lived. I spent a few days there in the old house where Lamartine's heroine Graziella lived. It is a calm meeting place of light, sky, land, a few rocky accents, the vault of an

arch. It is Virgil, and it is a canvas by Twombly: in every canvas, in fact, we shall find this emptiness of sky and water and
these very faint terrestrial marks (a boat, a promontory) which
float there (*apparent rari nantes*): the blue of the sky, the gray
of the sea, the pink of the dawn.

4

What happens in a painting by Twombly? A kind of Mediterranean effect. But this effect is not "frozen" in the ceremony
and the seriousness, the decorum of humanist works (even the
poems of a mind as intelligent as Valéry's remain imprisoned
by a kind of superior *propriety*). Into the event Twombly very
often introduces a *surprise* (*apodeston*). This surprise takes on
the appearance of an incongruity, a mockery, a deflation, as if the
humanist turgescence was suddenly pricked. In *Ode to Psyche*
(a drawing), a discreet series of measurements in one corner manages to "break" the noble solemnity of the title. In *Olympia*
occur sporadic, "clumsily" penciled motifs, like those children
produce when they want to draw butterflies. From the point of
view of "style," a lofty value which earned the respect of all
classical writers, what is more remote from the *Veil of Orpheus*
than these few childish lines worthy of an apprentice surveyor?
In *Untitled*, 1969, what a lovely gray! Two thin white lines
dangle across it (still the *Rarus*, the Japanese *Ma*); this could
be very Zen; but two barely legible numbers dance above the
two lines and refer the nobility of that gray to the faint mockery
of a page of calculations.

Unless . . . it is precisely by such surprises that Twombly's
canvases coincide with the purest Zen spirit. For there exists,
in the Zen attitude, a certain experience, sought without a rational method, which is extremely important: the *satori*. This
word has been most inadequately translated (because of our

Christian tradition) as *illumination*; sometimes, a little better, as *awakening*; it is probably, insofar as outsiders like ourselves can imagine, a kind of mental shock which grants access, regardless of all known intellectual means, to Buddhist "truth": an empty truth, unconnected with forms and causalities. What matters for us is that the Zen *satori* is sought with the help of techniques of surprise: not only irrational, but also, and especially, incongruous techniques, flouting the seriousness we attach to religious experiences: sometimes this will be a nonsensical answer to some lofty metaphysical question, sometimes a surprising gesture which violates the solemnity of a ritual (as in the case of that Zen master who stopped in the middle of a speech, took off his sandal, put it on his head, and left the room). Such essentially disrespectful incongruities are likely to unsettle the spirit of seriousness which often lends its mask to the good conscience of our mental habits. Exclusive of any religious perspective (obviously), certain canvases by Twombly contain such impertinences, such shocks, such minor *satori*.

Among the surprises Twombly provokes we must include all interventions of writing in the field of the canvas: each time Twombly produces a graphic sign, there occurs a shock, a disturbance of painting's "naturalness." Such interventions are of three kinds (let us say, for simplification's sake): first, marks of measurement, figures, tiny algorithms, everything that produces a contradiction between painting's sovereign uselessness and the utilitarian signs of computation; second, the canvases where the only event is a handwritten word; lastly, coextensive with these two types of intervention, there is the hand's constant "clumsiness"; in Twombly, the letter is the very contrary of an illuminated or printed letter; it seems to be formed without deliberation, and yet it is not really childish, for the child is diligent, presses down, rounds off, sticks out his tongue in his efforts; he works hard to join the code of the grown-ups; Twombly draws away from it, loosens, lags behind; his hand seems to levitate—as if the word has been written with his fingertips, not out of disgust or boredom, but out of a kind of whim which disappoints what is expected of a painter's "fine hand": this was the expression used in the seventeenth century to describe the copyist who had a proper script. And who could write better than a painter?

This scriptory "clumsiness" (though inimitable: try to imitate it) certainly has a plastic function in Twombly. But here, where we are not discussing Twombly in the language of art criticism, we shall insist on its critical function. By means of his "graphism," Twombly almost always introduces a contradiction into his canvas: the "poor," the "clumsy," the "awkward," coinciding with the "Rare," act as forces which break down the tendency of classical culture to turn antiquity into a repository of decorative forms: the Apollonian purity of the Greek reference, apparent in the luminosity of the canvas, the dawn-like peace of its space, are "shaken" (since this is the word used about *satori*) by the ungratefulness of the graphic elements. The canvas seems to be engaged *against* culture, whose rhetorical discourse it abandons, retaining only its beauty. It has been said that, contrary to the art of Paul Klee, Twombly's contains no aggression. This is true, if we take aggression in a Western sense, as the excited expression of a constrained body which explodes. Twombly's art is more an art of the shock than of violence, and it frequently happens that a shock is more subversive than violence: this is precisely the lesson of certain Eastern modes of behavior and of thought.

5

Drama, in Greek, is etymologically linked to the idea of "doing." *Drama* is both what is being done and what is being performed on the canvas: a "drama," yes, why not? For my part,

I see in Twombly's work two actions, or one action on two levels.

The action of the first type consists of a kind of performance of culture. What happens is "stories" which proceed from culture, and, as we have said, from classical culture: five days of Bacchanalia, the birth of Venus, the Ides of March, three dialogues of Plato, a battle, etc. These historical actions are not represented; they are evoked, by the power of the Name. In short, what is represented is culture itself, or, as we say now-adays, the inter-text, which is that circulation of anterior (or contemporary) texts in the artist's head (or hand). This repre-sentation is entirely explicit when Twombly takes works of the past (works consecrated as of the high culture) and puts them "*en abîme*" in some of his canvases: first of all, in titles (Raphael's *School of Athens*), then in tiny figures (virtually unrecognizable, moreover) placed in a corner, like images whose reference matters, but not their content (Leonardo, Poussin). In classical painting, "what happens" is the "subject" of the canvas; this subject is frequently anecdotal (Judith beheading Holophernes); but in Twombly's canvases, the "subject" is a concept: it is the classical text "in itself"—a strange concept, it is true, since it is desirable, the object of love, perhaps of nostalgia.

There is in French [and in English—Trans.] a useful lexical ambiguity: the "subject" of a work is sometimes its "object" (what it talks about, what it offers to reflection, the *quaestio* of the old rhetoric), sometimes the human being who thereby represents himself, who figures there as the implicit author of what is said (or painted). In Twombly, the "subject" is, of course, what the canvas is talking about; but since this subject-object is only a (written) allusion, the whole burden of the *drama* shifts to the one who produces it: the subject is Twom-bly himself. The "subject's" journey, however, does not stop there: because Twombly's art seems to involve little technical responsibility (this is, of course, only an illusion), the "subject" of the canvas is also the one who looks at it: you, me. Twombly's "simplicity" (which I have analyzed under the name of "Rare" or "Clumsy") summons, attracts the spectator: he wants to join the canvas, not in order to consume it aesthetically, but in order to produce it in his turn (to "re-produce" it), to try his hand at a making whose nakedness and clumsiness afford him an incredible (and quite misleading) illusion of facility.

It should be pointed out that the subjects who look at the canvas are varied, and that on the types of subject depends the discourse they (inwardly) produce in front of the object looked at (a "subject"—this is what modernity has taught us—is never constituted by anything but his language); of course, all these subjects can speak at once, one might say, in front of a Twombly canvas (let us note, in passing, that aesthetics as a discipline might be that science which studies not the work in itself but the work as the spectator, or the reader, makes it speak within himself: a typology of discourses, in a sense). Hence, there are several subjects who look at Twombly (and murmur him under their breath, each one in his head).

There is the subject of culture, the one who knows how Venus was born, who Poussin or Valéry is; this subject is talkative, he can talk fluently. There is the subject of specialization, the one who knows art history thoroughly and can discuss Twombly's place in it. There is the subject of pleasure, the one who enjoys himself in front of the canvas, experiences in its discovery a kind of jubilation, which, moreover, he is not good at expressing; this subject is therefore mute; he can only exclaim: "How beautiful this is!" over and over: that is one of language's minor torments: we can never explain why we find something beautiful; pleasure engenders a certain laziness of speech, and if we want to talk about a work, we have to substitute for the expression of enjoyment certain oblique, more rational discourses—with the hope that the reader will feel in them the euphoria afforded by the canvases we are talking about. A fourth subject is the subject of memory. On a canvas by Twombly, a certain smudge at first seems to me hurried, poorly formed, inconsequential: I do not understand it; but this smudge works in me, unknown to myself; after I have left the canvas, it returns, becomes a memory, a tenacious memory: everything has changed, the canvas makes me happy, retroactively. Actually, what I am consuming so happily is an absence: a paradox anything but paradoxical, if we remember that Mallarmé made it the very principle of poetry: "I say: a flower and . . . musically there rises the fragrant idea itself, the one missing from all bouquets."

The fifth subject is the subject of production: the one who wants to re-produce the canvas. Thus this morning, December 31, 1978, it is still dark, it is raining, everything is still when I sit down at my worktable again. I look at *Hérodiade* (1960), and I really have nothing to say about it, except the same platitude: that I like it. But suddenly something new appears, a desire: the desire to do *the same thing*: to go to another table (not the one where I write), to choose colors and to paint, to draw. Ultimately the question of painting is: "Do you want to do a Twombly?"

As a subject of production, the spectator of the canvas will then be exploring his own impotence—and at the same time, of course, as though by contrast, the artist's power. Even before having tried to draw anything at all, I realize that this background (or what gives me the illusion of being a background) is something I could never produce: I don't even know how it is done. Here is *Age of Alexander*: oh, that one smear of pink . . . ! I could never make it so light, rarefy the space around it; I couldn't *stop* filling in, continuing, in other words, *spoiling*; and from this, from my very mistakes, I realize how much wisdom there is in the artist's action: he prevents himself from *trying too hard*; his success is not unrelated to the erotics of the Tao: an intense pleasure comes from restraint. The same problem in V*iew* (1959): I could never *handle* the pencil, i.e., sometimes so heavily, sometimes so lightly, and I could never even learn to do so, because this art is not governed by any analogical principle, so that the *ductus* itself (that movement by which the medieval copyist guided each stroke of the letter according to a direction which was always the same) is here absolutely free. And what is inaccessible on the level of the stroke is still more so on the level of the surface. In *Panorama* (1955), the entire space crackles like a television screen before any image is flashed on it; now, I would not know how to get that irregularity of graphic distribution; for if I deliberately strove for the effect of disorder, I would produce only a *stupid* disorder. And from this I understand that Twombly's art is an incessant victory over the stupidity of all marks and lines: to make an *intelligent* stroke is ultimately what makes the painter different (from me). And in many other canvases, what I would persistently fail to obtain is the "scattering," the "thrown"— the decentering of marks and lines: no stroke seems endowed with an intentional direction, and yet the whole is mysteriously guided—oriented.

I return, in conclusion, to this notion of "Rarus" ("scattered"), which I consider more or less the key to Twombly's art. This art is paradoxical, even provocative (if it were not so delicate), in that its concision is not solemn. In general, what is succinct seems compact: rarity engenders density, and density gives birth to the enigma. In Twombly, there is a different development: of course there is a silence, or, to be more accurate, a very faint buzzing of the surface, but this ground itself is a positive power; inverting the usual relation of classical production, we might say that the line, the hatching, the shape, in short the graphic event, is what permits the surface or the canvas to exist, to signify, to take pleasure ("Being," says the Tao, "offers possibilities, it is by non-being that one makes use of them"). The space treated is no longer reckonable, though it does not cease to be plural: is it not according to this barely tenable opposition (since it excludes both number and unity, dispersion and center) that we must interpret Webern's dedication to Alban Berg: "*Non multa, sed multum*"?

There are paintings which are excited, possessive, dogmatic; they impose the product, give it the tyranny of a fetish. Twombly's art—this is its morality, and also its great historical singularity—*does not want to take anything*; it hangs together, it floats, it drifts between desire, which subtly animates the hand, and politeness, which is the discreet rejection of any desire to capture. If we wanted to situate this ethic, we could only go looking for it very far away, outside painting, outside the West, outside the historical period, at the very limit of meaning; we would have to say, with the Tao Tê Ching:

> *He produces without taking for himself,*
> *He acts without expectation,*
> *His work done, he is not attached to it,*
> *And since he is not attached to it,*
> *His work will remain.*

1979

Wilhelm von Gloeden

Is the Baron von Gloeden "camp"? Through Warhol's eyes, perhaps; but above all, in himself, he is "kitsch." As a matter of fact, kitsch implies the recognition of a high aesthetic value, but it adds that such taste can be perfectly dreadful, and that from this contradiction is born a fascinating monster. Which is indeed von Gloeden's case: his photographs interest, engage, amuse, amaze, and we feel that all our pleasure comes from an accumulation of contraries, as with any festivity related to carnival.

These contradictions are "heterologies," frictions of various opposed languages. For example: von Gloeden takes the code of Antiquity, overloads it, clumsily parades it (ephebes, shepherds, ivy and vine leaves, palms and olive trees, tunics, columns, steles), but (first distortion) he confuses Antiquity's signs, combining a vegetal Greece with Roman statuary and the "antique nude" from the Ecoles des Beaux-Arts: with no irony at all, apparently, he takes the most threadbare legends for ready cash. Nor is this all: he populates the Antiquity thus paraded (and by inference the pederasty thus postulated) with African bodies. Perhaps he is right, after all: didn't Delacroix report that the truth of classical drapery could be found only among the Arabs? Anyway, it is delectable, the contradiction between this whole literary apparatus of third-year Greek and the bodies of these young peasant gigolos (if any of these is still alive, may I be forgiven the expression, it is not an insult), with their heavy somber gaze and the blue-black glaze of sun-baked beetles.

The means to which the baron resorts, i.e., photography, deliriously accentuates this carnival of contradictions. It is quite paradoxical, for, after all, photography is reputed to be an exact, empirical art entirely in the service of such positive, rational values as authenticity, reality, objectivity: in our detective universe, is not a photograph the invincible *proof* of identities, facts, crimes? Further, von Gloeden's photography is "artistic" in its staging (poses and settings) but never in its technique: few dissolves, very little studied lighting. The body is simply there, uniting nakedness and truth, phenomenon and essence: the baron's photographs are of the genre known as *pitiless*. Thus, the entire sublime blur of legend enters into collision (we need this word to account for our astonishment and perhaps for our jubilation) with photography's realism; for what is a photo thus conceived if not an image *in which we see everything*, a collection of details without hierarchy, without "order" (that great classical principle)? Whereby these little Greek gods (already contradicted by their blackness) have rather dirty peasant hands with big rough fingernails, worn feet that are none too clean, and very visible swollen foreskins—no longer stylized, i.e., tapered and reduced: uncircumcised is what they are, and one sees only that: the baron's photos are at once sublime and anatomical.

This, then, is why von Gloeden's art is such an adventure of meaning: it produces a world (we should call it a "hominary," since we have bestiaries) at once true and fabulous, realistic and (crudely) fake, a counter-oneirism crazier than the craziest dreams. Need we suggest how close such an attempt comes, despite the "cultural" abyss, to certain experiments of contemporary art? But since art is a realm of recuperations (there is no getting away from it: art recuperates even its own contestation and makes it into a new art), it would be better to acknowledge in von Gloeden's photographs less an art than a force; that hard, thin force by which he resists all conformisms, those of art, of morality, even of politics (let us not forget the fascist confiscation of these images), the force we might call his *naïveté*. Today more than ever there is a great audacity in mingling so simply, as he did, the most "cultural" culture and the most luminous eroticism. Who has done so? Sade, Klossowski perhaps . . . Tirelessly, von Gloeden produced this mélange *without realizing it*. Whence the force of his vision, which astonishes us still: his *naïvetés* are awe-inspiring as feats of valor.

1978

That Old Thing, Art…

As all the encyclopedias remind us, during the fifties certain artists at the London Institute of Contemporary Arts became advocates of the popular culture of the period: comic strips, films, advertising, science fiction, pop music. These various manifestations did not derive from what is generally called an Aesthetic but were entirely produced by Mass Culture and did not participate in art at all; simply, certain artists, architects, and writers were interested in them. Crossing the Atlantic, these products forced the barrier of art; accommodated by certain American artists, they became works of art, of which culture no longer constituted the being, merely the reference: origin was displaced by citation. Pop art as we know it is the permanent theater of this tension: on one hand, the mass culture of the period is present in it as a revolutionary force which contests art; and on the other, art is present in it as a very old force which irresistibly returns in the economy of societies. There are two voices, as in a fugue—one says: "This is not Art"; the other says, at the same time: "I am Art."

Art is something which must be destroyed—a proposition common to many experiments of Modernity.

Pop art reverses values. "What characterizes pop is mainly its use of what is despised" (Lichtenstein). Images from mass culture, regarded as vulgar, unworthy of an aesthetic consecration, return virtually unaltered as materials of the artist's activity. I should like to call this reversal the "Clovis Complex": like Saint Remi addressing the Frankish king, the god of pop art says to the artist: "Burn what you have worshipped, worship what you have burned." For instance: photography has long been fascinated by painting, of which it still passes as a poor relation; pop art overturns this prejudice: the photograph often becomes the origin of the images pop art presents: neither "art painting" nor "art photograph," but a nameless mixture. Another example of reversal: nothing more contrary to art than the notion of being the mere reflection of the things represented; even photography does not support this destiny; pop art, on the contrary, accepts being an *imagery*, a collection of reflections, constituted by the banal reverberation of the American environment: reviled by high art, the copy returns. This reversal is not capricious, it does not proceed from a simple denial of value, from a simple rejection of the past; it obeys a regular historical impulse; as Paul Valéry noted (in *Pièces sur l'Art*), the appearance of new technical means (here, photography, serigraphy) modifies not only art's forms but its very concept.

Repetition is a feature of culture. I mean that we can make use of repetition in order to propose a certain typology of cultures. Popular or extra-European cultures (deriving from an ethnography) acknowledge as much, and derive meaning and pleasure from the fact (we need merely instance today's minimal music and disco); Occidental high culture does not (even if it has resorted to repetition more than we suppose, in the baroque period). Pop art, on the other hand, repeats—spectacularly. Warhol proposes a series of identical images (*White burning Car Twice*) or of images which differ only by some slight variation of color (*Flowers, Marilyn*). The stake of these repetitions (or of Repetition as a method) is not only the destruction of art but also (moreover, they go together) another conception of the human subject: repetition affords access, in effect, to a different temporality: where the Occidental subject experiences the ingratitude of a world from which the New—i.e., ultimately, Adventure—is excluded, the Warholian subject (since Warhol is a practitioner of these repetitions) abolishes the pathos of time in himself, because this pathos is always linked to the feeling that something has appeared, will die, and that one's death is opposed only by being transformed into a second something which does not resemble the first. For pop art, it is important that things be "finite" (outlined: no evanescence), but it is not important that they be finished, that work (is there a work?) be given the internal organization of a destiny (birth, life, death). Hence we must unlearn the boredom of the "endless" (one of Warhol's first films, *Four Stars*, lasted twenty-five hours; *Chelsea Girls* lasts three and a half). Repetition disturbs the person (that classical entity) in another fashion: by multiplying the same image, pop art rediscovers the theme of the Double, of the Doppelgänger; this is a mythic theme (the Shadow, the Man or the Woman without a Shadow); but in the productions of pop art, the Double is harmless—has lost all maleficent or moral power, neither threatens nor haunts: the Double is a Copy, not a Shadow: *beside*, not *behind*: a flat, insignificant, hence irreligious Double.

Repetition of the portrait induces an adulteration of the person (a notion simultaneously civic, moral, psychological, and of course historical). Pop art, it has also been said, takes the place of a machine; it prefers to utilize mechanical processes of reproduction; for example, it freezes the star (Marilyn, Liz) in her image *as star*: no more soul, nothing but a strictly imaginary status, since the star's being is the icon. The object itself, which in everyday life we incessantly personalize by incorporating into our individual world—the object is, according to pop art, no longer anything but the residue of a subtraction: everything left over from a tin can once we have mentally amputated all its possible themes, all its possible uses. Pop art is well aware that the fundamental expression of the person is style. As Buffon said (a celebrated remark, once known to every French school-boy): "Style is the man." Take away style and there is no longer any (individual) man. The notion of style, in all the arts, has therefore been linked, historically, to a humanism of the person. Consider an unlikely example, that of "graphism": manual writing, long impersonal (during Antiquity and the Middle Ages), began to be individualized in the Renaissance, dawn of the modern period; but today, when the person is a moribund idea, or at least a menaced one, under the pressure of the gregarious forces which animate mass culture, the personality of writing is fading out. There is, as I see it, a certain relation between pop art and what is called "script," that anonymous writing sometimes taught to dysgraphic children because it is inspired by the neutral and, so to speak, elementary features of typography. Further, we must realize that if pop art depersonalizes, it does not make anonymous: nothing is more identifiable than Marilyn, the electric chair, a telegram, or a dress, as seen by pop art; they are in fact *nothing but that*: immediately and exhaustively identifiable, thereby teaching us that identity is not the person: the future world risks being a world of identities (by the computerized proliferation of police files), but not of persons.

A final feature which attaches pop art to the experiments of Modernity: the banal conformity of representation to the thing represented. "I don't want a canvas," Rauschenberg says, "to look like what it isn't. I want it to look like what it is." The proposition is aggressive in that art has always regarded itself as an inevitable detour that must be taken in order to "render" the truth of the thing. What pop art wants is to desymbolize

the object, to give it the obtuse and matte stubbornness of a fact
(John Cage: "The object is a fact, not a symbol"). To say the
object is asymbolic is to deny it possesses a profound or proxi-
mate space through which its appearance can propagate vibrations of meaning: pop art's object (this is a true revolution of
language) is neither metaphoric nor metonymic; it presents
itself cut off from its source and its surroundings; in particular,
the pop artist does not stand *behind* his work, and he himself
has no depth: he is merely the surface of his pictures: no signified, no intention, anywhere. Now the fact, in mass culture,
is no longer an element of the natural world; what appears as
fact is the stereotype: what everyone sees and consumes. Pop
art finds the unity of its representations in the radical conjunction of these two forms, each carried to extremes: the stereotype and the image. Tahiti is a fact, insofar as a unanimous and
persistent public opinion designates this site as a collection of
palm trees, of flowers worn over one ear, of long hair, sarongs,
and languorous, enticing glances (Lichtenstein's *Little Aloha*).
In this way, pop art produces certain *radical images*: by dint of
being an image, the thing is stripped of any symbol. This is an
audacious movement of mind (or of society): it is no longer
the fact which is transformed into an image (which is, strictly
speaking, the movement of metaphor, out of which humanity
has made poetry for centuries), it is the image which becomes
a fact. Pop art thus features a philosophical quality of things,
which we may call *facticity*: the *factitious* is the character of
what exists as fact and appears stripped of any justification: not
only are the objects represented by pop art factitious, but they
incarnate the very concept of facticity—that by which, in spite
of themselves, they begin to signify again: they signify that they
signify nothing.

For meaning is cunning: drive it away and it gallops back.
Pop art seeks to destroy art (or at least to do without it), but
art rejoins it: art is the counter-subject of our fugue.

The attempt has been made to abolish the signified, and thereby the sign; but the signifier subsists, persists, even if it does not refer, apparently, to anything. What is the signifier? Let us say, to be quick about it: the thing perceived, augmented by a certain thought. Now, in pop art, this supplement exists— as it exists in all the world's arts.

First of all, quite frequently, pop art changes the level of our perception; it diminishes, enlarges, withdraws, advances, extends the multiplied object to the dimensions of a signboard, or magnifies it as if it were seen under a jeweler's *loupe*. Now, once proportions are changed, art appears (it suffices to think of architecture, which is an art of *the size of things*): it is not by accident that Lichtenstein reproduces a *loupe* and what it enlarges: *Magnifying Glass* is in a sense the emblem of pop art.

And then, in many works of pop art, the background against which the object is silhouetted, or even out of which it is made, has a powerful existence (rather of the kind clouds had in classical painting): there is an importance of the grid. This comes, perhaps, from Warhol's first experiments: serigraphs depend on textile (textile and grid are the same thing); it is as if our latest modernity enjoys this manifestation of the grid, at once consecrating the raw material (grain of the paper in Twombly's work) and the mechanization of reproduction (micro-pattern of the computer portraits). Grid is a kind of obsession (a thematics, criticism would have said not long ago); it participates in various exchanges: its perceptual role is inverted (in Lichtenstein's aquarium, water consists of polka dots); it is enlarged in a deliberately infantile fashion (Lichtenstein's sponge consists of holes, like a piece of Gruyère); the mechanical texture is exemplarily imitated (again, Lichtenstein's *Large Spool*). Here art appears in the emphasis on what should be insignificant.

Another emphasis (and consequently another return of art): color. Of course, everything found in nature and a fortiori in the social world is colored; but if it is to remain a factitious object, as a true destruction of art would have it, its color itself must remain *indeterminate*. Now, this is not the case: pop art's colors are intentional and, we might even say (a real denial), subject to a *style*: they are intentional first of all because they are always the same ones and hence have a thematic value; then because this theme has a value as meaning: pop color is openly chemical; it aggressively refers to the artifice of chemistry, in its opposition to Nature. And if we admit that, in the plastic domain, color is ordinarily the site of pulsion, these acrylics, these flat primaries, these lacquers, in short these colors which are never shades, since nuance is banished from them, seek to cut short desire, emotion: we might say, at the limit, that they have a moral meaning, or at least that they systematically rely on a certain frustration. Color and even substance (lacquer, plaster) give pop art a meaning and consequently make it an art; we will be convinced of this by noticing that pop artists readily define their canvases by the color of the objects represented: *Black Girl, Blue Wall, Red Door* (Segal), *Two Blackish Robes* (Dine).

Pop is an art because, just when it seems to renounce all meaning, consenting only to reproduce things in their platitude, it stages, according to certain methods proper to it and forming a style, an object which is neither the thing nor its meaning, but which is: its signifier, or rather: the Signifier. Art—any art, from poetry to comic strips—exists the moment our glance has the Signifier as its object. Of course, in the productions of art, there is usually a signified (here, mass culture), but this signified, finally, appears in an *indirect* position: obliquely, one might say; so true is it that meaning, the play of meaning, its abolition, its return, is never anything but a *question of place*. Moreover, it is not only because the pop artist stages the Signifier that his work derives from and relates to art; it is also because this work is *looked at* (and not only seen); however much pop art has depersonalized the world, platitudinized objects, dehumanized images, replaced traditional craftsmanship of the canvas by machinery, some "subject" remains. What subject? The one who looks, in the absence of the one who makes. We can fabricate a machine, but someone who looks at it is not a machine—he desires, he fears, he delights, he is bored, etc. This is what happens with pop art.

I add: pop is an art of the essence of things, it is an "ontological" art. Look how Warhol proceeds with his repetitions—initially conceived as a method meant to destroy art: he repeats the image so as to suggest that the object trembles before the lens or the gaze; and if it trembles, one might say, it is because it seeks itself: it seeks its essence, it seeks to put this essence before you; in other words, the trembling of the thing acts (this is its effect-as-meaning) as a pose: in the past, was not the pose—before the easel or the lens—the affirmation of an individual's essence? Marilyn, Liz, Elvis, Troy Donahue are not presented, strictly speaking, according to their contingency, but according to their eternal identity: they have an "eidos," which it is the task of pop art to represent. Now look at Lichtenstein: he does not repeat, but his task is the same: he reduces, he purifies the image in order to intercept (and offer) what? its rhetorical essence: here art's entire labor consists not, as in the past, in streamlining the stylistic artifices of discourse, but, on the contrary, in cleansing the image of everything in it which is not rhetoric: what must be expelled, like a vital nucleus, is the code essence. The philosophical meaning of this labor is that modern things have no essence other than the social code which manifests them—so that ultimately they are no longer ever "produced" (by Nature), but immediately "reproduced": reproduction is the very being of Modernity.

We come full circle: not only is pop art an art, not only is this art ontological, but even its reference is finally—as in the highest periods of classical art—Nature; not of course the vegetal, scenic, or human (psychological) Nature: Nature today is the social absolute, or better still (for we are not directly concerned with politics) the Gregarious. This new Nature is accommodated by pop art, and moreover, whether it likes it or not, or rather whether it admits it or not, pop art criticizes this Nature. How? By imposing a *distance* upon its gaze (and hence upon our own). Even if all pop artists have not had a privileged relation with Brecht (as was Warhol's case during the sixties), all of them practice, with regard to the object, that repository of the social relation, a kind of "distancing" which has a critical value. However, less naïve or less optimistic than Brecht, pop art neither formulates nor resolves its criticism: to pose the object "flat out" is to pose the object at a distance, but it is also to refuse to say how this distance might be corrected. A cold confusion is imparted to the consistency of the gregarious world (a "mass" world); the disturbance of our gaze is as "matte" as the thing represented—and perhaps all the more terrible for that. In all the (re-)productions of pop art, one question threatens, challenges: *"What do you mean?"* (title of a poster by Allen Jones). This is the millennial question of that very old thing: Art.

1980

[*Body*]

Réquichot and His Body

Je ne sais pas c'qui m'quoi.

The Body

Inside

Many painters have reproduced the human body, but that body was always someone else's. Réquichot paints only his own: not that exterior body the painter copies *looking at himself sidelong,* but his body from inside; his interior comes outside, but it is another body whose violent ectoplasm suddenly appears as a result of these two colors' confrontation: white of the canvas, black of closed eyes. A generalized revulsion then seizes the painter, revealing neither viscera nor muscles but only a machinery of thwarting and ecstatic movements; this is the moment when substance (raw material) is absorbed, abstracted in viscous or extra-acute vibration: painting (let us continue to use this word for all kinds of treatments) becomes a *noise* ("The extreme shrillness of noise is a form of sadism"). This excess of materiality is what Réquichot calls the *meta-mental*. The meta-mental is what denies the theological opposition of body and soul: it is the body without opposition and therefore, so to speak, without meaning; it is the *inside* assaulted like a slap from *within*.

Thereby representation is disturbed, and grammar, too: the verb *to paint* regains an odd ambiguity: its object (what one paints) is sometimes what is looked at (the model), sometimes what is covered (the canvas): Réquichot does not accept an object: he questions even as he corrupts himself: he paints himself like Rembrandt, he paints himself like a Redskin. The painter is simultaneously an artist (who represents something) and a savage (who daubs and abrades his body).

The Reliquaries

Yet the Reliquaries, being boxes at the bottom of which *there is something to see*, resemble certain endoscopic machines. Is it not the body's internal magma which is placed here, at the limit of our gaze, as a deep field? Does not a baroque and funereal concept govern the exhibition of the anterior body, *the body before the mirror-stage*? Are not the Reliquaries open wombs, profaned tombs ("What touches us very closely cannot become public without profanation")?

No, this aesthetic of vision and this metaphysic of secrecy are immediately confused if we know that Réquichot was reluctant to show his painting, and especially that it took him years to make a single Reliquary. This means that for him the box was not the (reinforced) frame of an exhibition but rather a kind of temporal space, the enclosure in which his body worked, worked itself over: withdrew and added itself, rolled and unrolled itself, discharged itself: *took pleasure*: the box is the

*From Nokto kéda taktafoni, "Reliquary," oil, bone, and
diverse materials. Private collection*

reliquary not of saints' bones but of Réquichot's pleasures. In the same way, on the Pacific coast we find ancient Peruvian tombs where the dead person is surrounded by terra-cotta statuettes: these represent neither relatives nor gods but only the dead person's preferred ways of making love: what death takes away are not his possessions, as in so many other religions, but the traces of his pleasure.

The Tongue

In certain collages (around 1960) appear many muzzles, snouts, and tongues of animals: respiratory anguish, says one critic. No, the tongue is language: not civilized speech, for that passes through the teeth (dentalized pronunciation is a sign of distinction: the teeth supervise speech), but the visceral, erectile language: the tongue is a phallus that talks. In one of Poe's tales it is the tongue of a magnetized corpse, not its teeth, that utters the unspeakable words: "I am dead": the teeth shape speech, they make it precise, fine, intellectual, truthful, but over the tongue, because it spreads and swells like a springboard, everything passes—language can explode, rebound, no longer be mastered: it is over the tongue of the magnetized corpse that the cries of "Death! Death!" explode without the magnetizer's being able to silence them and end the nightmare of this talking carcass; and it is also, within the body, on the level of the tongue that Réquichot represents a total language: in his lettrist poems and in his snout-collages.

The Rat-King

Réquichot's investigations concern a movement of the body which had fascinated Sade as well (though not the sadist Sade); this movement is *repugnance*: the body begins to exist where it *repugnates,* repulses, yet wants to devour what disgusts it and exploits that taste for distaste, thereby opening itself to a dizziness (vertigo is what does not end: vertigo disconnects meaning, postpones it).

The fundamental form of repugnance is agglomeration; it is not gratuitously, for mere technical experimentation, that Réquichot turns to collage; his collages are not decorative, they do not juxtapose, they conglomerate, extending over huge surfaces, thickening into volumes; in a word, their truth is etymological, they take literally the *colle,* the glue at the origin of their name; what they produce is the glutinous, alimentary paste, luxuriant and nauseating, where outlining, cutting-out—i.e., nomination— are done away with.

A rhetorical instance: what Réquichot's collages agglomerate are animals. Now, it seems that the conglomeration of creatures provokes in us a paroxysm of repugnance: swarming worms, nests of serpents, hives of wasps. A fabulous phenomenon (is it as yet scientifically proved? I haven't any idea) summarizes the entire horror of these animal agglomerations: this is the *rat-king:* "In their natural state," says an old zoological dictionary, "rats are occasionally subject to the strangest disease. A great number join together by the tail and thus form what is commonly known as the *rat-king* . . . The cause of this curious phenomenon is still unknown to us. It is supposed that there is a special exudation of the tail which keeps these organs stuck together. A *rat-king* has been preserved in Altenburg, consisting of twenty-seven individuals. Similar groups have been discovered in Bonn, Schnepfenthal, Frankfurt, Erfurt, and in Lindenau near Leipzig." Metaphorically, Réquichot has not stopped painting this rat-king, pasting together this collage which does not even have a name; for what exists, in Réquichot, is not the object, nor even its effect, but its trace: let us understand this word in its locomotor meaning: bursting out of the tube of paint, the worm is its own trace, much more repulsive than its body.

Erection

Disgust is a panic erection: it is the entire body-as-phallus which swells, hardens, and collapses. And this is what constitutes painting: it gets a hard-on. Perhaps we are here faced with an irreducible difference between painting and discourse: painting is "full"; the voice, on the contrary, establishes a distance, a void, in the body; every voice is "white"—succeeds in taking on color only by pitiable artifices. Hence, we must take literally this declaration of Réquichot's, describing his work not as an erotic action (which would be banal enough) but as an erectile movement *and what follows*: "I am talking about that simple rhythm which for me makes a canvas start up slowly, then gradually become more involving, and by a thrilling crescendo leads me to an effervescence on the order of an orgasm. At this climax, the painting abandons me, unless it is I, at the limits of my power, who let it go . . . If I then know that my painting is finished, my need to paint is not, and this paroxysm is followed by a great disappointment." Réquichot's work is this *detumescence* of the body (which he sometimes calls by the very word some use to designate pulsion: *drift*).

The Two Sources of Painting

Writing and Cooking

Toward the end of the eighteenth century, this is how neoclassical painters represented the birth of painting: love-struck, the daughter of a Corinthian potter reproduces her lover's silhouette by drawing the outline of his shadow on a wall. For this romantic image—which, moreover, is not a false one, since it adduces desire—let us substitute another myth, at once more abstract and more trivial; let us imagine, outside all history, a double origin of painting.

The first would be writing, the tracing of future signs, the exercise of the tip (of the brush, of the pencil lead, of the awl, of what striates and hollows out—even if it is the artifice of a line deposited by color). The second would be cooking, i.e., any practice which aims at transforming substance according to the complete scale of its consistencies, by various operations such as inspissation, liquefaction, granulation, lubrification, producing what in gastronomy is called the coated, the thickened, the creamy, the crisp, etc. Thus, Freud contrasts sculpture—*via di levare*—with painting—*via di porre*; but it is in painting itself that the opposition appears: the opposition between incision (the "line") and unction (the "coating").

These two origins could be linked to the two gestures of the hand, which sometimes scratches, sometimes levels, sometimes hollows out, sometimes smooths over; in a word, to the finger and to the palm, to the fingernail and to the mount of Venus. This double hand divides up the whole realm of painting, because the hand is the truth of painting, not the eye ("representation," or figuration, or the copy, are but a secondary and incorporated accident, an alibi, a transparency laid over the network of lines and coatings, a shadow cast, an inessential mirage). Another history of painting is possible, which is not that of works and artists but that of tools and substances; for a very long time, the artist, among us, was not distinguished by his instrument, which was, uniformly, the brush; when painting entered upon its historical crisis, the instruments were multiplied, and the raw materials as well: there has been an infinite journey of inscribing objects and of their supports; the limits of the pictural tool have been continually pushed back (even for Réquichot: razor, coal shovel, polystyrene rings). One consequence (still to be explored) is that the tool, no longer coded, partly escapes commerce: art-supply stores can no longer keep

up: they now distribute their merchandise only to docile amateurs; it is in the department stores, in the housewares section,
that Réquichot goes looking for his raw materials: commerce is
pillaged (to *pillage* means to appropriate without respect to
use). Painting, then, loses its aesthetic specificity, or rather that
(age-old) specificity proves fallacious: behind painting, behind
its splendid historical individuality (the sublime art of colored
figuration), is *something else*: the movements of the fingernails,
of the glottis, of the viscera, a projection of the body, and not
only a mastery of the eye.

Réquichot holds in his hand the fierce reins of painting. As
an original painter (here we are still speaking of a mythical
origin: neither theological nor psychological nor historical: pure
fiction), he constantly returns to writing and to food.

Cooking

Foodstuffs

Have you ever watched the preparation of a Swiss dish called
raclette? A hemisphere of raw cheese is held vertically above
the grille; it melts, swells, and sizzles; the knife gently scrapes
[*racle*] this liquid blister, this runny surplus, from the shape;
it falls, like a white dung; it hardens, it yellows on the plate;
with the knife, the amputated area is smoothed out; and then
the process begins all over again.

This is, strictly speaking, an operation of painting. For in
painting, as in cooking, *something must be allowed to drop
somewhere*: it is in this fall that matter is transformed (de-
formed): the drop spreads and the foodstuff softens: there is
production of a new substance (movement makes matter). In
Réquichot's work, all states of alimentary substance (ingested,
digested, evacuated) are present: the crystallized, the crackled,

the stringy, the granular—the dried, earthy excrement, the oily iridescence, the carbuncle, the intestine. And to crown this specter of the digestive bolus, in the large collages, in the last Reliquaries, the material origin is explicitly alimentary, taken from household magazines: here are Franco-Russian dishes, here are pastas, cutlets, strawberries, sausages (mixed with coils of hair, with dogs' muzzles); but it is the scrambling together which is culinary (and pictural): the strewing, the interlacing, the stew (Japanese sukiyaki is a painting systematically developed in time).

Here Réquichot brings us back to one of painting's mythic origins: a good half of it belongs to the nutritive (visceral) order. If we are to kill the alimentary sensuality of the thing painted, we must dismiss painting itself: you can neither eat nor vomit Joseph Kossuth's *Thing*; but also there is no painting left (no coating, no scratching): the painter's hand and the cook's are amputated at one and the same time. Réquichot, however, is *still* a painter: he eats (or doesn't eat), digests, vomits; his desire (for painting) is the very great representation of a need.

No Metaphor

We might still say that food is Réquichot's neurotic center (he did not like red meat, and let himself starve to death), but this center is not certain. For once food is imagined in its trajectory from aliment to excrement, from the mouth (the one that eats, but also the one that is eaten: the snout) to the anus, the metaphor shifts and another center appears: the cavity, the interior sheath, the intestinal reptile is an enormous phallus. Hence, to conclude, thematic inquiry becomes futile: we realize that Réquichot is saying only one thing, which is the very denial of all metaphor: the whole body is in its inside; this *inside* is thus both erotic and digestive. An inhuman anatomy governs pleasure and the work itself: this anatomy is to be found in the last abstract objects Réquichot produced: these are (all abstraction resembles something) seashells, uniting in themselves the spiral's "graphism" (a theme of writing) and digestive animality, for these molluscs (patellas, fissurellas, annelidae furnished with locomotor bristles) are gastropods: if they walked, it would be with their stomachs: it is the interior which produces movement.

Cast-off

Around 1949, at the beginning of his work, Réquichot made a charcoal drawing of a shoe: the holes in the uppers are empty; only a fragment of shoelace remains; for all its rather soft forms, this shoe is a *warped* object. Here begins, for Réquichot, a long epic of the *cast-off* (it was appropriate that the shoe should be at the origin of this epic: seeking to invert the civilized order, Fourier makes the worn-out shoe, a major cast-off equal to rags and refuse, into a flamboyant object). What is the cast-off? It is the name of what *has had* a name, it is the name of the denominated; we might develop here what will be said later on: the labor of de-nomination, of which Réquichot's oeuvre is the theater; better for now to reattach the cast-off to the foodstuff. The cast-off disfigures the foodstuff because it exceeds its function: it is what is not ingested; it is the foodstuff projected outside of hunger. Nature, i.e. the outskirts of farms, is full of cast-offs, the very ones which fascinated Réquichot and which he put into certain compositions (chicken and rabbit bones, feathers, whatever came to him from these "country encounters"). The things which enter into Réquichot's painting (the things themselves, not their simulacra) are always cast-offs, out-of-the-way supplements, abandoned objects: what has *fallen away* from its function: the vermicelli of painting cast straight onto the canvas as into the garbage pail upon emerging from the tube, magazine photographs cut up and disfigured, their origins unrecognizable (journalism's vocation is to be cast off), crusts (of bread, of paint). The cast-off is the only excrement the anorexic can permit himself.

Oil

Oil is that substance which augments the foodstuff without fragmenting it: which thickens without hardening it: magically, with the help of a thread of oil, the egg yolk assumes a growing volume, and this *to infinity*; it is in the same way that the organ grows, by intussusception. Now, oil is that same substance which serves for food and for painting. To abandon oil, for a painter, is to sacrifice painting itself, the culinary gesture which, mythically, establishes and sustains it. Réquichot has experienced the historical agony of painting (he could do this because he was a painter). This means that, on the one hand, he has been very far away from oil (in his collages, ring sculptures, ball-point drawings), but also that, on the other hand, he has been constantly tempted to return to it, as to a vital substance: the ancestral milieu of foodstuffs. Even his collages without oil obey the principle of thickened proliferation (that of an infinite mayonnaise); for years, Réquichot *grows* his Reliquaries as one develops a body organized by the slow ingestion of a juice.

Writing

Spiral

Where do letters come from? For ideographic writing, this is simple: they come from "nature" (the nature of a man, of a woman, of the rain, of a mountain); but that's just it: they are then immediately words, semanthemes, not letters. The letter

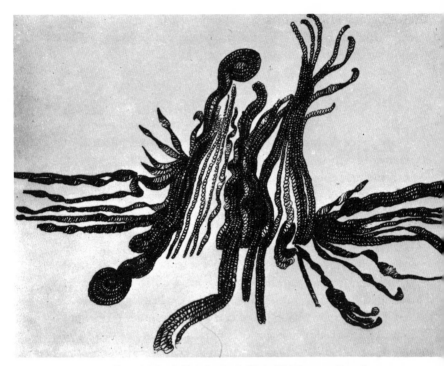

From Nokto kéda taktafoni, *"Spiral," ink on cardboard.*
Private collection

(the Phoenician letter, which is ours) is a form stripped of meaning: that is its first definition. The second is that the letter is not painted (deposited) but scratched, incised, hollowed out by the punch or the awl; its art of reference (and of origin) is not painting but glyptics.

In Réquichot's work, semiography no doubt appears around 1956, when he draws with a pen (let us take note of the instrument) certain clusters of coiled lines: sign, writing come with the spiral, which will not henceforth be absent from his work. The symbolism of the spiral is the opposite of that of the circle; the circle is religious, theological; the spiral, a kind of circle distended to infinity, is dialectical: on the spiral, things recur, but *at another level*: there is a return in difference, not repetition in identity (for Vico, an audacious thinker, world history followed a spiral). The spiral governs the dialectic of the old and the new; thanks to it, we need not believe: *everything has been said*, or: *nothing has been said*, but rather: nothing is first yet everything is new. This is what constitutes Réquichot's spiral: by repeating itself, it engenders a displacement. The same thing happens in poetic language (I mean: prosodic and/or metrical): since the signs of this language are very limited in number and infinitely free to combine, novelty here, more than elsewhere, consists of very close-set repetitions. In the same way Réquichot's spiral compositions (we might take for example his *War of Nerves*) explode in all directions, starting from a repeated and displaced element, the whorl (here related to lines, stems, splashes); they have the same mode of explosive generation as the poetic phrase. For Réquichot the spiral has visibly been a new sign, starting from which, once discovered, he could elaborate a new syntax, a new language. Yet this language—and in this it is a writing—is always *in the process of constituting itself*: the spiral is of course a sign in itself, but in order to exist this sign needs a movement, which is that of the hand: in writing, syntax, the source of all meaning is essentially the leverage of muscle—of meta-muscle, Réquichot would say: it is at the moment it bears down (however lightly) that it becomes intelligent; without *this weight which advances*, the pictural (or graphic) line remains stupid (the stupid line is one made *in order to resemble* or one made *in order not to resemble*: for example, the line made to undulate so as not to resemble a simple straight line). What constitutes writing, ultimately, is not the sign (analytic abstraction), but, much more paradoxically, *the cursivity of the discontinuous* (what is repeated is necessarily discontinuous). Make a loop: you produce a sign; but shift it forward, your hand still resting there on the receptive surface; you generate a writing: writing is the hand which bears down and advances or hangs back, *always in the same direction,* in short the hand which *plows* (whence the country metaphor which designates boustrophedonic writing according to the back-and-forth movement of oxen across the field). The corporal meaning of the repeated spiral is that the hand never leaves the paper until a certain pleasure is exhausted (meaning is transferred to the general figure: each of Réquichot's drawings is new).

Illegible

In 1930, the archaeologist Persson discovered in a Mycenean tomb a jar bearing certain "graphisms" on its rim; imperturbably, Persson translated the inscription, in which he had recognized certain words which resembled Greek; but later on, another archaeologist, Ventris, established that this was not writing at all, merely an incised pattern; moreover, at one end, the drawing ended in purely decorative curves. Réquichot takes the converse direction (on the same path): a spiral composition of September 1956 (that month when he constituted the reservoir of his final forms) ends (at the bottom) in a line of writing. Thus is born a special semiography (already practiced by Klee, Ernst, Michaux, and Picasso): illegible writing. Fifteen days before his death, Réquichot writes in two nights six indecipherable texts which will remain so forever; yet no doubt buried under some future cataclysm, these texts will find a Persson to translate them; for History alone institutes the legibility of a writing; as for its Being, writing derives that not from its meaning (from its communicative function) but from the rage, the tenderness, or the rigor with which its strokes and curves are drawn.

Illegible testament, Réquichot's last letters say several things: first of all that meaning is always contingent, historical, *invented* (by some overconfident archaeologist): nothing separates writing (which we believe communicates) from painting (which we believe expresses): both consist of the same tissue, which is perhaps quite simply, as in very modern cosmogonies: speed (Réquichot's illegible writings are as runaway as certain of his canvases). Another thing: what is illegible is nothing but *what has been lost*: to write, to lose, to rewrite, to establish the infinite play of *under* and *over*, to bring the signifier closer, to make it a giant, a monster of presence, to diminish the signified to imperceptibility, to unbalance the message, to retain memory's form but not its content, to make the impenetrable *definitive*—in a word, to put all writing, all art in a palimpsest, and to make this palimpsest inexhaustible, what *has been written* continually returning in what *is written* in order to make it superlegible—i.e., illegible. It is, in short, by the same movement that Réquichot has written his illegible letters and created the pictural palimpsest, cutting out and sewing together certain canvases, taking down and respattering his *tachiste* paintings, introducing the Book (by its flyleaves) into his large compositions with Sample Papers. All this super-writing, a meaningless scribbling, opens out on oblivion: it is an impossible memory: "On islands off the Norwegian coast," Chateaubriand writes, "have been exhumed certain urns engraved with indecipherable characters. To whom do these ashes belong? The winds know nothing of them."

Representation

Substance

On Réquichot's worktable (indistinguishable from a kitchen counter), bunches of curtain rings bought at some department store: they will make, later on, the *Plastic Sculptures*, the *Glued Rings*.

Usually (I mean: if we refer to the history of art), the work proceeds from a pure raw material, which has not yet served for anything else (powder, clay, stone). Hence it is, classically, the raw material's first degree of transformation. The artist can then mythically identify himself with a demiurge, who creates something out of nothing: this is the Aristotelian definition of art (*techné*), and it is also the classical image of the Titanesque creator: Michelangelo creates the work as his God creates man. All such art utters the Origin.

Réquichot's rings, when he takes them, are *already* utilitarian (manufactured) objects, which happen to be perverted from their function: the work then departs from a previous past, the myth of Origin is shaken, painting's theological crisis begins (with the first collages, the "ready-mades"). This brings the pictural (or sculptural) work—the transformation of raw material will soon require another name—closer to the (so-called literary) Text; for the Text, too, takes utilitarian words, "manufactured" with a view to ordinary communication, in order to produce a new object, outside usage and hence outside commerce.

The final (perhaps even the unforeseeable) consequence of this distortion is to accentuate art's materialist nature. It is not substance itself which is materialist (a stone when framed is merely a pure fetish), it is, so to speak, the infinitude of its transformations; a little symbolism leads to divinity, but the desperate symbolism which governs the artist's work separates him from it: he knows that substance is infallibly symbolic—in perpetual displacement; his (social) function is to tell, to remind, to teach everyone that *substance is never in its place* (neither in the place of its origin nor in the place of its usage) —which is perhaps a way of suggesting (an essentially materialist affirmation): that there is no substance.

(The substance treated by the artist finds a place only at the moment when he frames it; exhibits it, sells it—it is the place

established by alienation: where the symbol's infinite displacement ceases.)

The Loupe

Just as in a palimpsest there is writing in writing, so in a
"picture" (it matters little whether or not the word is accurate)
there are several pictures: not only (in Réquichot) because
canvases are rewritten or replaced as partial objects within new
ensembles, but because there are as many works as there are
levels of perception: isolate, enlarge, and treat a detail, you
create a new work, you cross over centuries, schools, styles, out
of the very old you can make the very new. Réquichot has
practiced this technique on himself: "Looking at a picture very
closely, you can see future pictures in it: it has happened to
me, I've cut up big ones and tried to isolate the parts that look
interesting." The potential instrument of painting (for that—
perhaps tiny—part of itself which concerns the eye and not the
hand) might be the *loupe* or even the turntable, which permits
changing the object by making it turn (Réquichot has in this
way utilized dog muzzles intact, without any adjunction, but
by *turning them*): all this, not to see better or to see more
completely, but to see *something else*: size is an object in itself:
does it not suffice to establish a major art, architecture? The
loupe and the turntable produce that supplement which disturbs
meaning, i.e., recognition (to understand, to read, to receive a
language is to recognize; the sign is what is recognized; Réquichot belongs to that race of artists *who do not recognize*).
To change the level of perception produces a shock which
shakes up the classified, named world (the recognized world)
and consequently liberates a veritable hallucinatory energy. As
a matter of fact, if art (let us continue to use this convenient
word to designate any unfunctional activity) had for its goal

only to make us see better, it would be nothing but a technique of analysis, an ersatz science (which realistic art has claimed to be); but in seeking to produce that *something else* which is in the thing, it subverts an entire epistemology: it is this *limitless* work which rids us of a common hierarchy: first of all, ("true") perception, then nomination, lastly association (the artist's "noble," "creative" share); for Réquichot, on the contrary, there is no privilege granted to the first perception: perception is *immediately* plural—that which, once again, dispenses with idealist classification; the mental is only *the body raised to another level of perception*: what Réquichot calls the "meta-mental."

Name

Let us take two modern treatments of the object. In the ready-made, the object is *real* (art begins only at its periphery, its framing, its museography)—hence it has been possible to refer it to petit-bourgeois realism. In so-called conceptual art, the object is *named*, rooted in the dictionary—which is why it would be better to say "denotative art" than "conceptual art." In the ready-made, the object is so real that the artist can permit himself the eccentricity or the uncertainty of denomination; in conceptual art, the object is so precisely named that it no longer needs to be real: it can be reduced to a dictionary entry (Joseph Kossuth's *Thing*). These two apparently opposed treatments derive from one and the same activity: classification.

In Hindu philosophy, classification has an illustrious name: it is *Maya*: not the world of "appearances," the veil which hides some intimate truth, but the principle which causes all things to be classified, measured by man, not by nature; once an opposition appears, there is Maya: the network of forms (objects) is Maya, the paradigm of names (language) is Maya (the

Brahman does not deny Maya, he does not oppose the One to the Many, he is not a monist—for to unite is also Maya; what he seeks is the end of opposition, the extinction of measurement; his project is not to withdraw himself from any class, but from classification itself).

Réquichot's effort is not Maya: it seeks neither object nor language. What it aims at is to undo the Name; from work to work, it proceeds to a generalized ex-nomination of the object. This is a singular project which separates Réquichot from the sects of his time. This project is not simple: ex-nomination of the object necessarily passes through a phase of exuberant super-nomination: we must outbid Maya before exhausting it: this is the *thematic* moment which is today out of fashion. A thematic critique· of Réquichot is not only possible but inevitable; his forms "resemble" something, summon up a procession of names, according to the method of metaphor; he himself knew this: "My paintings: you can find crystals in them, branches, grottoes, algae, sponges . . ." Here analogy is irrepressible (a kind of precocious pleasure), but from the point of view of language, it is already ambiguous: it is because the drawn (painted or composed) form has no name that several are sought for it and imposed upon it; metaphor is the only way of naming the un-namable (it then very specifically becomes a catachresis): the chain of names is valid for the name which is missing. What happens in analogy (at least the kind which Réquichot practices) is not its term, its supposed signified ("this blotch signifies a sponge"), it is the temptation of the name, whatever it may be: extravagant polysemy is the first (initiatory) episode of an *ascesis*: the one which leads outside the dictionary, outside meaning.

The thematics suggested by Réquichot is deceptive because as a matter of fact it cannot be mastered: *metaphor does not stop*, the labor of nomination inexorably continues, constrained to proceed forever, never to be fixed, constantly undoing the

names found, concluding nowhere, if not at a perpetual ex-
nomination: because *this* resembles not everything but *succes-
sively* something, *this* resembles nothing. Or again: *this* resembles, yes, but what? "Something which has no name." The
analogy thus fulfills its own denial, and the gap of the name is
maintained to infinity: *What is that?*

This question (the one the Sphinx asked Oedipus) is always
a cry, the demand of a desire: quick, a Name, let me be re-
assured! Let Maya cease being lacerated, let it be reconstituted
and restored in a rediscovered language: let the picture give me
its Name! But—this precisely defines Réquichot—the Name is
never given: we enjoy only our desire, not our pleasure.

Perhaps that is what abstraction really is: not the painting
produced by certain painters around the idea of *line* (popular
opinion wants the line to be abstract, Apollonian; the image of
an abstract magma, as in Réquichot, seems incongruous), but
this dangerous debate between object and language, whose
script Réquichot has provided us: he has created abstract *objects*: *objects* because they seek a name, and *abstract* because
they are unnamable: once the object is here (and not the line),
it seeks to engender a name, to produce a filiation—that of
language: isn't language what is bequeathed to us by an anterior
order? In his work, Réquichot proceeds to an exheredation of
the object, he severs the inheritance from the name. From the
signifier's very substance he removes any orgin: these "accidents" (from which certain collages of his are woven) are what?
Canvases painted long ago, then rolled up and put away:
disinherited.

Réquichot's project is doubly determined (indeterminable):
on the one hand, on the avant-garde game board, he explores
the crisis of language, disturbs formulation to the point of
breaking down denotation; on the other hand, he *personally*
pursues the definition of his own body and discovers that this
definition begins where the Name stops, i.e., *inside* (only doc-

tors can name, far from any reality, the inside of the body—that body which is only its inside). All of Réquichot's painting might carry this legend, written by the painter himself: "I don't know what thinks me"—*Je ne sais pas c'qui m'quoi.*

Representation

How does the painter know that his work is done? That he should stop, put the object down, move on to another work? As long as the painting is strictly figurative, *finish* is conceivable —was even constituted as an aesthetic value—since it was a matter of achieving a resemblance (or at least an effect): once *this* (the illusion) is achieved, I can drop *that* (the canvas); but, in later painting, perfection (*to perfect* means *to finish*) ceases to be a value: the work is infinite (as was, already, Balzac's *Unknown Masterpiece*), and yet, at a certain moment, one does leave off (either in order to exhibit or to destroy): the measure of a work of art no longer resides in its finality (the finished product which it constitutes) but in the labor it exhibits (the production into which it seeks to bear its "reader"): in the process of its creation (and reading), its end is transformed. Now this is something like what happens in psychoanalytic therapy: it is the very idea of "cure," initially very simple, which gradually grows more complicated, transforms itself and becomes distant: the work of art is interminable, like the cure: in both cases, it is less a matter of obtaining a result than of modifying a problem, i.e., a subject: gaining release from the imprisoning finality of the point of departure.

As we see, the difficulty of finishing—to which Réquichot has often testified—implicates representation itself, unless it is the abolition of the figure, brought about by a whole interplay of historical determinants, which compels the non-realization of art's *end* (goal and term). The entire conflict may reside in the two meanings of the word *representation*. In the current one, which is the one from which the classical work derives, representation designates a copy, an illusion, an analogical figure, a resemblance-product; but in the etymological meaning, representation is merely the return of what has been presented; in it, the present reveals its paradox, which is to have *already* taken place (since it does not escape the code): thus, what is most irrepressible in the artist (in this case, Réquichot), i.e., the explosion of pleasure, is constituted only with the help of that which is *already* in language, which is language; and it is here that, despite the apparently inexpiable war of Old and New, the two meanings unite: from one end of its history to the other, art is merely the varied conflict of image and name: sometimes (at the figurative pole), the exact Name governs and the sign imposes its law upon the signifier; sometimes (at the "abstract" pole—which puts it very badly indeed), the Name escapes, the signifier, continually in explosion, tries to undo the stubborn signified which seeks to return in order to form a sign (Réquichot's originality derives from the fact that, transcending the abstract solution, he has understood that, in order to undo the Name, Maya, he must submit to exhausting it: asemy passes through an exuberant, desperate polysemy: *the name does not stay in place*).

In short, there is a moment, a level of theory (of the Text, of art) where the two meanings coincide; it is possible to assert that the most figurative of paintings never represents (copies) anything but only seeks a Name (the name of the scene, of the object); but it is also possible (although today more scandalous) to say that the least figurative "painting" still represents something: either language itself (this is, one might say, the position of the canonical avant-garde) or the inside of the body, the body as inside, or still better: enjoyment: this is what Réquichot does (as painter of enjoyment, Réquichot is singular nowadays: out of fashion—for the avant-garde is not often given to enjoyment).

The Artist

Beyond What?

Must we reinstate Réquichot in the history of paintings? Réquichot himself has seen the futility of this question: "Going beyond van Gogh or Kandinsky isn't much good, nor is *wanting* to go beyond them: all that is only a historical transcendence . . ." What is called the "history of painting" is only a cultural sequence, and any sequence participates in an imaginary History: the sequence is in fact what constitutes the image-repertoire of our History. Is it not, in fact, an odd automatism to put the painter, the writer, the artist in the enfilade of his kind? A filial image which, once again, imperturbably identifies antecedence with origin: we must find Fathers and Sons for the artist, so that he can acknowledge the latter and kill the former, uniting two *beaux rôles*: gratitude and independence: this is what we call: "going beyond."

Yet there is quite often in a single painter a whole history of painting (we need merely change the levels of perception: Nicolas de Staël is in three square centimeters of Cézanne). In the sequence of his works, Réquichot has performed that devouring progress: he has skipped no image, making himself historical at top speed, by an accumulation of abrupt liberations; he has passed through many painters who have preceded, surrounded, and even followed him, but this apprenticeship was not artisanal, it sought no ultimate mastery; it was infinite, not by mystical dissatisfaction, but by a persistent return of desire.

Perhaps this is how we must read painting (at least, Réquichot's): outside any cultural sequence. Thereby we have some chance of squaring the circle: withdrawing painting from the ideological suspicion which today marks any *penultimate* work, and still leaving upon it the imprint of its historical responsibility (of its insertion in a crisis of History), which is, in Réquichot's case, to participate in the agony of painting. The result of combining these two contradictory movements is, in effect, a *remainder*. What remains is *our right to the enjoyment of the work.*

Amateur

Disfiguring the word, one would like to be able to say that Réquichot was an *amateur*. The amateur is not necessarily defined by a lesser knowledge, an imperfect technique (in which case Réquichot is not an amateur), but rather by this: he is *the one who does not exhibit*, the one who does not make himself heard. The meaning of this occultation is as follows: the amateur seeks to produce only his own enjoyment (but nothing forbids it to become ours *in addition*, without his knowing it), and this enjoyment is shunted toward no hysteria. Beyond the amateur ends pure enjoyment (withdrawn from any neurosis) and begins the image-repertoire, i.e., the artist: the artist can enjoy, of course, but once he exhibits and makes himself heard, once he has a public, his enjoyment must come to terms with an *imago*, which is the discourse the Other offers about what he does. Réquichot did not exhibit his canvases (they are still widely unknown): "Every glance at what I make is a usurpation of my thought and of my heart . . . What I make is not made to be seen . . . Your opinions and your praise seem to me intruders who disturb and distort the genesis, the anxiety, the delicate perception of the mental in which something is germinating, trying to grow . . ." Réquichot's singularity is to have carried out his work simultaneously at the highest and the lowest level: as the arcanum of enjoyment and as a modest hobby not to be exhibited.

Faust

The artist (here no longer in opposition to the amateur):
what a worn-out word! How does it happen that if we apply it
to Réquichot it loses its romantic and bourgeois overtones?
First of all, because of this: Réquichot's painting starts from
his body: the body's inside works within it uncensored; whence
this paradox: this oeuvre is *expressive,* it expresses Réquichot
(Réquichot expresses himself in it, in the literal sense of the
word, presses on the canvas the violent juice of his interior
synesthesia), and therefore seems, in a first impulse, to participate in the subject's idealist aesthetic (an aesthetic nowadays harshly contested); but in a second impulse, since this
subject is precisely seeking to abolish the age-old contrast between "soul" and "flesh," since he makes every effort to put
before us a new substance, an unheard-of, revulsed, *disorganized*
body (no more organs, no more muscles, no more nerves, nothing but vibrations of pain and of pleasure), it is the subject
himself (the subject of classical ideology) *who is no longer
here*: the body dismisses the subject and Réquichot's painting
then joins the extreme avant-garde: *the one which is not classifiable* and whose psychotic character society denounces because
thereby at least society can name it.

And then—another reason not to erase the "artist" in him—
Réquichot conceived his work, his labor—all his labor—as an
experiment, a risk. ("You have to paint, not to make an oeuvre,
but to know how far an oeuvre can go.") There was nothing
humanist about this experiment, there was no question of test-
ing the limits of man in the name of humanity; it was deliberately autarchic, its end always remained an agonizing enjoyment;
and even so, it was not an individualistic experiment, for it included—even by superfluity—the notion of a certain totality: a

totality of making, first of all: Réquichot exercised and revised
all the techniques of modernity, not hesitating to incorporate
into his work a certain mathesis of painting and never neglecting
what his predecessors might teach him; competition of the arts
as well: just as the Renaissance painters were *also*, very frequently, engineers, architects, hydraulic engineers, Réquichot
utilized another signifier, writing: he wrote poems, letters, a
private diary, and a text entitled, precisely, *Faustus*: for Faust is
still the eponymous hero of this race of artists: their knowledge
is apocalyptic: they carry out at one and the same time the
exploration of making and the catastrophic destruction of the
product.

Sacrifice

To be modern is to know *what is no longer possible*. Réquichot knew that "painting" cannot return (except perhaps,
someday, to another place, i.e., *spirally*), and he participated
in its destruction (by his collages, his sculptures). Yet Réquichot
was a painter (delighting in the density of oil, in the fluidity of
ink, in the scarifications of a talon, willingly traversing the
painters of the past, entering the inter-text of cubism, of abstraction, of *tachisme*). Doomed by historical necessity and by
what we might call the pressure of a responsible enjoyment to
kill, if not what he loved, at least what he knew and *knew how
to make*, he worked in a condition of sacrifice. However, this
sacrifice had nothing oblatory about it; Réquichot offered the
apocalypse of his knowledge, of his creation, of his "culture"
to no one—to no idea, to no law, to no history, to no progress,
to no faith. He worked at a loss; he knew he could not reach
his spectator as he himself had been reached; he therefore
practiced a strictly suicidal economy and decided that any
communication of his work (a mocking communication) would

redeem nothing of what he had invested in it. If now, by the care of a friend, we can see some of Réquichot's work, we must realize that this enormous sacrifice of violence and of enjoyment was not made for us. Réquichot wanted to lose *for nothing*: he contested any exchange. Historically, this is a sumptuary oeuvre, entirely subjected to that unconditional loss of which Bataille has written.

At Auction

Every aesthetic (but thereby destroying its very idea) comes down to this question: *Under what conditions does the work, the text, find a taker?* Based (today) on a subversion of any exchange, the work (even today) does not escape exchange, and it is here that, determined to liquidate every signified, it still possesses a *meaning*. At auction, who will bid for Réquichot? His value is protected neither by tradition nor by fashion nor by the avant-garde. From a certain point of view, his work is "null and void" (two pieces at the Museum of Modern Art in Paris, only one of which has been exhibited). And it is for this reason that his work is one of the sites where the *last subversion* is achieved: of this oeuvre, History can recuperate nothing except its own crisis.

To Talk about Painting?

At random, let us compare Réquichot to one of the sects which have followed him. In so-called conceptual art (reflexive art), there is, in principle, no place for delectation; these artists are well aware, lacking anything else, that in order to cauterize the ideological gangrene once and for all, it is desire which must be eliminated, for desire is always feudal. The work (if we can still call it this) is no longer formal, but merely visual, simply and directly articulating a perception and a nomination (form is what is *between* the thing and its name, form is what delays the name); which is why it would be better to say that this art is denotative rather than conceptual. Now here is the consequence of this purification; art is no longer fantasmatic; there is certainly a scenario (since there is exhibition), but this scenario is without subject: the operator and the reader can no more put themselves into a conceptual composition than the user of language can put himself into a dictionary. Thereby, all of criticism falls as well, for it can no longer thematize, poeticize, interpret; literature is foreclosed at the very moment when there is no longer any painting. Art then comes to the point of taking its own theory in hand; it can no longer do anything but *speak itself*, reducing itself to the speech which it *might* offer upon itself, if it consented to exist: desire being expelled, discourse returns in force: art becomes *talkative* at the very moment it ceases to be erotic. Ideology and its defects are banished, certainly; but at the price of *aphanasis*, the loss of desire, in a word, castration.

Réquichot's path is contrary: he exhausts art's idealism not by the reduction of form but by its exasperation; he does not sterilize the fantasm, he overloads it to the point of collapse; he does not collectivize the artist's labor (indifferent, even, to exhibiting it), he super-individualizes it, seeks that extreme point where the violence of expulsion will transform the subject's neurotic consistency into that *something else* which society locates in the realm of psychosis. Conceptual art (which we are simply taking as an example of an art contrary to Réquichot's) seeks to establish a *this side* of form (the dictionary); Réquichot wants to reach the *other side* of language; to do so, instead of filtering out the symbolic, he radicalizes it: he *displaces*—and it is here that he sides with the symbol. ("The so-called *blotches* of my paintings—I'm not trying to make them

fall in the right places; I'd rather they fell in the wrong ones.")
Hence, it is still possible to talk about Réquichot; his art can
be *spoken*: erotic (because it is his body he displaces), or
wicked, or violent, or dirty, or elegant, or viscous, or obsessed,
or powerful; in short, he can receive the linguistic mark of the
fantasm, as read by the Other—i.e., the *adjective*. For it is my
desire which, permitting the Other to speak of me, establishes,
with one and the same movement, adjective and criticism.

The Signature

Réquichot

For a good while now I have been writing not *on* Réquichot
but *around* him; this name "Réquichot" has become the emblem of my present writing; I no longer hear in it anything but
the familiar sound of my own work; I say *Réquichot* as I have
said *Michelet, Fourier,* or *Brecht.* And yet, awakened from its
usage, this name (like any name) is strange: so French, even
so rural, there is in it, by its hissing sound, by its diminutive
termination (in French), something gourmand (quiche!),
something of the farm (clogs), something friendly (the little
chap): there is something in it of the name of a *good classmate.*
We can transfer this instability of the major signifier (the
proper name) to the signature. In order to disturb the law of the
signature, there may be no need to suppress it, to imagine an
anonymous art; it is sufficient to displace its object: *Who signs
what?* Where does my signature stop? At what support? At the
canvas (as in classical painting)? At the object (as in the
ready-made)? At the event (as in the happening)? Réquichot
has perceived this infinity of the signature, which releases its
appropriative link, for the further the support extends, the

further the signature is removed from the subject: to sign is only to cut off, to cut oneself off, to cut off the other. Why, Réquichot supposed, could I not sign, beyond my canvas, the muddy leaf which has moved me, or even the path where I saw it stuck? Why not put my name on the mountains, the cows, the faucets, the factory chimneys (*Faustus*)? The signature is no more than the fulguration, the inscription of desire: the utopic and caressing imagination of a society without artists (for the artist will always be *humiliated*), in which, however, each of us would sign the objects of his pleasure. Réquichot, quite alone, has momentarily prefigured this sublime society of *amateurs*. To recognize Réquichot's signature is not to admit him to the cultural pantheon of painters, it is to possess an additional sign in the chaos of the enormous Text which is written without interruption, without origin, and without end.

1973

Right in the Eyes

A sign is what repeats itself. Without repetition there is no sign, for we could not *recognize* it, and recognition establishes the sign. Now, Stendhal notes, the gaze can say everything but cannot repeat itself, "word for word." Hence, the gaze is not a sign, yet it signifies. What is this mystery? It is that the gaze belongs to that realm of signification whose unit is not the sign (discontinuity) but *signifying* [*signifiance*], whose theory Benveniste has proposed. In opposition to language, an order of signs, the arts in general derive from *signifying*. Nothing surprising, then, that there should be a kind of affinity between the gaze and music, or that classical painting has lovingly reproduced so many kinds of gaze—imploring, imperious, frowning, pensive, etc. *Signifying* doubtless has a specific semantic core, without which the gaze could not mean something: literally, gaze cannot be *neutral*, except to signify neutrality; and if it is "vague," the vagueness is evidently full of duplicity; but this core is surrounded by a halo, a field of infinite expansion in which meaning *overflows*, is diffused without losing its *impress* (the action of impressing itself): and this is in fact what happens when we hear music or look at a picture. The "mystery" of the gaze, the disturbance which constitutes it, is obviously situated in this "overflow" zone. Here, then, is an object (or an entity) whose being inheres in its *excess*. Let us examine such overflows a little.

Science interprets the gaze in three (combinable) ways: in terms of information (the gaze informs), in terms of relation (gazes are exchanged), in terms of possession (by the gaze, I touch, I attain, I seize, I am seized): three functions: optical, linguistic, haptic. But always the gaze *seeks*: something, someone. It is an *anxious* sign: singular dynamics for a sign: its power overflows it.

In front of where I live, on the other side of the street, level with my windows, there is an apparently unoccupied apartment; however, from time to time, as in the best detective stories, there is a presence—a light late at night, an arm which opens and closes a shutter . . . From the fact that I see no one and that I myself am looking (peering), I induce that I am not looked at—and I leave my curtains open. But it may be just the contrary: perhaps I am being constantly, intensely gazed at by whoever is *lurking* over there. The lesson of this fable would be that, by dint of gazing, one forgets one can be gazed at oneself. Or again, in the verb "to gaze," the frontiers of active and passive are uncertain.

Neuropsychology has clearly established how the gaze is born. In the first days of life, there is an ocular reaction toward soft light; at the end of a week, the infant tries to see, focuses his eyes, but in a still somewhat vague and hesitant manner; two weeks later, he can focus on a nearby object; at six weeks, vision is firm and selective: the gaze is formed. Can we not say that these six weeks are the ones in which the human "soul" is born?

. . .

As signifying's site, the gaze provokes a synesthesia, an in-division of (physiological) meanings which share their impressions, so that we can attribute to one, poetically, what happens to another (Baudelaire: "There are odors succulent as young flesh"): hence, all the senses can "gaze" and, conversely, the gaze can smell, listen, grope, etc. Goethe: "The hands want to see, the eyes want to caress."

We say, scornfully: "His gaze was evasive . . ." as if it was proper for the gaze to be direct, imperious. Yet psychoanalytic economy tells us something quite different: "In our relation to things as constituted by the path of vision and ordered in the figures of representation, something shifts, passes, is transmitted from stage to stage, in order to be—invariably, to some degree—elided: this is what is called the gaze." And again: "In a general way, the relation of the gaze to what one wants to see is a relation of deception. The subject presents himself as other than he is, and what he is allowed to see is not what he wants to see. Thereby the eye can function as an object, i.e., on the level of privation" (Lacan, *Séminaire* XI).

To return, however, to the direct, imperious gaze: which does not evade, hesitate, freeze, flinch. Analysis has also foreseen this case: such a gaze can be the *fascinum*, the wicked spell, the evil eye, whose effect is "to arrest movement and to kill life" (*Séminaire* XI).

According to an old experiment, when a film was shown for the first time to natives of the African bush, they paid no attention to the scene represented (the central square of their village) but only to the hen crossing this square in one corner of the screen. One might say: it was the hen that gazed at them.

A massacre in Cambodia: the dead lie heaped up on the stairs of a half-demolished house; sitting on a step above them, a young boy looks at the photographer. The dead have delegated to the living the responsibility of gazing at me; and it is in the boy's gaze that I see they are dead.

At the Rijksmuseum in Amsterdam, there is a series of pictures painted by the so-called Master of Alkmaar. These are scenes of everyday life, people gathered together for reasons which change from picture to picture; in each group, there is one figure, always the same: lost in the crowd, which is represented as though unaware of being observed, only this person, each time, gazes at the painter (and hence at me) right in the eyes. This figure is Christ.

Richard Avedon's incomparable art consists (among other things) in this: all the subjects he photographs, planted in front of me, look at me right in the eyes. Does this produce an effect of "frankness"? No, the pose is artificial (it is obvious that it is a pose), the situation is not psychological. The effect produced is of "truth": the character is "true"—often intolerably so. Why this truth? As a matter of fact, the portrait is looking at no one, and I know it; it is only gazing at the lens, i.e., at another enigmatic eye: the eye of truth (just as Venice maintained, in order to receive anonymous denunciations, various "Mouths of Truth"). The gaze, rendered here in an emphatic manner by the photographer (in the past, this could be done by the painter), acts as the very organ of truth: its space of action is located *beyond appearance*: it implies at least that this "beyond" exists, that what is "perceived" (gazed at) is truer than what is simply shown.

At a particular moment, the psychoanalyst (Lacan, *Séminaire* I) defines imaginary inter-subjectivity as a three-term structure: (1) I see the other; (2) I see him seeing me; (3) he knows I see him. Now, in the lover's relation, the gaze is not so devious, so to speak, it lacks one of these trajectories. No doubt, in this relation, on the one hand, I see the other, with intensity; I see only the other, I scan the other, I want to penetrate the secret of this body I desire; and on the other hand, I see the other seeing me: I am intimidated, dazzled, passively constituted by the other's all-powerful gaze; and this panic is so great that I cannot (or will not) recognize that the other knows I see him (which would dis-alienate me): I see myself *blind* in front of the other.

"I gaze at you as one gazes at the impossible."

For months at a time, the tick can remain inert on a tree, waiting for some warm-blooded animal (sheep, dog) to pass under the branch; then it drops off, sticks to the animal's hide, sucks its blood: its perception is selective: all it knows of the world is warm blood. In the same way, in the past, the slave was perceived only as an instrument, not as a human figure. How many gazes are thus merely instruments of a single finality: I gaze at what I am looking for, and finally, if one may advance this paradox, I see only what I gaze at. However, in certain exceptional cases, and how delightful they are, the gaze is obliged to pass unexpectedly from one finality to another: two codes intersect without warning in the closed field of the gaze, and there occurs a disturbance of "reading." Thus, walking in a Moroccan *souk* and looking at a handicrafts vendor, I see clearly that this vendor reads in my eyes only the gaze of a possible purchaser, for like the tick he perceives strollers only as a single species, customers. But if my gaze insists (for how many additional seconds? that would be a good problem in semantics), his "reading" suddenly vacillates: if it were in him and not in his merchandise that I was interested? If I left the first code in order to enter the second (that of complicity)? It is this friction of the two codes that I, in my turn, read in his gaze. All this forms a fleeting fabric of successive meanings. And for a semantician, even one strolling through the *souk*, nothing is more stimulating than to see in a gaze the mute birth of a meaning.

As we have seen apropos of Avedon, it is not excluded that a photographed subject should gaze at you—i.e. gaze at the lens: the direction of the gaze (one might say: its *address*) is not pertinent in photography. But it is so in the cinema, where it is forbidden for an actor to look at the camera, i.e., at the spectator. I am not far from considering this ban as the cinema's distinctive feature. This art *severs* the gaze: one of us gazes at the other, does only that: it is my right and my duty to gaze; the other never gazes; he gazes at everything, except me. If a single gaze from the screen came to rest on me, the whole film would be lost. But this is only the literal truth. For it can happen that, on another, invisible level, the screen—like the African hen—does not cease gazing at me.

1977
*Unpublished by RB, this text
may not have been completed*

II

Music's Body

Listening

Hearing is a physiological phenomenon; *listening* is a psychological act. It is possible to describe the physical conditions of hearing (its mechanisms) by recourse to acoustics and to the physiology of the ear; but listening cannot be defined only by its object or, one might say, by its goal. Along the scale of living beings (the ancient naturalists' *scala viventium*), and throughout human history, listening's object, considered in its most general type, varies or has varied. Therefore, simplifying to the extreme, we shall propose three types of listening.

According to the first, a living being orients its hearing (the exercise of its physiological faculty of hearing) to certain *indices*; on this level, nothing distinguishes animal from man: the wolf listens for a (possible) noise of its prey, the hare for a (possible) noise of its hunter, the child and the lover for the approaching footsteps which might be the mother's or the beloved's. This first listening might be called an *alert*. The second is a *deciphering*; what the ear tries to intercept are certain *signs*. Here, no doubt, begins the human: I listen the way I read, i.e., according to certain codes. Finally, the third listening, whose approach is entirely modern (which does not mean it supplants the other two), does not aim at—or await—certain determined, classified signs: not what is said or emitted, but who speaks, who emits: such listening is supposed to develop in an inter-subjective space where "I am listening" also means "listen to me"; what it seizes upon—in order to transform and restore to the endless interplay of transference—is a general "signifying" no longer conceivable without the determination of the unconscious.

I

There is no sense which humanity does not share with the animal world. Still, it is quite apparent that phylogenetic development and, within human history itself, technological development have modified (and will modify further) the hierarchy of the five senses. Anthropologists report that a living being's nutritive behavior is linked to touch, taste, smell, and affective behavior to touch, smell, sight; hearing seems essentially linked to evaluation of the spatio-temporal situation (to which humanity adds sight, animals smell). Based on hearing, listening (from an anthropological viewpoint) is the very sense of space and of time, by the perception of degrees of remoteness and of regular returns of phonic stimulus. For the mammal, its territory is marked out by odors and sounds; for the human being—and this is a phenomenon often underestimated—the appropriation of space is also a matter of sound: domestic space, that of the house, the apartment—the approximate equivalent of animal territory—is a space of familiar, *recognized* noises whose ensemble forms a kind of household symphony: differentiated slamming of doors, raised voices, kitchen noises, gurgle of pipes, murmurs from outdoors: Kafka has described very precisely (is not literature an incomparable storehouse of knowledge?) this domiciliary symphony in his journal: "I am sitting in my room, i.e., the noise headquarters of the whole apartment; I hear all the doors slamming, etc."; and we know the anguish of the hospitalized child who no longer hears the familiar noises of the maternal refuge. It is against the auditive background that *listening* occurs, as if it were the exercise of a function of *intelligence*, i.e., of selection. If the auditive background invades the whole of phonic space (if the ambiant noise is too loud), then selection or intelligence of space is no longer possible, listening is injured; the ecological phenomenon which is today called pollution—and which is becoming a black myth of our technological civilization—is precisely the intolerable corruption of human space, insofar as humanity needs to *recognize itself* in that space: pollution damages the senses by which the living being, from animal to man, recognizes its territory, its habitat: sight, smell, hearing. And indeed there is an audio-pollution which everyone, from hippie to pensioner, feels (through certain myths of nature) is deleterious to the living being's very intelligence, which is, *stricto sensu*, its power of communicating effectively with its *Umwelt*: pollution prevents listening.

It is doubtless by this notion of territory (or of appropriated, familiar, domestic space) that we can best grasp the function of listening, insofar as territory can be essentially defined as the space of security (and as such, as space to be defended): listening is that preliminary attention which permits intercepting whatever might disturb the territorial system; it is a mode of defense against surprise; its object (what it is oriented toward) is menace or, conversely, need; the raw material of listening is the index, because it either reveals danger or promises the satisfaction of need. From this double function, defensive and predatory, there remain, in civilized listening, certain traces: think of all those horror films which rely on our listening for the alien, on our bewildered expectation of the irregular noise which will disturb our aural comfort, the security of the house: at this stage, listening has as its essential partner the unaccustomed, i.e., danger or windfall; and conversely, when listening is oriented toward assuaging fantasy, it immediately becomes hallucinated: I believe I am really hearing what I would like to hear as a promise of pleasure.

Morphologically, on the species level, the ear seems made for this capture of the fleeting index: it is motionless, fixed, poised like that of an animal on the alert; like a funnel leading to the interior, it receives the greatest possible number of impressions and channels them toward a supervisory center of selection and decision; the folds and detours of its shell seem eager to multiply the individual's contact with the world yet to reduce this very multiplicity by submitting it to a filtering trajectory; for it is essential—and this is the role of such initial listening—that what was confused and undifferentiated become distinct and pertinent—that all nature assume the special form of danger or prey; listening is the very operation of this metamorphosis.

2

Long before writing was invented, even before parietal figuration was practiced, something was produced which may fundamentally distinguish man from animal: the intentional reproduction of a rhythm: there have been found on cave walls of the Mousterian epoch certain rhythmic incisions—and everything suggests that these first rhythmic representations coincide with the appearance of the first human habitations. Of course, we *know* nothing about the birth of phonic rhythm; but it would be logical to speculate (let us not reject the delirium of origins) that to produce a rhythm (incisions or beats) and to build a house are contemporary activities: humanity's operational characteristic is an extensively repeated rhythmic percussion, as is attested by broken-stone "choppers" and hammered polyhedral "balls": by rhythm, the pre-anthropic creature enters the humanity of the Australanthropes.

By rhythm, too, listening ceases to be a purely supervisory activity and becomes creation. Without rhythm, no language is possible: the sign is based on an oscillation, that of the *marked* and the *non-marked*, which we call a paradigm. The best legend which accounts for the birth of language is the Freudian story of the child who mimes his mother's absence and presence as a game during which he throws away and pulls back a spool attached to a thread: he thereby creates the first symbolic game, but he also creates rhythm. Let us imagine this child listening for noises which can tell him of the mother's desired return: he is in the first stage of listening, that of indices; but when he stops directly supervising the appearance of the index and begins miming its regular return himself, he is making the awaited index into a sign: he shifts to the second stage of listening, which is that of meaning: what is listened for is no longer the *possible* (the prey, the threat, or the object of desire which occurs without warning), it is the *secret*: that which, concealed in reality, can reach human consciousness only through a code, which serves simultaneously to encipher and to decipher that reality.

Listening is henceforth linked (in a thousand varied, indirect forms) to a hermeneutics: to listen is to adopt an attitude of decoding what is obscure, blurred, or mute, in order to make available to consciousness the "underside" of meaning (what is experienced, postulated, intentionalized as hidden). The communication implied by this second listening is religious: it *ligatures* the listening subject to the hidden world of the gods, who, as everyone knows, speak a language of which only a few enigmatic fragments reach men, though it is vital—cruelly enough—for them to understand this language.

To listen is the evangelical verb par excellence: listening to the divine word is what faith amounts to, for it is by such listening that man is linked to God: Luther's Reformation was largely made in the name of listening: the Protestant church is exclusively a site of listening, and the Counter-Reformation itself, in order not to be left behind, placed the pulpit in the center of the church (in Jesuit buildings) and made the faithful into "listeners" (to a discourse which itself revives the old rhetoric as an art of "forcing" listening).

By a single impulse, this second listening is religious *and* deciphering: it intentionalizes at once the sacred and the secret (to listen in order to decipher history, society, the body, is *still*, under various lay alibis, a religious attitude). What is it that listening, then, seeks to decipher? Essentially, it would appear, two things: the future (insofar as it belongs to the gods) or transgression (insofar as transgression is engendered by God's gaze).

By her noises, Nature shudders with meaning: at least this is how, according to Hegel, the ancient Greeks listened to her. The oaks of Dodona, by the murmur of their boughs, uttered prophecies, and in other civilizations as well (derived more directly from ethnography) noises have been the immediate raw materials of a divination, cledonomancy: to listen is, in an institutional manner, to try to find out what is happening (it is impossible to note all the traces of this archaic finality in our secular existence).

But, also, listening is *taking soundings*. As soon as religion is internalized, what is plumbed by listening is intimacy, the heart's secret: Sin. A history and a phenomenology of interiority (which we perhaps lack) should here join a history and a phenomenology of listening. For at the very heart of a civilization of Sin (our Judeo-Christian civilization, different from civilizations of Shame), interiority has developed steadily. What the first Christians listen to are still exterior voices, those of demons or angels; it is only gradually that the object of listening is internalized to the point of becoming pure conscience. For centuries, all that was required of the guilty person, whose penitence involved the acknowledgment of his sins, was only that he make public confession: private listening by a priest was regarded as an abuse and was roundly condemned by bishops. Auricular confession, from mouth to ear, in the secrecy of the confessional, did not exist in the Patristic age; it was born (around the seventh century) from the excesses of public confession and from the advances of individualist conscience: "for a public sin, public confession; for a private sin, private confession": limited listening, walled in and virtually clandestine ("one to one"), has thus constituted a "progress" (in the modern sense of the word), since it has assured the protection of the individual—of his rights to be an individual—against group control; private listening to sin has thus developed (at least originally) in the margins of the ecclesiastical institution: among the monks, successors of the martyrs, or among heretics like the Cathars, or even in less institutionalized religions like Buddhism, where private listening, "brother to brother," is practiced regularly.

Thus formed by the very history of the Christian religion, listening brings two subjects into relation; even when it is a crowd (a political assembly, for example) which must put itself in a listening situation, this is in order to receive a message from only one person, who seeks to make the singularity (the emphasis) of this message heard. The injunction to listen is the total interpellation of one subject by another: it places above everything else the quasi-physical contact of these subjects (by voice and ear): it creates transference: *"listen to me"* means *touch me, know that I exist*; in Jakobson's terminology, *"listen to me"* is a phatic expression, an operator of individual communication; the archetypal instrument of modern listening, the telephone, collects the two partners into an ideal (and under certain circumstances, an intolerable) inter-subjectivity, because this instrument has abolished all senses except that of hearing: the order of listening which any telephonic communication inaugurates invites the Other to collect his whole body in his voice and announces that I am collecting all of myself in my ear. Just as the first listening transforms noise into index, this second listening metamorphoses man into a dual subject: interpellation leads to an interlocution in which the listener's silence will be as active as the locutor's speech: *listening speaks,* one might say: it is at this (either historical or structural) stage that psychoanalytic listening intervenes.

3

The unconscious, structured like a language, is the object of a special and at the same time exemplary listening: that of the psychoanalyst.

"The analyst must bend his own unconscious," Freud writes, "like a receptive organ toward the emerging unconscious of the patient, must be as the receiver of the telephone to the disc. As the receiver transmutes the electric vibrations induced by the sound waves back again into sound waves, so is the physician's unconscious mind able to reconstruct the patient's unconscious which has directed his associations, from the communications derived from it." It is, in effect, from unconscious to unconscious that psychoanalytic listening functions, from a speaking unconscious to another which is presumed to hear. What is thus spoken emanates from an unconscious knowledge transferred to another subject, whose knowledge is presumed. It is this latter subject that Freud addresses, attempting to establish something he regards as the corollary to the fundamental psychoanalytic rule imposed upon the patient: "We must make no effort to concentrate the attention on anything in particular, but to maintain in regard to all that one hears the same measure of calm quiet attentiveness—of 'evenly hovering' attention as I once before described it. In this way a strain which could not be kept up for several hours daily and a danger inseparable from deliberate attentiveness are avoided. For as soon as attention is deliberately concentrated in a certain degree, one begins to select from the material before one; one point will be fixed in the mind with particular clearness and some other consequently disregarded, and in this selection one's expectations or one's inclinations will be followed. This is just what must not be done; if one's expectations are followed in this selection, there is the danger of never finding anything but what is already known, and if one follows one's inclinations, anything which is to be perceived will most certainly be falsified. It must not be forgotten that the meaning of the things one hears, at all events for the most part, is only recognizable later on. It will be seen, therefore, that the principle of evenly distributed attention is the necessary corollary to the demand on the patient to communicate everything that occurs to him without criticism or selection. If the physician behaves otherwise, he is throwing aside most of the advantage to be gained by the patient's obedience to the 'fundamental rule of psychoanalysis.' For the physician the rule may be expressed thus: All conscious exertion is to be withheld from the capacity for attention, and one's 'unconscious memory' is to be given full play; or to express it in terms of technique pure and simple: one has simply to listen and not to trouble to keep in mind anything in particular."*

An ideal rule, by which it is difficult if not impossible to abide. Freud himself derogates from it. Either because of his

---

* Sigmund Freud, "Recommendations for Physicians on the Psychoanalytic Method of Treatment," 1912. Translated by Joan Rivière.

concern for an aspect of theory, as in the case of Dora (seeking to prove the importance of her incestuous feelings toward her father, Freud neglects the role played by Dora's homosexual feelings for Frau K.). It was also a theoretical concern which influenced the course of the Wolf Man's treatment, when Freud's expectations were so imperious (he was eager to offer additional proofs in his argument with Jung) that all material concerning the primal scene was obtained under pressure of a limit-date he himself had set. Or else because his own unconscious representations interfered in the conduct of therapy (in the Wolf Man's treatment, Freud associates the color of a butterfly's wings with that of a woman's garment—worn by a girl he himself had been in love with at the age of seventeen).

The originality of psychoanalytic listening is to be found in that oscillating movement which links neutrality and commitment, suspension of orientation and theory: "The rigor of unconscious desire, the logic of desire, are revealed only to someone who respects both these apparently contradictory requirements, order and singularity" (S. Leclaire). This oscillation (which reminds us of the movement generating sound) engenders for the psychoanalyst something like a resonance permitting him to "cock an ear" toward the essential: the essential being not to miss (and to make the patient miss) "access to the singular and sensitive insistence of a major element of his unconscious." What is thus designated as a major element offering itself to the psychoanalyst's listening is a term, a word, a group of letters referring to body movement: a signifier.

In this hostelry of the signifier where the subject can be heard, the principal body movement is the one the voice originates from. The voice, in relation to silence, is like writing (in the graphic sense) on blank paper. Listening to the voice inaugurates the relation to the Other: the voice by which we recognize others (like writing on an envelope) indicates to us their way of being, their joy or their pain, their condition; it bears an image of their body and, beyond, a whole psychology (as when we speak of a warm voice, a white voice, etc.). Sometimes an interlocutor's voice strikes us more than the content of his discourse, and we catch ourselves listening to the modulations and harmonics of that voice without hearing what it is saying to us. This dissociation is no doubt partly responsible for the feeling of strangeness (sometimes of antipathy) which each of us feels on hearing his own voice: reaching us after traversing the masses and cavities of our own anatomy, it affords us a distorted image of ourselves, as if we were to glimpse our profile in a three-way mirror.

"The act of hearing is not the same, depending on whether it aims at the coherence of the verbal chain . . . or accommodates itself in speech to phonic modulation, to some goal of acoustic analysis, tonal, phonetic, even of musical power."* The singing voice, that very specific space in which a tongue encounters a voice and permits those who know how to listen to it to hear what we can call its "grain"—the singing voice is not the breath but indeed that materiality of the body emerging from the throat, a site where the phonic metal hardens and takes shape.

Corporality of speech, the voice is located at the articulation of body and discourse, and it is in this interspace that listening's back-and-forth movement might be made. "To listen to someone, to hear his voice, requires on the listener's part an attention open to the interspace of body and discourse and which contracts neither at the impression of the voice nor at the expression of the discourse. What such listening offers is precisely what the speaking subject does not say: the unconscious texture which associates his body-as-site with his discourse: an active texture which reactualizes, in the subject's speech, the totality

* Jacques Lacan, *Ecrits*, 1966.

of his history" (Denis Vasse). Here is the project of psycho-analysis: to reconstruct the subject's history in his speech. From this point of view, the psychoanalyst's listening is a posture oriented toward origins, insofar as these origins are not con-sidered as historical. The psychoanalyst, attempting to grasp the signifiers, learns to "speak" the language which is his pa-tient's unconscious, just as the child, plunged into the bath of language, grasps the sounds, the syllables, the consonances, the words, and learns to speak. Listening is this means of trap-ping signifiers by which the *infans* becomes a speaking being.

To hear the language which is the other's unconscious, to help him to reconstruct his history, to lay bare his unconscious desire: the psychoanalyst's listening leads to a recognition: that of the other's desire. Listening, then, involves a risk: it cannot be constructed under the shelter of a theoretical appa-ratus, the analysand is not a scientific object from whom the analyst, deep in his armchair, can project himself with objec-tivity. The psychoanalytic relation is effected between two subjects. The recognition of the other's desire can therefore not be established in neutrality, kindliness, or liberality: to recognize this desire implies that one enters it, ultimately find-ing oneself there. Listening will exist only on condition of accepting the risk, and if it must be set aside in order for there to be *analysis*, it is by no means with the help of a theoretical shield. The psychoanalyst cannot, like Ulysses bound to his mast, "enjoy the spectacle of the sirens without risks and with-out accepting its consequences . . . There was something mar-velous in that song, secret, simple, and everyday, which had to be immediately recognized . . . a song from the abyss which, once heard, opened an abyss in each word and lured one to vanish into it."* The myth of Ulysses and the sirens does not tell us what a successful listening might be; we can sketch it *a*

* Maurice Blanchot, *Le Livre à venir*, 1959.

contrario between the reefs the navigator-psychoanalyst must avoid at all costs: plugging one's ears like the men of the crew, employing deception and giving evidence of cowardice like Ulysses, or answering the sirens' invitation and vanishing. What is thereby revealed is a listening no longer immediate but displaced, conducted in the space of another navigation, "which is that of narrative, the song no longer immediate but recounted." Narrative, a mediate, delayed construction: Freud does just this in writing up his "cases." Councilor Schreber, Dora, Little Hans, and the Wolf Man are so many narratives (someone has even alluded to "Freud the novelist"); in writing them as such (the strictly medical observations are not written in narrative form), Freud did not act by chance, but according to the very theory of the new listening: it has concerned itself with images.

In dreams, the sense of hearing is never solicited. The dream is a strictly visual phenomenon, and it is by the sense of sight that what is addressed to the ear will be perceived: a matter, one might say, of acoustic images. Thus, in the Wolf Man's dream the wolves' "ears were cocked like those of dogs when they are alert to something." The "something" toward which the wolves' ears are cocked is obviously a sound, a noise, a cry. But, beyond this "translation" the dream makes between listening and looking, links of complementarity are formed. If Little Hans is afraid of horses, it is not only that he is afraid of being bitten: "I was afraid," he says, "because the horse was making a row with his feet." The "row" (in German: *Krawall*) is not only the disordered movements which the horse, lying on the ground, makes as it kicks, but also all the noise these movements occasion. (The German term *Krawall* is translated as "tumult, riot, row"—all words associating visual and acoustic images.)

4

It was necessary to make this brief detour into the realm of psychoanalysis, otherwise we should fail to understand how modern listening no longer quite resembles what has here been called *listening to indices* and *listening to signs* (even if these two forms of listening subsist concurrently). For psychoanalysis—at least in its recent development, which takes it as far from a simple hermeneutics as from the location of an original trauma, a facile substitute for Sin—modifies whatever notion we can have of listening.

First of all, whereas for centuries listening could be defined as an intentional act of audition (to listen is to *want* to hear, in all conscience), today it is granted the power (and virtually the function) of playing over unknown spaces: listening includes in its field not only the unconscious in the topical sense of the term, but also, so to speak, its lay forms: the implicit, the indirect, the supplementary, the delayed: listening grants access to all forms of polysemy, of overdetermination, of superimposition, there is a disintegration of the Law which prescribes direct, unique listening; by definition, listening was *applied*; today we ask listening to *release*; we thereby return, but at another loop of the historical spiral, to the conception of a *panic* listening, as the Greeks, or at least as the Dionysians, had conceived it.

In the second place, the roles implied by the act of listening no longer have the same fixity as in the past; there is no longer, on one side, someone who speaks, gives himself away, confesses, and, on the other, someone who listens, keeps silent, judges, and sanctions; this does not mean that the analyst, for instance, speaks as much as his patient; it is because, as has been said, his listening is active, it assumes the responsibility of taking its place in the interplay of desire, of which all language is the theater: we must repeat, *listening speaks*. Whence a movement appears: the sites of speech are less and less protected by the institution. Traditional societies knew two modes of listening, both alienated: the arrogant listening of a superior, the servile listening of an inferior (or of their substitutes); today this paradigm is contested, still crudely, it is true, and perhaps inadequately: it is believed that, in order to liberate listening, it suffices to begin speaking oneself—whereas a free listening is essentially a listening which circulates, which permutates, which disaggregates, by its mobility, the fixed network of the roles of speech: it is not possible to imagine a free society, if we agree in advance to preserve within it the old modes of listening: those of the believer, the disciple, and the patient.

In the third place, what is listened to here and there (chiefly in the field of art, whose function is often utopian) is not the advent of a signified, object of a recognition or of a deciphering, but the very dispersion, the *shimmering* of signifiers, ceaselessly restored to a listening which ceaselessly produces new ones from them without ever arresting their meaning: this phenomenon of shimmering is called *signifying* [*signifiance*], as distinct from signification: "listening" to a piece of classical music, the listener is called upon to "decipher" this piece, i.e., to recognize (by his culture, his application, his sensibility) its construction, quite as coded (predetermined) as that of a palace at a certain period; but "listening" to a composition (taking the word here in its etymological sense) by John Cage, it is each sound one after the next that I listen to, not in its syntagmatic extension, but in its raw and as though vertical *signifying*: by deconstructing itself, listening is externalized, it compels the subject to renounce his "inwardness." This is valid, *mutatis mutandis*, for many other forms of contemporary art, from "painting" to the "text"; and this, of course, does not proceed without some laceration; for no law can oblige the subject to take his pleasure where he does not want to go (whatever the reasons might be for his resistance), no law is in a position to constrain our listening: freedom of listening is as necessary as freedom of speech. That is why this apparently modest notion (*listening* does not figure in the encyclopedias of the past, it belongs to no acknowledged discipline) is finally like a little theater on whose stage those two modern deities, one bad and one good, confront each other: power and desire.

1976
In collaboration with Roland Havas

Musica Practica

There are two musics (or so I've always thought): one you listen to, one you play. They are two entirely different arts, each with its own history, sociology, aesthetics, erotics: the same composer can be minor when listened to, enormous when played (even poorly)—take Schumann.

The music you play depends not so much on an auditive as on a manual (hence much more sensuous) activity; it is the music you or I can play, alone or among friends, with no audience but its participants (i.e., with no risk of theater, no hysterical temptation); it is a muscular music; in it the auditive sense has only a degree of sanction: as if the body was listening, not the "soul"; this music is not played "by heart"; confronting the keyboard or the music stand, the body proposes, leads, coordinates—the body itself must transcribe what it reads: it fabricates sound and sense: it is the scriptor, not the receiver; the decoder. Initially linked to the (aristocratic) leisure class, such music has dwindled into a mundane rite with the advent of bourgeois democracy (the piano, the jeune fille, the salon, the nocturne); subsequently it has vanished altogether (who plays the piano today?). To find a *musica practica* in our Western societies we must look for it among another public, in another repertoire, on another instrument (young people, songs, the guitar). Concurrently, a passive, receptive music— one of resonance rather than of presentation—has become *music proper* (of the concert, the festival, the record, the radio): playing no longer exists; musical activity is no longer manual, muscular, kneading, but only liquid, effusive, "lubricant," to borrow Balzac's word. The performer, too, has changed. The musical amateur—a role defined by a style much more than by a technical imperfection—is no longer to be found; the professionals, pure specialists whose formation is entirely esoteric for the public (who still knows the problems of musical pedagogy?), no longer offer that style of the perfect amateur whose value we could still recognize in a Lipati, in a Panzéra, because it stirred in us not satisfaction but desire—the desire to *make* such music. In short, first there was the performer, the *actor* of music, then the interpreter (the great romantic voice), finally the technician, who relieves the auditor of every activity, however vicarious, and abolishes in the musical order the very notion of *praxis*.

It seems to me that Beethoven's oeuvre is linked to this historical problem, not as the simple expression of a moment (the transition from amateur to interpreter), but as the powerful genre of a civilization's discontent, of which Beethoven both combined the elements and sketched the solution. This ambiguity is that of Beethoven's two historical roles: the mythic role which the entire nineteenth century assigned to him, and the modern role which our century is beginning to grant him (here I am referring to Boucourechliev's study).

For the nineteenth century, if we except a few idiotic images such as that of Vincent d'Indy, who more or less turns Beethoven into a kind of reactionary and anti-Semitic dolt, Beethoven was the first *free* man of music. For the first time, an artist was glorified for having several successive *manners*; he was granted the privilege of metamorphosis; he was entitled to be dissatisfied with himself or, more profoundly, with his language—he was able, in the course of his life, to change his codes (this is what we are told by the naïve and enthusiastic image Lenz has given of Beethoven's three manners); and once the oeuvre becomes the trace of a movement, of an itinerary, it thereby appeals to the notion of a destiny; the artist seeks his "truth," and this search becomes an order in itself, a totally legible message, despite the variations of its content— or at least whose legibility feeds on a kind of totality of the artist: his career, his loves, his ideas, his character, his remarks become features of meaning: a Beethovenian biography is born (we should be able to say: a bio-mythology); the artist is produced as a complete hero, endowed with a discourse (rare phenomenon for a musician), with a legend (some dozen anecdotes), with an iconography, with a race (that of the Titans of Art: Michelangelo, Balzac), and with a fatal disease (the deafness of the man who created for the pleasure of our ears). Certain specifically structural features have come to be integrated into this system of meaning, the romantic Beethoven (ambiguous features, simultaneously musical and psychological): the development of paroxysmal contrasts in intensity (the significant opposition of *pianos* and *fortes*, whose historical importance is perhaps inadequately acknowledged, since after all it marks only an infinitesimal portion of music as a whole and corresponds to the invention of an instrument whose name has its own significance, the *pianoforte*), the explosion of melody, received as the symbol of creative ferment and anxiety, the energetic redundance of strokes and clausulae (naïve image of fate knocking), the experience of limits (abolition or inversion of the traditional parts of the discourse), the production of musical chimeras (the voice welling up out of the symphony): everything which could readily be transformed metaphorically into pseudo-philosophical values nonetheless admissible in musical terms, since they were still deployed under the authority of the West's fundamental code: tonality.

Now, it happens that this romantic image (of which, in short, the meaning is a certain *discord*) produces an uneasiness of execution: the amateur cannot master Beethoven's music, not so much because of the technical difficulties as because of the very breakdown of the code of the anterior *musica practica*; according to this code, the fantasmatic (i.e., corporeal) image which guided the performer was that of a song (which one "spins out" within oneself); with Beethoven, the mimetic pulsion (does not the musical fantasm consist in situating *oneself* as subject in the scenario of performance?) becomes orchestral; hence, it escapes the fetishism of a single element (voice or rhythm): the body seeks to be total; thereby, the notion of an intimist or family *praxis* is destroyed: to *want* to play Beethoven is to project oneself as an orchestra conductor (the dream of how many children? the tautological dream of how many conductors whose performances are a prey to the signs of panic possession?). Beethoven's oeuvre abandons the amateur and seems, initially, to summon up the new romantic deity, the interpreter. Yet here there occurs a new disappointment: who (what soloist, what pianist?) plays Beethoven well? One might say that this music merely offers a choice between a "role" and its absence, the illusory demiurge and the docile platitude, sublimated under the name of simplification.

Perhaps this is because there is something *inaudible* in Beethoven's music (for which audition is not the *exact* mode). Here we meet the second Beethoven. It is not possible that a musician be deaf by pure contingency or poignant fate (which is the same thing). Beethoven's deafness designates the *lack* where all signification is lodged: it appeals to a music not abstract or interior, but endowed, one might say, with sensuous intelligibility, with an intelligibility somehow perceptible to the senses. This category is specifically revolutionary, inconceivable in terms of the old aesthetics; the oeuvre which accepts it cannot be received according to pure sensuality, which is always cultural, nor according to an intelligible order which would be that of (rhetorical or thematic) development; without it, neither the modern text nor contemporary music can be accepted. As we know since Boucourechliev's analyses, this Beethoven is exemplarily the one of the *Diabelli Variations*. The operation which permits us to grasp this Beethoven (and the category he inaugurates) can no longer be either execution or hearing, but reading. This does not mean that we must sit down with a Beethoven score and from it obtain an interior hearing (which would still remain tributary to the old animist fantasm); it means that, whether as an abstract or sensuous foreclosure—it matters little which—we must assume with regard to this music the state, or better the activity, of a *performer* who can displace, regroup, combine, dispose, in a word (if it is not too worn-out) can *structure* (which is quite different from constructing or reconstructing, in the classical sense of the words). Just as the reading of the modern text (at least as we can postulate it, can require it) does not consist in receiving, in knowing, or in feeling this text, but in writing it anew, in traversing its writing by a new inscription, in the same way, to read this Beethoven is to perform, to *operate* his music, to lure it (as it lends itself) into an unknown *praxis*.

Hence we can rediscover, modified according to the movement of historical dialectics, a certain *musica practica*. What is the use of composing if it merely confines the product in the enclosure of the concert or the solitude of radio reception? To compose is, at least by tendency, to offer for *doing*, not to offer for hearing but for writing: the modern site of music is not the concert hall but the stage, where the musicians transmigrate, in an often dazzling interplay, from one auditive source to another: it is we who are playing, still vicariously, it is true; but we can imagine that—eventually?—the concert will be exclusively a studio, a workshop, an atelier from which nothing—no dream, no image-repertoire, in a word no "soul"—will overflow and where all musical *doing* will be absorbed into a *praxis* with nothing *left over*. It is this utopia which a certain Beethoven, one not played, teaches us to formulate—whereby it is possible to foresee in him a musician still to come.

1970

The Grain of
the Voice

Language, according to Benveniste, is the only semiotic system capable of *interpreting* another semiotic system (though there are doubtless certain limit-works, in which a system feigns self-interpretation: *The Art of the Fugue*). How then does language manage, when it must interpret music? Alas, badly—very badly, it seems. If we examine the current practice of music criticism (or of conversations "on" music: often the same thing), we see that the work (or its performance) is invariably translated into the poorest linguistic category: the adjective. Music is, by a natural inclination, what immediately receives an adjective. The adjective is inevitable: this music is *this*, that execution is *that*. No doubt, once we make an art into a subject (of an article, a conversation), there is nothing left for us to do but "predicate" it; but in the case of music, this predication inevitably takes the most facile and trivial form: the epithet. Of course this epithet, to which we turn and return out of weakness or fascination (parlor game: discuss a piece of music without using a single adjective), has an economic function: the predicate is always the rampart by which the subject's image-repertoire protects itself against the loss that threatens it: the man who furnishes himself or is furnished with an adjective is sometimes wounded, sometimes pleased, but always *constituted*; music has an image-repertoire whose function is to reassure, to constitute the subject, who hears it (would this be because music is dangerous—an old Platonic notion? Leading to ecstasy, to loss, as many examples from ethnography and popular culture would tend to show?), and this image-repertoire immediately comes to language by the adjective. A historical dossier should be compiled here, for adjectival criticism (or predicative interpretation) has assumed, down through the ages, certain institutional aspects: the musical adjective becomes somehow legal whenever an *ethos* of music is postulated, i.e., whenever a regular (natural or magical) mode of signification is attributed to music: among the ancient Greeks, for whom it was the musical *language* (and not the contingent work), in its denotative structure, which was immediately adjectival, each mode being linked to a coded expression (harsh, austere, proud, virile, solemn, majestic, warlike, educative, proud, ceremonious, mourning, proper, dissolute, voluptuous); and among the Romantics, from Schumann to Debussy, who substitute or add to the simple indication of movements (*allegro, presto, andante*) certain poetic, emotive, increasingly refined predicates—given in the vernacular, so as to diminish the coded imprint and to develop the "free" character of the predication (*sehr kräftig, sehr präcis, spirituel et discret*, etc.).

Are we doomed to the adjective? Are we faced with this dilemma: the predicable or the ineffable? To know whether there are (verbal) means of talking about music without adjectives, we would have to consider a little more closely all of music criticism, which, I believe, has never been done and which, even so, we have neither the intention nor the means of doing here. What we can say is this: it is not by struggling against the adjective (shifting this adjective that comes to the tip of our tongue toward some substantive or verbal periphrasis) that we are likely to exorcise musical commentary and to liberate it from the predicative fatality; rather than trying to change directly the language used about music, it would be better to change the musical object itself, as it presents itself to speech: to modify its level of perception or of intellection: to shift the fringe of contact between music and language.

It is this shift that I should like to sketch here, not with regard to all music, but only with regard to a portion of vocal music (art song, lied, or *mélodie*); a very specific space (genre) in which *a language encounters a voice*. I shall immediately give a name to this signifier on the level of which, I believe, the temptation of ethos can be liquidated—and the adjective therefore dismissed: this name will be the *grain*: the grain of the voice, when the voice is in a double posture, a double production: of language and of music.

What I shall attempt to say about the *"grain"* will, of course, be only an apparently abstract approach, the impossible accounting of an individual enjoyment which I constantly experience when I listen to singing. In order to disengage this "grain" from the acknowledged values of vocal music, I shall employ a double opposition: the theoretical one of the pheno-text and the geno-text (Kristeva's terms), and the paradigmatic one of two singers, one of whom I like very much (though he is no longer to be heard) and the other very little (though he is heard more than anyone else): Panzéra and Fischer-Dieskau (who will, of course, be no more than ciphers here: I am not deifying the first and I have nothing against the second).

Listen to a Russian bass (a church bass: for opera, the entire voice shifts to dramatic expressivity: a voice in which the grain signifies little): something is there, manifest and persistent (you hear only *that*), which is past (or previous to) the meaning of the words, of their form (the litany), of the melisma, and even of the style of performance: something which is directly the singer's body, brought by one and the same movement to your ear from the depths of the body's cavities, the muscles, the membranes, the cartilage, and from the depths of the Slavonic language, as if a single skin lined the performer's inner flesh and the music he sings. This voice is not personal: it expresses nothing about the singer, about his soul; it is not original (all Russian basses have this same voice, more or less), and at the same time it is individual: it enables us to hear a body which, of course, has no public identity, no "personality," but which is nonetheless a separate body; and above all this voice directly conveys the symbolic, over and above the intelligible, the expressive: here, flung before us all in a heap, is the Father, his phallic status. That is what the "grain" would be: the materiality of the body speaking its mother tongue: perhaps the letter; almost certainly what I have called *signifying* [*signifiance*].

It is here in song, then (pending the extension of the distinction to all music), that we first discern the two texts of which Julia Kristeva writes. The *pheno-song* (if I may be permitted to make this transposition) covers all the phenomena, all the features which derive from the structure of the sung language, from the coded form of the melisma, the idiolect, the composer, the style of interpretation: in short, everything which, in the performance, is at the service of communication, of representation, of expression: what is usually spoken of, what forms the tissue of cultural values (the substance of acknowledged tastes, of fashions, of critical discourse), what is directly articulated around the ideological alibis of a period (an artist's "subjectivity," "expressivity," "dramaticism," "personality"). The *geno-song* is the volume of the speaking and singing voice, the space in which the significations germinate "from within the language and in its very materiality"; this is a signifying function alien to communication, to representation (of feelings), to expression; it is that culmination (or depth) of production where melody actually *works on* language—not what it says but the voluptuous pleasure of its signifier-sounds, of its letters: explores how language works and identifies itself with that labor. Geno-song is, in a very simple word which must be taken quite seriously: the *diction* of language.

From the point of view of pheno-song, Fischer-Dieskau is certainly an irreproachable artist; everything in the (semantic and lyric) structure is respected; and yet nothing seduces, nothing persuades us to enjoyment; this is an excessively expressive art (the diction is dramatic, the caesuras, the checks and releases of breath intervene as in the upheavals of passion) and thereby it never transcends culture: here it is the soul that accompanies the song, not the body: for the body to accompany the musical diction, not by an impulse of emotion but by a "gesture-notice"*—that is what is difficult, especially since all musical pedagogy teaches not the culture of the "grain" of the voice but the emotive modes of its emission: this is the myth of *breath*. How many singing teachers have we heard prophesy that the whole art of song was in the mastery, the proper management of breathing! Now, the breath is the *pneuma*, the soul swelling or breaking, and any exclusive art of the breath is likely to be a secretly mystical art (a mysticism reduced to the demands of the long-playing record). The lung, a stupid organ (the lights of catfood!), swells but does not become erect: it is in the throat, site where the phonic metal hardens and assumes its contour, it is in the facial mask that *signifying* breaks out, producing not the soul but enjoyment. In Fischer-Dieskau's performance, I seem to hear only the lungs, never the tongue, the glottis, the teeth, the sinuses, the nose. Panzéra's entire art, on the contrary, was in the letters, not in the bellows (a simple

---

* "This is why the best way to read me is to accompany the reading with certain appropriate body movements. *Contra* non-spoken writing, *contra* non-written speech. *Pro* gesture-notice" (Philippe Sollers, *Lois*).

technical feature: we did not hear him *breathe*, but only *shape* the phrase). An extreme thought controlled the prosody of enunciation and the phonic economy of the French language; certain prejudices (generally resulting from oratorical and ecclesiastical diction) were reversed. The consonants, which are too readily assumed to constitute the armature of our language (though it is not a Semitic language) and which we are always supposed to "articulate," to separate, to emphasize *in order to fulfill the clarity of meaning*—these consonants Panzéra frequently recommended *skating over*, restoring to them the erosion of a language which has lived, functioned, and worked for a very long time, to make it into the simple springboard of the admirable vowels: here was the "truth" of language, not its functionality (clarity, expressivity, communication); and the range of the vowels received what was *signifying* (which is everything that can be voluptuous in meaning): the opposition of *é* and *è* (so necessary in conjugation); the virtually *electronic* purity, I should say, so taut, raised, exposed, tenuous was its sound, of the most French vowel of all, the *ü*, which our language does not inherit from Latin; in the same way, Panzéra held his *r*'s beyond the singer's norms—without rejecting those norms: his *r* was certainly rolled, as in any classical art of song, but such rolling had nothing peasant-like or Canadian in it; it was an artificial roll, the paradoxical state of a letter sound at once quite abstract (by its metallic brevity of the vibration) and quite material (by its obvious implantation in the moving throat). Such phonetics (Am I alone in hearing it? Am I hearing voices in the voice? But is it not the truth of the voice to be hallucinated? Is not the entire space of the voice an infinite space? No doubt this was the meaning of Saussure's work on anagrams)—such phonetics does not exhaust *signifying* (which is inexhaustible); at least it imposes a limit on those efforts of *expressive reduction* made by a whole culture upon the poem and its melody.

It should not be excessively difficult to date, to specify this

culture historically. Fischer-Dieskau reigns today almost exclusively over the long-playing song discography; he has re-
corded everything: if you like Schubert and you don't like
Fischer-Dieskau, Schubert is inaccessible to you nowadays: an
example of that *positive* censorship (by repletion) which characterizes mass culture without its ever being criticized for it;
perhaps this is because Fischer-Dieskau's art, expressive, dramatic, *emotionally clear*, conveyed by a voice without "grain,"
without signifying weight, corresponds perfectly to the requirements of an *average* culture; this culture, defined by the
extension of listening and the disappearance of practice (no
more amateur performers), is eager for art, for music, provided
that such art and such music be clear, that they "translate" an
emotion and represent a signified (the poem's "meaning"):
an art which vaccinates enjoyment (by reducing it to a known,
coded emotion) and reconciles the subject with what, in music,
can be said: with what is said of it, predicatively, by the Acad-
emy, by Criticism, by Opinion. Panzéra does not belong to
this culture (he could not have done so, having sung before
the advent of the long-playing record; I doubt, moreover, that
his art, if he were singing nowadays, would be acknowledged
or even simply *perceived*); his reign—very widespread between
the wars—was that of an exclusively bourgeois art (i.e., in no
way petit-bourgeois), concluding the fulfillment of its internal
development, separated from History—by a very familiar distortion; and it is perhaps, precisely and less paradoxically than
it would seem, because this art was *already* marginal, mandarin,
that it could show traces of *signifying [signifiance]*, could escape
the tyranny of signification.

The "grain" of the voice is not—or not only—its timbre; the
signifying it affords cannot be better defined than by the *friction* between music and something else, which is the language
(and not the message at all). The song must speak, or better
still, must *write*, for what is produced on the level of geno-song

is ultimately writing. This sung writing of the language is, to my sense, what the French *mélodie* has occasionally attempted to achieve. I know of course that the German lied, too, has been intimately linked with the German language by the intermediary of the romantic poem; I know that Schumann's poetic culture was vast and that this same Schumann once said of Schubert that if he had lived to be old he would have set all of German literature to music; but all the same I think that the historical meaning of the lied must be sought in its music (if only by reason of its folk origins). On the contrary, the historical meaning of the French *mélodie* is a certain culture of the French language. We know that the romantic poetry of our country is more oratorical than textual; but what our poetry has not been able to do in and of itself, the *mélodie* has sometimes accomplished in collaboration with it; it has worked on the language through the poem. This work (in the specificity here granted to it) is not apparent in the general run of melodic production, overindulgent as it is of minor poets, of the model of the petit-bourgeois ballad, of salon practice; but it is incontrovertible in several works: anthologically (let us say: virtually at random) in certain *mélodies* by Fauré and Duparc, massively in the late (prosodic) Fauré and in Debussy's vocal oeuvre (even if *Pelléas* is often sung badly: dramatically). What is involved in these works is much more than a musical style, it is a practical reflection (so to speak) on the language; there is a gradual assumption of the language to the poem, of the poem to the *mélodie*, and of the *mélodie* to its performance. This means that the French *mélodie* derives very little from the history of music and a great deal from the theory of the text. The signifier must, here again, be redistributed.

Let us compare two sung deaths—both very famous—that of Boris, that of Mélisande. Whatever Musorgsky's intentions, Boris's death is *expressive*, or one might even say, hysterical; it is overloaded with affective, historical content; every performance of this death has to be dramatic: this is the triumph of the pheno-text, the smothering of *signifying* under the signified: soul. Mélisande, on the contrary, dies only *prosodically*; two extremes are linked, braided: the perfect intelligibility of the denotation, and the pure prosodic contour of the enunciation: between the two a beneficent void, which constituted the repletion of Boris: *pathos*, i.e., according to Aristotle (why not?), passion *as men speak it, imagine it,* the accepted notion of death, *endoxal* death. Mélisande dies *without any noise*; let us understand this expression in its cybernetic sense: nothing comes to disturb the signifier, and hence nothing compels redundancy; there is production of a music-language whose function is to prevent the singer from being expressive. As for the Russian bass, what is symbolic (death) is immediately cast (without mediation) before us (this in order to forestall the accepted notion according to which what is not expressive has to be cold, intellectual; Mélisande's death is "moving"; this means that it moves something in the chain of the signifier).

The French *mélodie* has disappeared (one might even say that it sank like a stone) for a good many reasons, or at least this disappearance has assumed a good many aspects; it doubtless succumbed under the image of its salon origin, which is somewhat the parody of its class origin; classical music of mass culture (radio, records) has left it behind, preferring either the more emotive orchestra (Mahler's triumph) or instruments less bourgeois than the piano (harpsichord, trumpet). But, above all, this death accompanies a much greater historical phenomenon, one which has little connection with the history of music or with that of musical taste: the French are abandoning their language, not of course as a normative set of noble values (clarity, elegance, correctness)—or at least we scarcely concern ourselves much about that, for those are institutional values—but as a space of pleasure, of enjoyment, a site where the language works upon *itself for nothing*, i.e., in perversion (let us recall here the singularity—the solitude—of Philippe Soller's recent text *Lois*, which re-presents the prosodic and metrical work of the language).

The "grain" is the body in the singing voice, in the writing hand, in the performing limb. If I perceive the "grain" of this music and if I attribute to this "grain" a theoretical value (this is the assumption of the text in the work), I cannot help making a new scheme of evaluation for myself, individual no doubt, since I am determined to listen to my relation to the body of someone who is singing or playing and since that relation is an erotic one, but not at all "subjective" (it is not the psychological "subject" in me who listens; the enjoyment that subject seeks is not going to reinforce him—to express him— but on the contrary will destroy him). This evaluation will be made outside of the law: it will baffle the law of culture but also the law of anti-culture; it will develop beyond the subject all the value which is hidden behind "*I like*" or "*I don't like.*" Singers, particularly, will be ranked in two categories which we might call prostitutive, since it is a matter of my choosing what does not choose me: hence, I shall freely exalt some little-known, secondary, forgotten, even dead artist, and I shall turn away from some consecrated star (let us not furnish examples, they would doubtless have only a biographical value), and I shall shift my choice to every genre of vocal music, including popular music, where I shall have no difficulty recognizing the distinction between pheno-song and geno-song (certain artists in this genre have a "grain" which others, however celebrated, do not). Further, aside from the voice, in instrumental music, the "grain" or its lack persists; for if there is no longer a language here to afford *signifying* in its extreme form and scope, there is at least the artist's body which once again compels me to an evaluation: I will not judge a performance according to the rules of interpretation, the constraints of style (which are quite illusory, moreover), almost all of which belong to the pheno-song (I shall not go into ecstasy over the "rigor," the "brilliance," the "warmth," the "respect for the score," etc.), but according to the image of the body (the figure) which is given me: I hear without a doubt—the certitude here of the body, of the body's enjoyment—that Wanda Landowska's harpsichord comes from her inner body, and not from the minor digital knitting of so many harpsichordists (to the point where I hear a different instrument); and with regard to piano music, I know immediately which part of the body it is that plays: if it is the arms, as all too often it is, muscular as a dancer's calf, or the talons (regardless of the wrist flourishes), or if on the contrary it is the only erotic part of a pianist's body: the pads of the fingers, whose "grain" I hear so rarely (need I remark that there seems to be, nowadays, under the pressure of long-playing records and their mass sales, a flattening out of technique, which is paradoxical: all playing is flattened out *into perfection*: there is nothing left but pheno-text).

All of this has been said about "classical" music (in the broadest possible sense); but it goes without saying that the mere consideration of the musical "grain" could lead to another history of music than the one we know (which is purely pheno-textual): if we were to succeed in refining a certain "aesthetic" of musical enjoyment, we should doubtless attach less importance to the tremendous break in tonality which modernity had produced.

1972

Music, Voice,

Language

There will be something a little paradoxical about the reflections which follow: they have for their object a unique and special endeavor: that of a singer of French art songs whom I loved a great deal, Charles Panzéra. How can I involve the auditors of a Colloquium whose theme is a general one in what is perhaps only a very personal taste, my enthusiasm for a singer absent from the musical scene for the last twenty-five years and thereby, no doubt, unknown to most of you?

In order to justify or at least excuse so egoistic an enterprise, and one no doubt unsuitable to the customs of such Colloquia, I should like to remind you of this: any interpretation, it seems to me, any discourse of interpretation is based on a positing of values—upon an evaluation. However, most of the time, we conceal this basis: either by idealism or by "scientism," we disguise our evaluation: we proceed *"indifferent* [= without difference] *as to what is valid in itself, as to what is valid for everyone"* (Nietzsche, Deleuze).

It is from this *indifference* of values that music wakens us.

About music, no discourse can be sustained but that of difference—of evaluation. As soon as someone speaks about music—or a specific music—as a value *in itself*, or on the contrary—though this is the same thing—as soon as someone speaks about music as a value *for everyone*—i.e., as soon as we are told we must love all music—we feel a kind of ideological cope falling over the most precious substance of evaluation, music: this is "commentary." Because commentary is unendurable, we see that music compels us to evaluation, imposes difference upon us—or else we fall into futile discourse, the discourse of music-in-itself or of music for everyone.

Hence, it is very difficult to speak about music. Many writers have spoken well about painting; none, I think, has spoken well about music, not even Proust. The reason for this is that it is very difficult to unite language, which belongs to the order of the general, with music, which belongs to the order of difference.

If then, on occasion, one can risk talking about music, as I am doing today, it must not be in order to "commend" scientifically or ideologically, i.e., *generally*—according to the category of the general—but in order openly and actively to affirm a value and to produce an evaluation. Now my evaluation of music involves the voice, and very specifically the voice of a singer I have known, one whose voice has remained in my life the object of a constant love and of a recurrent meditation which has often carried me, beyond music, toward the text and toward language—the French language.

The human voice is, as a matter of fact, the privileged (eidetic) site of difference: a site which escapes all science, for there is no science (physiology, history, aesthetics, psychoanalysis) which exhausts the voice: no matter how much you classify and comment on music historically, sociologically, aesthetically, technically, there will always be a remainder, a supplement, a lapse, something non-spoken which designates itself: the voice. This always *different* object is assigned by psychoanalysis to the category of objects of desire: there is no human voice which is not an object of desire—or of repulsion: there is no neutral voice—and if sometimes that neutrality, that whiteness of the voice occurs, it terrifies us, as if we were to discover a frozen world, one in which desire was dead. Every relation to a voice is necessarily erotic, and this is why it is in the voice that music's difference is so apparent—its constraint to evaluate, to affirm.

I myself have a lover's relation to Panzéra's voice: not to his raw, physical voice, but to his voice as it passes over language, over our French language, like a desire: no voice is raw; every voice is steeped in what it says. I love this voice—I have loved it all my life. At twenty-two or twenty-three, wanting to learn to sing and knowing no teacher, I intrepidly applied to the best singer of art songs of the period between the wars—to Panzéra. This man generously worked with me until illness kept me from continuing my apprenticeship to singing. Since then, I have not stopped listening to his voice, on the rare, technically imperfect records he has made: Panzéra's historical misfortune is that he ruled over French art songs between the wars but no testimony to this reign can be directly transmitted to us: Panzéra stopped singing at the very advent of the long-playing record; we have only some 78 rpm's of his work, or imperfect rerecordings. Nonetheless, this circumstance retains its ambiguity: for if listening to these records may disappoint today, it is because these records are imperfect, and perhaps more generally because history itself has modified our tastes, so that this way of singing has lapsed into the indifference of the out-of-fashion, but also, more topically, because this voice participates in my affirmation, my evaluation, and because it is therefore possible that I am the only one to love it.

We lack, I believe, a historical sociology of the French *mélodie*, that specific form of music which developed, by and large, from Gounod to Poulenc but of which the eponymous heroes are Fauré, Duparc, and Debussy. This *mélodie* (our word is not a good one) is not exactly the French version of the German lied: through romanticism, the lied, however culti- vated its form, participates in a German form of existence at once popular and national. The ecology, one might say, of the French *mélodie* is different: its milieu of birth, formation, and consumption is not popular, and it is national (French) only because other cultures are not much concerned with it; this milieu is the bourgeois salon.

It would be easy, by reason of this origin, to reject the French *mélodie* today, or at least to ignore it. But History is complex, dialectical, especially if we shift to the level of values: as Marx had clearly seen in detaching the "Greek miracle" from the social archaism of Greece, or Balzacian realism from Balzac's theocratic convictions. We must do the same thing with the French *mélodie*: seek out how it can interest us, despite its origins. Here, for my part, is how I should define the French *mélodie*: it is the field [*champ* or *chant*] of celebration of the cultivated French language. At the period when Panzéra sings these songs, such celebration is coming to its end: the French language is no longer a *value*; it is entering upon a mutation (whose characteristics have not yet been studied, or even con- sciously perceived); a new French language is being born today, not exactly by the action of the "working classes," but under the action of an age class (marginal classes have today become political realities), the young; there is, separate from our lan- guage, a young parlance, whose musical expression is *Pop*.

In Panzéra's period, music's relation to the old French lan- guage is in its extreme refinement, which is its last refinement. A certain French language is dying out: this is what we hear in Panzéra's singing: it is the perishable which glistens so heart- breakingly in this singing; for an entire art of speaking the lan- guage has taken refuge here: *diction* is to be found among singers, not among actors subservient to the petit-bourgeois aesthetic of the Comédie-Française, which is an aesthetic of *articulation* and not of *pronunciation*, as was Panzéra's (to which we shall return).

Panzéra's musical phonetics involves, it seems to me, the following features: (1) vocalic purity, particularly apparent in the French vowels par excellence: the *ü*, a forward, *exterior* vowel, one might say (as if it summons the Other to enter my voice), and the closed *é*, which serves us, semantically, to oppose future to conditional, imperfect to *passé simple*; (2) the distinct and fragile beauty of the *a*'s, the most difficult vowel of all when it must be sung; (3) the grain of the nasals, a little harsh, as though spiced; (4) the *r*, rolled of course, but in no way obedient to the somewhat heavy roll of peasant speech, for it is so pure, so brief, that it merely affords the *idea* of a rolled *r*, as if its—symbolic—role is to virilize gentleness without abandoning it; (5) lastly, the patina of certain consonants, at certain moments: consonants which have "alighted" rather than fallen, sounding "induced" rather than marked.

This last feature is not only deliberate but indeed theorized by Panzéra himself: it constituted part of his teaching, this necessary patina of certain consonants, and served him, according to a project of *evaluation* (once again), to oppose *articulation* and *pronunciation*: articulation, he used to say, is the simulacrum and the enemy of pronunciation; one must *pronounce*, never *articulate* (contrary to the stupid watchword of so many singing manuals); for articulation is the negation of *legato*; it seeks to give each consonant the same phonic intensity, whereas in a musical text a consonant is never the same: each syllable—far from being the result of an Olympian code of phonemes, given in itself and once and for all—must be set (like a precious stone) in the general meaning of the phrase.

And it is here, on this purely technical point, that the scope of Panzéra's aesthetic (and I should add: ideological) options suddenly appears. Articulation, in effect, functions abusively as *a pretense of meaning*: claiming to serve meaning, it basically misreads it: of the two contrary excesses which kill meaning, the vague and the emphatic, the latter is the most serious and the most consistent: *to articulate* is to encumber meaning with a parasitical clarity, useless without being, for all that, sumptuous. And such clarity is not innocent; it involves the singer in a highly ideological art of expressivity—or, to be even more precise, of *dramatization*: the melodic line is broken into fragments of meaning, into semantic sighs, into effects of hysteria. On the contrary, *pronunciation* maintains the perfect coalescence of the line of meaning (the phrase) and of the line of music (the *phrased*, as we call it in French: *le phrasé*); in the arts of articulation, language, poorly understood as a theater, a staging of meaning that is slightly kitsch, explodes into the music and deranges it inopportunely, unseasonably: language thrusts itself forward, it is the intruder, the nuisance of music; in the art of pronunciation, on the contrary (Panzéra's), it is music which enters the language and rediscovers there what is musical, what is "amorous."

For this rare phenomenon to occur, for music to enter language, there must be, of course, a certain *physique* of the voice (by *physique* I mean the way in which the voice behaves in the body—or in which the body behaves in the voice). What has always struck me in Panzéra's voice is that through a perfect mastery of all the nuances imposed by a good reading of the musical text—nuances which require knowing how to produce *pianissimi* and extremely delicate "dis-timbres"—this voice was always *secured*, animated by a quasi-metallic strength of desire: it is a "raised" voice—*aufgeregt* (a Schumannian word)—or even better: an erected voice—a voice which gets an erection. Except in the most successful *pianissimi*, Panzéra always sang with his entire body, *full-throatedly*: like a schoolboy who goes out into the countryside and sings for himself, as we say in French *à tue-tête* [to kill the head]—to kill everything bad, depressed, anguished in his head. In a sense, Panzéra always sang with *the naked voice, à voix nue*. And it is here that we can understand how Panzéra, while honoring the art of the French *melodié* with a last luster, subverts that art; for to sing *à voix nue* is the very mode of the traditional folk song (today often edulcorated by unwarranted accompaniments): Panzéra, in secret, sings the cultivated song as though it were a folk song (the singing exercises he assigned were always borrowed from old French songs). And here, too, we recognize the aesthetic of meaning I so love in Panzéra. For if the folk song was traditionally sung *à voix nue*, that is because it was important *to understand the story*: something is being told, which I must receive without disguise: nothing but the voice and the telling: that is what the folk song wants; and that—whatever the detours imposed by culture—was what Panzéra wanted.

Then what is music? Panzéra's art answers: a *quality of language*. But this quality of language in no way derives from the sciences of language (poetics, rhetoric, semiology), for in becoming a quality, what is promoted in language is what it does not say, does not articulate. In the unspoken appears pleasure, tenderness, delicacy, fulfillment, all the values of the most delicate image-repertoire. Music is both what is expressed and what is implicit in the text: what is pronounced (submitted to inflections) but is not articulated: what is at once outside meaning and non-meaning, fulfilled in that *signifying* [*signifiance*], which the theory of the text today seeks to postulate and to situate. Music, like signifying, derives from no metalanguage but only from a discourse of value, of praise: from a lover's discourse: every "successful" relation—successful in that it manages to say the implicit without articulating it, to pass over articulation without falling into the censorship of desire or the sublimation of the unspeakable—such a relation can rightly be called *musical*. Perhaps a thing is valid only by its metaphoric power; perhaps that is the value of music, then: to be a good metaphor.

Unpublished text of a lecture; 1977

The Romantic Song

Once again, tonight, I am listening to the opening phrase of the andante of Schubert's first trio—a perfect phrase, at once unitary and divided, an *amorous* phrase, if ever there was one— and once again I realize how difficult it is to talk about what one loves. What is there to say about what one loves except: *I love it*, and to keep on saying it? My difficulty is all the greater in that today the romantic song is no longer the object of any great argument: it is not an avant-garde art, there is no need to do battle for it; nor is it a remote or alien art, a mis- understood or little-known art for whose resurrection we must militate; it is neither fashionable nor frankly out of fashion: we might call it simply untimely [*inactuel*]. But perhaps it is just here that its subtlest provocation is to be found: and it is out of this untimeliness that I should like to make another timeliness.

All discourse about music must begin, it would seem, with the obvious. About the Schubertian phrase I mentioned, I can say only this: *it sings*, it sings simply, terribly, at the limits of the possible. But is it not surprising that this assumption of song to its essence, this musical action by which song seems to manifest itself in all its glory, should occur precisely without the collabora- tion of the organ which constitutes song, i.e., the voice? It would seem that the human voice is here all the more present in that it has delegated itself to other instruments, the strings: the substitute becomes more real than the original, the violin and the cello "sing" better—or, to be more exact, sing *more*— than the soprano or the baritone, because, if there is a signification of sensuous phenomena, it is always in displacement, in substitution, i.e., ultimately, in *absence*, that it is most brilliantly manifest.

The romantic song does not abolish the voice: Schubert wrote 650 lieder, Schumann 250: but it abolishes *voices*, and perhaps this is its revolution. Here we must recall that the classification of human voices—like any classification elaborated by a society —is never innocent. In the peasant choirs of old rural societies, the men's voices answered to the women's voices: by this simple division of the sexes, the group mimed the preliminaries of exchange, of the matrimonial market. In our Western society, through the four vocal registers of the opera, it is Oedipus who triumphs: the whole family is there, father, mother, daughter, and son, symbolically projected, whatever the detours of the anecdote and the substitutions of roles, into bass, mezzo, soprano, and tenor. It is precisely these four family voices which the romantic lied, in a sense, *forgets*: it does not take into account the sexual marks of the voice, for the same lied can be sung by a man or by a woman; no vocal "family," nothing but a human subject—*unisexual*, one might say, precisely insofar as it is *amorous*: for love—passion, romantic love—is no respecter of sexes or of social roles. There is a historic phenomenon which is perhaps not insignificant: it is *precisely* when the castrati disappear from musical Europe that the romantic lied appears and immediately sheds its brightest light: the publicly castrated creature is succeeded by a complex human subject whose imaginary castration will be interiorized.

Perhaps, however, the romantic song did know the temptation of a division of voices. But this division, which sometimes haunts it, is no longer that of sexes or of social roles. It is another division: it opposes the dark voice of super-nature, or of demonic nature, to the pure voice of the soul, not insofar as it is religious but simply human, all too human. The diabolic evocation and the maiden's prayer here belong to the order of the sacred, not of the religious: what is suggested, what is here vocally put before us, is the anguish of something that threatens to divide, to separate, to dissociate, to dismember the body. The dark voice, voice of Evil or of Death, is a voice without site, a voice without origin: it resonates everywhere (in the Wolf's Glen of *Freischütz*) or becomes motionless, suspended (in Schubert's *Death and the Maiden*): in every case, it no longer refers to the body, which is distanced in a kind of non-site.

This dark voice is the exception, of course. For the most part, the romantic lied originates in the heart of a finite, collected, centered, intimate, familiar site which is the singer's—and hence the listener's—body. In opera, it is the sexual timbre of the voice (bass/tenor, soprano/mezzo) which is important. In the lied, on the contrary, it is the tessitura (the ensemble of sounds which *best* suit a given voice): here no excessive notes, no high C, no overflow or outburst into sharps or flats, no shrieks, no physiological prowess. The tessitura is the modest space of the sounds each of us can produce and within the limits of which he can fantasize the reassuring unity of his body. All romantic music, whether vocal or instrumental, utters this song of the natural body: it is a music which has a meaning only if I can always sing it, in myself, with my body: a vital condition which is denatured by so many modern interpretations, too fast or too personal, through which, under cover of *rubato*, the interpreter's body abusively substitutes itself for mine and *robs* it (*rubare*) of its breathing, its emotion. For *to sing*, in the romantic sense, is this: fantasmatically to enjoy my unified body.

What, then, is this body which sings the lied? What is it that, in my body, sings the lied to me listening?

It is everything that resounds in me, frightens me, or makes me desire. It matters little where this wound, or this joy, comes from: for the lover as for the child, it is always the affect of the lost, abandoned subject that the romantic song sings. Schubert loses his mother at fifteen; two years later his first great song, *Gretchen at the Spinning Wheel*, utters the tumult of absence, the hallucination of the return. The romantic "heart," an expression in which we no longer perceive anything but an edulcorated metaphor, is a powerful organ, extreme point of the interior body where, simultaneously and as though contradictorily, desire and tenderness, the claims of love and the summons of pleasure, violently merge: something raises my body, swells it, stretches it, bears it to the verge of explosion, and immediately, mysteriously, depresses it, weakens it. This movement must be perceived *beneath* the melodic line; this line is pure and, even at the climax of melancholy, always utters the euphoria of the unified body; but it is caught up in a phonic volume which often complicates and contradicts it: a stifled pulsion, marked by respirations, tonal or modal modulations, rhythmic throbbings, a mobile swelling of the entire musical substance, comes from the separated body of the child, of the lover, of the lost subject. Sometimes this subterranean movement exists in the pure state: I believe I can hear it quite nakedly in a brief prelude by Chopin (the first one): something swells, does not yet sing, aspires to utter itself, and then disappears.

I know of course that historically the romantic lied occupies the whole nineteenth century and that it proceeds from Beethoven's *An die Ferne Geliebte* to Schönberg's *Gurrelieder*, by way of Schubert, Schumann, Brahms, Wolf, Mahler, Wagner, and Strauss (without forgetting some of Berlioz's *Nuits d'Été*). But the argument I am sustaining here is not musicological: I am discussing the lied of Schumann and Schubert, because that is for me the incandescent core of the romantic song.

Who listens to this lied? It is not the bourgeois salon, social site where the "romance," a coded expression of love quite distinct from the lied, will gradually refine itself and engender the French *mélodie*. The lied's space is affective, scarcely socialized: sometimes, perhaps, a few friends—those of the Schubertiades; but its true listening space is, so to speak, the interior of the head, of *my head*: listening to it I sing the lied with myself, for myself. I address myself, within myself, to an Image: the image of the beloved in which I lose myself and from which my own image, abandoned, comes back to me. The lied supposes a rigorous interlocution, but one that is imaginary, imprisoned in my deepest intimacy. Opera casts external conflicts—social, familial—into what we might call separate voices; in the lied, the only reactive force is the irremediable absence of the beloved: I struggle with an image, which is both the image of the desired, lost other, and my own image, desiring and abandoned. Every lied is secretly an object of dedication: I dedicate what I sing, what I listen to; there is a *diction* of the romantic song, an articulated address, a kind of secret declaration which we hear very clearly in certain variations of Schumann's *Kreisleriana*, because here no poem comes to invest it, to *fill* it. In short, the lied's interlocutor is the Double—my Double, which is Narcissus: a corrupt double, caught in the dreadful scene of the cracked mirror, as Schubert's unforgettable *Döppelgänger* puts it.

The world of the romantic song is the lover's world, the world which the amorous subject has in his head: a single beloved, but a whole population of figures. These figures are not persons but little scenes, each of which consists, in turn, of a memory, a landscape, a movement, a mood, of anything which may be the starting point of a wound, of a nostalgia, of a felicity. Take *Die Winterreise*: *Goodnight* states the gift the lover makes of his own departure, a gift so furtive the beloved will not even be troubled by it, and I, too, withdraw, my footsteps in his. *Cold Tears* utters the right to weep; *Frost* that very particular cold of abandonment; the *Linden Tree*, the splendid romantic tree, the tree of fragrance and somnolence, speaks the lost peace; *On the River* the pulsion of inscribing—of writing—the perfect love; lastly, the *Hurdy-Gurdy Man* recalls the lover's great summing up of the figures of discourse. This faculty—this decision—to elaborate an ever-new speech out of brief fragments, each of which is both intense and mobile, uncertainly located, is what, in romantic music, we call the *Fantasy*, Schubertian or Schumannian: *Fantasieren*: at once to imagine and to improvise: in short, to hallucinate, i.e., to produce the novelistic without constructing a novel. Even the lieder cycles do not narrate a love story, but only a journey: each moment of this journey is in a sense turned back on itself, blind, closed to any general meaning, to any notion of fate, to any spiritual transcendence: in short, a pure *wandering*, a becoming without finality: at one stroke, and to infinity, to begin everything all over again.

It is possible to situate the art of the romantic song within the history of music: to say how it was born, how it ended, through what tonal framework it passed. But to evaluate it as a moment of civilization is more difficult. Why the lied? By what historical and social determinants was there constituted, in the last century, a poetic and musical form so typical and so fruitful? The difficulty of answering may derive from this paradox: that History has produced, in the lied, an object which is *always* anachronic. The lied inherits this untimeliness from the lover's emotion, of which it is the pure expression. Love— Passion—is historically ineffable because it is always, so to speak, half historical: appearing at certain periods, disappearing at others: sometimes yielding to the determinations of History, sometimes resisting them, as if it had lasted forever and were to last eternally. Amorous passion, that *intermediary* phenomenon (as Plato called it), may derive its historical opacity from the fact that it in fact appears down through the centuries, only in marginal subjects or in marginal groups dispossessed by History, alien to the strong, gregarious society which surrounds, besets, and excludes them, alienated as they are from all power: among the Udrits of the Arab world, the Troubadours of courtly love, the Précieux of our seventeenth century, and the poet-musicians of romantic Germany. Whence, too, the social ubiquity of the lover's sentiment, which can be sung by all classes, from peasantry to aristocracy: we recognize this trans-social character in the very style of the Schubertian lied, which has been able to be, at the same time or in alternation, both elitist and popular. The status of the romantic song is by nature uncertain: out of date without being repressed, marginal without being eccentric. This is why, despite this music's intimist and docile appearances, we can classify it without insolence among the *extreme arts*: the subject who expresses himself in it is singular, untimely, deviant—a madman, one might say, if, by an ultimate elegance, he did not reject madness's glorious mask.

1976

Loving Schumann

There is a kind of French prejudice, writes Marcel Beaufils in his study of Schumann's piano music, against Schumann: he is readily seen as a kind of "thicker Fauré." I do not suppose we need attribute this lukewarm estimation to some opposition between "French clarity" and "German sentimentality"; to judge by current discography and radio programs, the French these days delight in the affecting musicians of "heavy" romanticism, Mahler and Bruckner. No, the reason for this lack of interest (or this minor interest) is historical (and not psychological).

Schumann is very broadly a piano composer. Now the piano, as a social instrument (and every musical instrument, from the lute to the saxophone, implies an ideology), has undergone for a century a historical evolution of which Schumann is the victim. The human subject has changed: interiority, intimacy, solitude have lost their value, the individual has become increasingly gregarious, he wants collective, massive, often paroxysmal music, the expression of *us* rather than of *me*; yet Schumann is truly the musician of solitary intimacy, of the amorous and imprisoned soul that *speaks to itself* (whence the abundance of *parlando* in his work, like that of the splendid sixth variation of the *Kreisleriana*), in short of the child who has no other link than to the Mother.

Listening to the piano has also changed. It is not merely that we have shifted from a private, at the very most a family, listening to a public listening—each record, even when listened to at home, presenting itself as a concert event and the piano becoming a field of achievements—it is also that virtuosity itself, which certainly existed in Schumann's time, since he wanted to become a virtuoso equal to Paganini, has suffered a mutilation; it no longer has to match the worldly hysteria of concerts and salons, it is no longer Lisztian; now, because of the record, it has become a somewhat chilly prowess, a perfect achievement (without flaw, without accident), in which there is nothing to find fault with, but which does not exalt, does not *carry away*: far from the body, in a sense. Hence, for today's pianist, enormous esteem but no fervor and, I should say, referring to the word's etymology, no sympathy. Now Schumann's piano music, which is difficult, does not give rise to the image of virtuosity (in effect, virtuosity is an image, not a technique); we can play it neither according to the old delirium nor according to the new style (which I should readily compare to the "nouvelle cuisine"— undercooked). This piano music is intimate (which does not mean *gentle*), or again, *private*, even individual, refractory to professional approach, since to play Schumann implies a technical *innocence* very few artists can attain.

Finally, what has changed, and fundamentally, is the piano's *use*. Throughout the nineteenth century, playing the piano was a class activity, of course, but general enough to coincide, by and large, with listening to music. I myself began listening to Beethoven's symphonies only by playing them four hands, with a close friend as enthusiastic about them as I was. But nowadays listening to music is dissociated from its practice: many virtuosos, listeners, *en masse*: but as for practitioners, amateurs— very few. Now (here again) Schumann lets his music be fully heard only by someone who plays it, even badly. I have always been struck by this paradox: that a certain piece of Schumann's delighted me when I played it (approximately), and rather disappointed me when I heard it on records: then it seemed mysteriously impoverished, incomplete. This was not, I believe, an infatuation on my part. It is because Schumann's music goes much farther than the ear; it goes into the body, into the muscles by the beats of its rhythm, and somehow into the viscera by the voluptuous pleasure of its *melos*: as if on each occasion the piece was written only for one person, the one who plays it; the true Schumannian pianist—*c'est moi.*

Then is this an egoistic music? Intimacy is always a little egoistic; that is the price which must be paid if we want to renounce the arrogances of the universal. But Schumann's music involves something radical, which makes it into an existential, rather than a social or moral experience. This radicality has some relation to madness, even if Schumann's music is continuously "well-behaved" insofar as it submits to the code of tonality and to the formal regularity of melismata. Madness here is incipient in the vision, the economy of the world with which the subject, Schumann, entertains a relation which gradually destroys him, while the music itself seeks to construct itself. Marcel Beaufils puts all this very well: he clarifies and names those points where life and music change places, the one being destroyed, the other constructed.

This is the first point: for Schumann the world is not unreal, reality is not null and void. His music, by its titles, sometimes by certain discreet effects of description, continuously refers to concrete things: seasons, times of the day, landscapes, festivals, professions. But this reality is threatened with disarticulation, dissociation, with movements not violent (nothing harsh) but brief and, one might say, ceaselessly "mutant": nothing lasts long, each movement interrupts the next: this is the realm of the *intermezzo*, a rather dizzying notion when it extends to all of music, and when the matrix is experienced only as an exhausting (if graceful) sequence of interstices. Marcel Beaufils is right to set at the source of all Schumann's piano music the literary theme of the Carnival; for the Carnival is truly the theater of this decentering of the subject (a very modern temptation) which Schumann expresses in his fashion by the carousel of his brief forms (from this point of view, the *Album for the Young*, if played in sequence, is not so well-behaved as it appears).

In this fragmented world, distorted by whirling appearances (the whole world is a Carnival), a pure and somehow terribly motionless element occasionally breaks through: pain. "If you asked me the name of my pain, I could not tell you. I think it is pain itself, and I could not designate it better." This pure pain without object, this essence of pain, is certainly a madman's pain; we believe that only the mad (insofar as we can name madness and demarcate ourselves from it) quite simply *suffer*. Schumann experienced this absolute pain of the madman premonitorily on the night of October 17, 1833, when he was seized by the most dreadful fear: that, precisely, of losing his reason. Such pain cannot be expressed musically; music can only express the pathos of pain (its social image), not its being; but music can fleetingly express, if not pain, at least purity—the unprecedented quality of purity: to offer the listener a pure sound is an entire musical action by which modern music has often profited (from Wagner to Cage). Schumann, of course, had not conducted such experiments; and yet: Marcel Beaufils very rightly points out the enigmatic B natural which opens the song *Mondnacht* and which vibrates in us so "supernaturally." It is in this perspective, it seems to me, that we must listen, in Schumann's music, to the positions of tonality. Schumannian tonality is simple, robust; it does not have the marvelous sophistication of Chopin's (notably in the Mazurkas). But precisely: its simplicity is an insistence: for many Schumannian pieces, the tonal range has the value of a single sound which keeps vibrating until it maddens us; the tonic is not endowed with a "cosmic widening" (like the first E flat of *Rheingold*), but rather with a massiveness which insists, imposing its solitude to the point of obsession.

The third point where Schumann's music encounters his madness is rhythm. Marcel Beaufils analyzes this very well; he shows its importance, its originality, and finally its dissolution (for example, through the generalization of syncopations). Rhythm, in Schumann, is a violence (Beaufils shows how it does violence to the theme, rendering it "barbarous," which Chopin did not like at all); but (as with pain) this violence is pure, it is not "tactical." Schumannian rhythm (listen carefully to the basses) imposes itself like a texture of beats; this texture can be delicate (Beaufils shows that the lovely though little-known *Intermezzi* are differentiated and extended studies of pure rhythm), yet it has something atypical about it (as is proved by the fact that we never consider Schumann a composer of rhythm: he is imprisoned in melody). To put it differently: rhythm, in Schumann, singularly enough, is not in the service of a dual, oppositional organization of the world.

Here we touch on Schumann's singularity, I believe: that point of fusion at which his fate (madness), his thought, and his music converge. This point Beaufils has seen: "His universe is without struggle," he says. This is, at first glance, a very paradoxical diagnosis for a musician who so often suffered, and so cruelly, from opposition to his projects (marriage, vocation) and whose music always shudders with the leaps of desire (despondencies, hopes, desolations, intoxications). And yet Schumann's "madness" (this is not, obviously, a psychiatric diagnosis, which would horrify me in many respects) arises (or at least can be said to arise) from the fact that he "lacks" a conflictual (I should say in my language: *paradigmatic*) structure of the world: his music is based on no simple and, one might say, no "natural" (naturalized by anonymous culture) confrontation. No Beethovenian Manichaeism, or even Schubertian fragility (tender melancholy of a subject who sees death facing him). This is a music at once dispersed and unary, continually taking refuge in the luminous shadow of the Mother (the lied, copious in Schumann's work, is, I believe, the expression of this maternal unity). In short, Schumann lacks conflict (necessary, it is said, to the proper economy of the "normal" subject), precisely insofar as—paradoxically—he multiplies his "moods," his "humors" (another important notion of the Schumannian aesthetic: humoresques, *mit Humor*): in the same way, he destroys the pulsion (let us play on words; let us also say: the pulsation) of pain by experiencing it in a pure mode, just as he exhausts rhythm by generalizing syncopation. For him, only the external world is differentiated, but according to the Carnival's superficial fits and starts. Schumann ceaselessly "attacks," but he always does so in the void.

Is this why our period grants him what is doubtless an "honorable" place (of course he is a "great composer"), but not a favored one (there are many Wagnerites, many Mahlerians, but the only Schumannians I know are Gilles Deleuze, Marcel Beaufils, and myself)? Our period, especially since the advent, by recordings, of mass music, wants splendid images of great conflicts (Beethoven, Mahler, Tchaikovsky). Loving Schumann, as Beaufils and his publisher give evidence that they do, is in a way to assume a philosophy of Nostalgia, or, to adopt a Nietzschean word, of Untimeliness, or again, to risk this time the most Schumannian word there is: of Night. Loving Schumann, doing so in a certain fashion *against* the age (I have sketched the motifs of this solitude), can only be a responsible way of loving: it inevitably leads the subject who does so and says so to posit himself in his time according to the injunctions of his desire and not according to those of his sociality. But that is another story, whose narrative would exceed the limits of music.

1979

Rasch

... there is nothing clearer than the following
passage I read somewhere: Musices seminarium
accentus, *accent is the nursery of melody.*

—Diderot

In Schumann's *Kreisleriana* (Opus 16; 1838), I actually hear
no note, no theme, no contour, no grammar, no meaning, nothing which would permit me to reconstruct an intelligible structure of the work. No, what I hear are blows: I hear what beats
in the body, what beats the body, or better: I hear this body that
beats.

Here is how I hear Schumann's body (indeed, he had a body,
and what a body! His body was *what he had most of all*):
   in the first variation, it curls up into a ball, then it weaves,
   in the second, it stretches out; and then it wakes up: it pricks,
it knocks, it glows,
   in the third, it rises, it extends: *aufgeregt,*
   in the fourth, it speaks, it declares: someone declares himself,

in the fifth, it showers, it comes undone, it shudders, it rises: running, singing, beating,

in the sixth, it speaks, it spells out, what is spoken intensifies until it is sung,

in the seventh, it strikes, it beats,

in the eighth, it dances, but also it begins snarling all over again, beating . . .

I hear it said: Schumann wrote so many short pieces *because he didn't know how to develop*. A repressive criticism: what you *refuse* to do is what you *can't* do.

The truth is more likely this: the Schumannian body does not *stay in place* (a major rhetorical transgression). It is not a meditative body. It sometimes makes a meditative gesture, but does not assume meditation's bearing, infinite persistence, and faint posture of subsidence. This is a pulsional body, one which pushes itself back and forth, turns to something else—thinks of something else; this is a stunned body (intoxicated, distracted, and at the same time ardent). Whence the *envy* (let us retain this word's physiological meaning: from *invidia*, looking askance) of the *intermezzo*.

The intermezzo, consubstantial with the entire Schumannian oeuvre, even when the episode does not bear its name, has as its function not to distract but to displace: like a vigilant sauce chef, it keeps the discourse from "setting," from thickening, from spreading, from returning obediently into the culture of development; it is this renewed act (as every speech-act is renewed) by which the body stirs and disturbs the hum of artistic speech. At the limit, there are only intermezzi: what interrupts is in its turn interrupted, and this begins all over again.

One might say that the intermezzo is *epic* (with the meaning Brecht gave this word): by its interruptions, its head movements, the body begins to *criticize* (to put in crisis) the discourse which, under cover of art, others have tried to put over on it, without it.

. . .

The second variation begins by a scene of stretching (*a*); and then something (intermezzo 1) suddenly comes down the staircase of notes (*b*). Is this a matter of contrast? It would be convenient to say so: we could then remove the surface of the paradigmatic structure and recognize musical semiology, which makes the meaning of unit-oppositions appear. But does the body know contraries? Contrast is a simple rhetorical state: plural, lost, panicked, the Schumannian body knows (at least here) only bifurcations; it does not construct itself, it keeps diverging according to an accumulation of interludes; it has only that *vague* idea (the vague can be a phenomenon of structure) of meaning which we call *signifying* [*signifiance*]. The sequence of intermezzi has as its function not to make contrasts speak but rather to fulfill a radiant writing, which is then recognizable much closer to painted space than to the spoken chain. Music, in short, at this level, is an image, not a

(a)

(b)

language, in that every image is radiant, from the rhythmic incisions of pre-history to the frames of comic strips. The musical text *does not follow* (by contrasts or amplification), it explodes: it is a continuous *big bang*.

It is not a matter of beating fists against the door, in the presumed manner of fate. What is required is that *it beat* inside the body, against the temple, in the sex, in the belly, against the skin from inside, at the level of that whole sensuous emotivity which we call, both by metonymy and by antiphrasis, the "heart." "To beat" is the very action of the heart (there is no "beating" except the heart's), which occurs at this paradoxical site of the body: central and decentered, liquid and contractile, pulsional and moral; but it is also the emblematic word of two languages: linguistics (in the grammatical example *"Peter beats Paul"*) and psychoanalysis (*"A child is being beaten"*).

Schumannian beating is panic, but it is also coded (by rhythm and tonality); and it is because the panic of the blows apparently keeps within the limits of a docile language that it is ordinarily not perceived (judging by most interpretations of Schumann). Or rather: nothing can determine if these beats are censored by most people, who do not want to hear them, or are hallucinated by one man alone, who hears nothing but them. We recognize here the very structure of the *paragram*: a second text is heard, but at the limit—like Saussure listening for his anagrammatic verses—*I alone hear them*. It seems, then, that only Yves Nat and I (if I may say so) hear the formidable

(c)

beating of the seventh variation (c). This uncertainty (of reading, of listening) is the very status of the Schumannian text, collected contradictorily in an excess (that of hallucinated evidence) and an evasion (the same text can be played insipidly). In methodological terms one can say (or repeat): no model in the text: not because it is "free," but because it is "different."

The beat—corporal and musical—must never be *the sign of a sign*: the accent is not expressive.

Interpretation is then merely the power to read the anagrams of the Schumannian text, to reveal the network of accents beneath the tonal, rhythmic, melodic rhetoric. The accent is the music's truth, in relation to which all interpretation declares itself. In Schumann (to my taste), the beats are played too timidly; the body which takes possession of them is almost always a mediocre body, trained, streamlined by years of Conservatory or career, or more simply by the interpreter's insignificance, his indifference: he plays the accent (the beat) like a simple rhetorical mark; what the virtuoso then displays is the platitude of his own body, incapable of "beating" (as is the case with Rubinstein). It is not a question of strength, but of rage: the body must pound—not the pianist (this has been glimpsed here and there by Nat and Horowitz).

On the level of the beats (of the anagrammatic network), each listener *executes* what he hears. Hence, there is a site of the musical text where every distinction between composer, interpreter, and auditor is abolished.

The beat's ecstatic recurrence—that would be the origin of the refrain.

The beat can assume this or that figure, which is not necessarily that of a violent, furious accent. However, whatever it is, since it is of the order of enjoyment, no figure can be predicated

(d)

romantically (even and above all if it is proposed by a romantic composer); we cannot say that a certain figure is gay or melancholy, somber or joyous, etc.; the figure's precision, its distinction, is linked not to states of the soul but to subtle movements of the body, to all that differential coenesthesia, that histological fabric out of which the self-experiencing body is made. The third variation, for example, is not "animated" (*molto animato*): it is "raised (*aufgeregt*), lifted up, stretched out, erected; one might also say—but this will be the same thing—that it progresses through a series of tiny revulsions, as if, at each incision, something were coming undone, were turning back, were being severed, as if all the music were entering the sudden wave of the swallowing throat (*d*).

Hence, we must call *beat* whatever makes any site of the body flinch, however briefly, even if this flinching seems to take the romantic forms of a pacification. Pacification, at least in the *Kreisleriana*, is always a *stretching out*: the body stretches, distends, extends toward its extreme form (to stretch out is to attain the limit of a dimension, the very gesture of the undeniable body which here wins itself back). Is there a better-dreamed-of stretching (as we have seen) than that of the second variation (*e*)? Here everything converges: the melodic form, the suspense harmony (*f*). Sometimes the body even curls itself up into a ball in order to stretch itself out all the better later on: in the second variation (*g*) or in the disguised intermezzo of the third, whose long stretching will vary—by broadening or relaxing?—the pricked, swallowed, revulsed body of the beginning (*h*).

What does the body *do*, when it enunciates (musically)? And Schumann answers: my body strikes, my body collects itself, it explodes, it divides, it pricks, or on the contrary and without warning (this is the meaning of the intermezzo, which

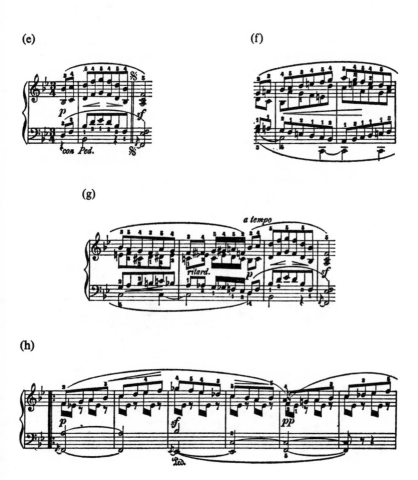

always comes *like a thief*), it stretches out, it weaves (like the Arachnean interlude of the first variation) (*i*). And sometimes —why not?—it even speaks, it declaims, it doubles its voice: *it speaks but says nothing*: for as soon as it is musical, speech—or its instrumental substitute—is no longer linguistic but corporeal; what it says is always and only this: *my body puts itself in a state of speech*: *quasi parlando* (*j* and *k*).

Quasi parlando (I take the indication from one of Beethoven's *Bagatelles*): this is the movement of the body *which is about to speak*. This *quasi parlando* governs an enormous share of the Schumannian oeuvre; it overflows the work for voice (which

(i)

(j)

(k)

paradoxically may not participate in it at all): the instrument (the piano) speaks without saying anything, in the fashion of a mute who reveals on his face the inarticulate power of speech. All these *quasi parlandos* which mark so many pianistic oeuvres come from poetic culture; hence, what his poets have given Schumann, even more perhaps than their poems, is the gesture of a voice; this voice speaks in order to say nothing but the measure (the meter) which permits it to exist—to emerge—as signifier.

Such are the *figures of the body* (the "somathemes"), whose texture forms musical *signifying* (hence, no more grammar, no more musical semiology: issuing from professional analysis—identification and arrangement of "themes," "cells," "phrases" —it risks bypassing the body; composition manuals are so many ideological objects, whose meaning is to annul the body).

These figures of the body, which are musical figures, I do not always manage to name. For this operation requires a metaphorical power (how would I utter my body except in images?), and this power can occasionally fail me: "it" stirs in me, but I do not find the right metaphor. As with the fifth variation, of which a certain episode (event, rather) obsesses me, but whose corporeal secret I cannot transfix: "it" is inscribed within me, but I don't know where: in what part, in what region of the body and of language (*l*)? As body (as *my* body), the

(l)

musical text is riddled with losses: I struggle to join a language, a nomination: *my kingdom for a word! ah, if I could only write!* Music, then, is what struggles with writing.

When writing triumphs, it takes up where science, impotent to restore the body, leaves off: only the metaphor is exact; and it would suffice that we be *writers* for us to be able to account for these musical beings, these corporeal chimeras, in a perfectly *scientific* fashion.

"Soul," "feeling," "heart" are romantic names for the body. Everything is clearer, in the romantic text, if we translate the effusive moral term by a pulsional corporeal one—whereby there is no harm done: romantic music is saved, once the body returns to it—as soon as, through music, in fact, the body returns to music. By restoring the body to the romantic text, we correct the ideological reading of this text, for this reading, that of our current opinion, never does anything but *invert* (this is the gesture of any ideology) the body's motions into movements of the soul.

Classical semiology has not been interested in the referent; this was possible (and doubtless necessary) because in the articulated text there is always the screen of the signified. But, in music, a field of *signifying* and not a system of signs, the referent is unforgettable, for here the referent is the body. The body passes into music without any relay but the signifier. This passage—this transgression—makes music a madness: not only Schumann's music, but all music. In relation to the writer, the composer is always mad (and the writer can never be so, for he is condemned to meaning).

And the tonal system—what does it become in this semantics of the musical body, in this "art of beats" which is what music would ultimately be? Let us imagine for tonality two contradictory (and yet concomitant) statuses. On the one hand, the whole tonal apparatus is a demure screen, an illusion, a veil of *Maya*, in short a *language*, intended to articulate the body not according to its own beats (its own articulations) but according to a known organization which deprives the subject of any possibility of delirium. On the other hand, contradictorily, or dialectically, tonality becomes the ready servant of the beats which on another level it claims to domesticate.

Here are several of the "services" tonality performs for the body: by dissonance, it permits the beat, here and there, to "toll," to "tilt"; by modulation (and tonal return), it can complete the figure of the beat, give it its specific form; *it curls up into a ball*, says the first variation; but it curls up into a ball all the better if we return to the source after having left it (*m*); finally (to remain with the Schumannian text), tonality provides the body the strongest, the most constant of oneiric figures: the ascent (or the descent) of the stairs: there is, we know, a scale of tones, and by traversing this scale (according to very diverse moods) the body lives in breathlessness, haste, desire, anguish, the approach of orgasm, etc. (*n*).

(m)

(n)

In short, tonality can have an *accentual* function (it participates in the paragrammatical structure of the musical text).
When the tonal system disappears (today), this function passes
to another system, that of timbres. "Timbrality" (the network
of timbre colors) assures the body the entire richness of its
"beats" (chimes, slides, tollings, poundings, streamings, echo-
ings, scatterings, etc.). It is then the "beats"—sole structural
elements of the musical text—which constitute music's trans-
historical continuity, whatever the system (itself perfectly
historical) the beating body uses to produce utterance.

Indications of movements, of atmosphere, are in general flattened out by the Italian code (*presto, animato,* etc.), which is
here a purely technical code. Restored to another language
(original or unknown), music's words open the theater of the
body. I do not know whether Schumann was the first musician
to connote his texts in the vernacular (such information is
usually missing from our histories of music); but I believe that
the explosion of the mother tongue into the musical text is an
important phenomenon. To remain with Schumann (the man
with two wives—two mothers?—the first of whom sang and the
second, Clara, visibly gave him abundant speech: a hundred
lieder in 1840, the year of his marriage), the explosion of the
Muttersprache in musical writing is really the declared restora-
tion of the body—as if, on the threshold of melody, the body
discovered itself, assumed itself in the double depth of the beat
and of language; as if, with regard to music, the mother tongue
occupied the place of the *chora* (a notion adapted from Plato
by Julia Kristeva): the indicating word is the receptable of
signifying.
  Read, listen to some of these Schumannian words, and see
all that they tell about the body (nothing to do with any kind
of metronomic movement):
  Bewegt: something begins moving (not too fast), something

stirs without direction, like shifting branches, like a rustling agitation of the body

Aufgeregt: something wakens, rises, lifts itself (like a mast, an arm, a head), something provokes, irritates (and of course: something gets a hard-on)

Innig: you take yourself deep inside, you collect yourself at the limit of this depth, your body is internalized, loses itself inside, toward its own land

Ausserst innig: you conceive yourself in a limit state; by dint of inwardness, *inside* turns around, as if there were an *outside* of the inside, though this were not, still, the exterior

Ausserst bewegt: it stirs, it throbs so powerfully that it might even crack—but doesn't crack

Rasch: directed speed, exactitude, precise rhythm (contrary to haste), rapid strides, surprise, the movement of a serpent through leaves

Rasch: this, say the publishers, signifies only: *quick, fast* (*presto*). But I who am not German and who, confronted by this foreign tongue, possess only a stupefied listening, I add to it the truth of the signifier: as if I had a limb swept away, *torn off* by the wind, whipped toward a site of dispersion which is precise but unknown.

In a famous text,* Benveniste sets in opposition two realms of signification: the *semiotic*, an order of articulated signs each of which has a meaning (such as the natural language), and the *semantic*, an order of discourse no unit of which signifies in itself, although the ensemble is given a capacity for signifying. Music, Benveniste says, belongs to semantics (and not to semiotics), since sounds are not signs (no sound, in itself, has meaning); hence, Benveniste continues, music is a language which has a syntax but no semiotics.

* Benveniste, *Problèmes de linguistique générale* II, 1974.

What Benveniste does not say, but what perhaps he would not contradict, is that musical *signifying*, in a much clearer fashion than linguistic *signification*, is steeped in desire. Hence, we change logics. In Schumann's case, for instance, the order of beats is rhapsodic (there is weaving, patchwork of inter-mezzi): the syntax of the *Kreisleriana* is that of a quilt: the body, one might say, accumulates its expenditure—*signifying* takes on the frenzy but also the sovereignty of an economy which destroys itself as it develops; it therefore relates to a semanalysis, or one might say to a second semiology, that of the body in a state of music; let the first semiology manage, if it can, with the system of notes, scales, tones, chords, and rhythms; what we want to perceive and to follow is the effervescence of the beats.

By music, we better understand the Text as *signifying* [*signifiance*].

1975